A New Measure of Competition in the Financial Industry

The 2008 credit crisis started with the failure of one large bank: Lehman Brothers. Since then the focus of both politicians and regulators has been on stabilising the economy and preventing future financial instability. At this juncture, we are at the last stage of future-proofing the financial sector by raising capital requirements and tightening financial regulation. Now the policy agenda needs to concentrate on transforming the banking sector into an engine for growth. Reviving competition in the banking sector after the state interventions of the past years is a key step in this process.

This book introduces and explains a relatively new concept in competition measurement: the performance-conduct-structure (PCS) indicator. The key idea behind this measure is that when a firm's efficiency is more highly rewarded in terms of market share and profit, the competitive pressure is stronger. The book begins by explaining the financial market's fundamental obstacles to competition, presenting a brief survey of the complex relationship between financial stability and competition. The theoretical contributions of Hay and Liu, and Boone provide the theoretical underpinning for the PCS indicator, while its application to banking and insurance illustrates its empirical qualities. Finally, this book presents a systematic comparison between the results of this approach and (all) existing methods as applied to 46 countries, over the same sample period.

This book presents a comprehensive overview of the knowns and unknowns of financial sector competition for commercial and central bankers, policy-makers, supervisors and academics alike.

Jacob A. Bikker is Research Coordinator, Supervisory Policy Division, Strategy Department, De Nederlandsche Bank, Amsterdam, the Netherlands, and Professor in Banking and Financial Regulation, Utrecht School of Economics, Utrecht University, the Netherlands.

Michiel van Leuvensteijn is Senior Policy Advisor, Group Strategy and Policy Division, All Pensions Group (APG), Amsterdam, the Netherlands.

Routledge International Studies in Money and Banking

1. **Private Banking in Europe**
   Lynn Bicker

2. **Bank Deregulation and Monetary Order**
   George Selgin

3. **Money in Islam**
   A study in Islamic political economy
   Masudul Alam Choudhury

4. **The Future of European Financial Centres**
   Kirsten Bindemann

5. **Payment Systems in Global Perspective**
   Maxwell J. Fry, Isaak Kilato, Sandra Roger, Krzysztof Senderowicz, David Sheppard, Francisco Solis and John Trundle

6. **What is Money?**
   John Smithin

7. **Finance**
   A characteristics approach
   Edited by David Blake

8. **Organisational Change and Retail Finance**
   An ethnographic perspective
   Richard Harper, Dave Randall and Mark Rouncefield

9. **The History of the Bundesbank**
   Lessons for the European Central Bank
   Jakob de Haan

10. **The Euro**
    A challenge and opportunity for financial markets
    Published on behalf of Société Universitaire Européenne de Recherches Financières (SUERF)
    Edited by Michael Artis, Axel Weber and Elizabeth Hennessy

11. **Central Banking in Eastern Europe**
    Edited by Nigel Healey and Barry Harrison

12. **Money, Credit and Prices Stability**
    Paul Dalziel

13. **Monetary Policy, Capital Flows and Exchange Rates**
    Essays in memory of Maxwell Fry
    Edited by William Allen and David Dickinson

14. **Adapting to Financial Globalisation**
    Published on behalf of Société Universitaire Européenne de Recherches Financières (SUERF)
    Edited by Morten Balling, Eduard H. Hochreiter and Elizabeth Hennessy

15. **Monetary Macroeconomics**
A new approach
Alvaro Cencini

16. **Monetary Stability in Europe**
Stefan Collignon

17. **Technology and Finance**
Challenges for financial markets, business strategies and policy makers
Published on behalf of Société Universitaire Européenne de Recherches Financières (SUERF)
Edited by Morten Balling, Frank Lierman and Andrew Mullineux

18. **Monetary Unions**
Theory, history, public choice
Edited by Forrest H. Capie and Geoffrey E. Wood

19. **HRM and Occupational Health and Safety**
Carol Boyd

20. **Central Banking Systems Compared**
The ECB, the pre-Euro Bundesbank and the Federal Reserve System
Emmanuel Apel

21. **A History of Monetary Unions**
John Chown

22. **Dollarization**
Lessons from Europe and the Americas
Edited by Louis-Philippe Rochon and Mario Seccareccia

23. **Islamic Economics and Finance: A Glossary, 2nd Edition**
Muhammad Akram Khan

24. **Financial Market Risk**
Measurement and analysis
Cornelis A. Los

25. **Financial Geography**
A banker's view
Risto Laulajainen

26. **Money Doctors**
The experience of international financial advising 1850–2000
Edited by Marc Flandreau

27. **Exchange Rate Dynamics**
A new open economy macroeconomics perspective
Edited by Jean-Oliver Hairault and Thepthida Sopraseuth

28. **Fixing Financial Crises in the 21st Century**
Edited by Andrew G. Haldane

29. **Monetary Policy and Unemployment**
The U.S., Euro-area and Japan
Edited by Willi Semmler

30. **Exchange Rates, Capital Flows and Policy**
Edited by Peter Sinclair, Rebecca Driver and Christoph Thoenissen

31. **Great Architects of International Finance**
The Bretton Woods era
Anthony M. Endres

32. **The Means to Prosperity**
Fiscal policy reconsidered
Edited by Per Gunnar Berglund and Matias Vernengo

33. **Competition and Profitability in European Financial Services**
Strategic, systemic and policy issues
Edited by Morten Balling, Frank Lierman and Andy Mullineux

34. **Tax Systems and Tax Reforms in South and East Asia**
Edited by Luigi Bernardi, Angela Fraschini and Parthasarathi Shome

35. **Institutional Change in the Payments System and Monetary Policy**
Edited by Stefan W. Schmitz and Geoffrey E. Wood

36. **The Lender of Last Resort**
Edited by F.H. Capie and G.E. Wood

37. **The Structure of Financial Regulation**
Edited by David G. Mayes and Geoffrey E. Wood

38. **Monetary Policy in Central Europe**
Miroslav Beblavý

39. **Money and Payments in Theory and Practice**
Sergio Rossi

40. **Open Market Operations and Financial Markets**
Edited by David G. Mayes and Jan Toporowski

41. **Banking in Central and Eastern Europe 1980–2006**
A comprehensive analysis of banking sector transformation in the former Soviet Union, Czechoslovakia, East Germany, Yugoslavia, Belarus, Bulgaria, Croatia, the Czech Republic, Hungary, Kazakhstan, Poland, Romania, the Russian Federation, Serbia and Montenegro, Slovakia, Ukraine and Uzbekistan
Stephan Barisitz

42. **Debt, Risk and Liquidity in Futures Markets**
Edited by Barry A. Goss

43. **The Future of Payment Systems**
Edited by Stephen Millard, Andrew G. Haldane and Victoria Saporta

44. **Credit and Collateral**
Vania Sena

45. **Tax Systems and Tax Reforms in Latin America**
Edited by Luigi Bernardi, Alberto Barreix, Anna Marenzi and Paola Profeta

46. **The Dynamics of Organizational Collapse**
The case of Barings Bank
Helga Drummond

47. **International Financial Co-operation**
Political economics of compliance with the 1988 Basel Accord
Bryce Quillin

48. **Bank Performance**
A theoretical and empirical framework for the analysis of profitability, competition and efficiency
Jacob A. Bikker and Jaap W.B. Bos

49. **Monetary Growth Theory**
Money, interest, prices, capital, knowledge and economic structure over time and space
Wei-Bin Zhang

50. **Money, Uncertainty and Time**
Giuseppe Fontana

51. **Central Banking, Asset Prices and Financial Fragility**
Éric Tymoigne

52. **Financial Markets and the Macroeconomy**
Willi Semmler, Peter Flaschel, Carl Chiarella and Reiner Franke

53. **Inflation Theory in Economics**
Welfare, velocity, growth and business cycles
Max Gillman

54. **Monetary Policy Over Fifty Years**
Heinz Herrman (Deutsche Bundesbank)

55. **Designing Central Banks**
David Mayes and Geoffrey Wood

56. **Inflation Expectations**
Peter J.N. Sinclair

57. **The New International Monetary System**
Essays in honour of Alexander Swoboda
Edited by Charles Wyplosz

58. **Taxation and Gender Equity**
A comparative analysis of direct and indirect taxes in developing and developed countries
Edited by Caren Grown and Imraan Valodia

59. **Developing Alternative Frameworks for Explaining Tax Compliance**
Edited by James Alm, Jorge Martinez-Vazquez and Benno Torgler

60. **International Tax Coordination**
An interdisciplinary perspective on virtues and pitfalls
Edited by Martin Zagler

61. **The Capital Needs of Central Banks**
Edited by Sue Milton and Peter Sinclair

62. **Monetary and Banking History**
Edited by Geoffrey E. Wood, Terence Mills and Nicholas Crafts

63. **New Approaches to Monetary Economics and Theory**
Interdisciplinary perspectives
Edited by Heiner Ganßmann

64. **Social Banks and the Future of Sustainable Finance**
Edited by Olaf Weber and Sven Remer

65. **Policy Makers on Policy**
The Mais lectures
Edited by Forrest H. Capie and Geoffrey E. Wood

66. **Prediction Markets**
Theory and applications
Edited by Leighton Vaughan Williams

67. **Towards a Socioanalysis of Money, Finance and Capitalism**
Beneath the surface of the financial industry
Edited by Susan Long and Burkard Sievers

68. **Doing Money**
Heiner Ganßmann

69. **Banking Regulation and the Financial Crisis**
Jin Cao

70. **Banking Crises, Liquidity and Credit Lines**
A macroeconomic perspective
Gurbachan Singh

71. **New Paradigms in Financial Economics**
How would Keynes reconstruct economics?
Kazem Falahati

72. **Risk, Risk Management and Regulation in the Banking Industry**
The risk to come
Peter Pelzer

73. Financial Systems in Troubled Waters
Information, strategies, and governance to enhance performances in risky times
Edited by Alessandro Carretta and Gianluca Mattarocci

74. Reforming the Governance of the Financial Sector
Edited by David G. Mayes and Geoffrey Wood

75. Money in Economic Theory
Hasse Ekstedt

76. New Perspectives on Emotions in Finance

The sociology of confidence, fear and betrayal
Edited by Jocelyn Pixley

77. Global Finance in Emerging Market Economies
Todd A. Knoop

78. Monetary Policy in Theory and Practice
Facing the internal vs external stability dilemma
Nicolas Barbaroux

79. New Contributions to Monetary Analysis
The foundations of an alternative economic paradigm
Edited by Faruk Ülgen (with the collaboration of Matthieu Méaulle, Rémi Stellian and Ramón Tortajada)

80. Money and its Origins
Shahzavar Karimzadi

81. Cultures of Expertise in Global Currency Markets
Leon Wansleben

82. The Global Financial Crisis and the New Monetary Consensus
Marc Pilkington

83. A New Measure of Competition in the Financial Industry
The performance-conduct-structure indicator
Edited by Jacob A. Bikker and Michiel van Leuvensteijn

A New Measure of Competition in the Financial Industry

The performance-conduct-structure indicator

Edited by Jacob A. Bikker and Michiel van Leuvensteijn

Routledge
Taylor & Francis Group
LONDON AND NEW YORK

First published 2015
by Routledge
2 Park Square, Milton Park, Abingdon, Oxon OX14 4RN

and by Routledge
711 Third Avenue, New York, NY 10017

Routledge is an imprint of the Taylor & Francis Group, an informa business

British Library Cataloguing in Publication Data
A catalogue record for this book is available from the British Library

Library of Congress Cataloging in Publication Data
A new measure of competition in the financial industry : the performance-conduct-structure indicator / edited by Jacob Bikker and Michiel van Leuvensteijn.
pages cm. – (Routledge international studies in money and banking)
Includes bibliographical references and index.
1. Banks and banking. 2. Financial services industry. 3. Competition.
4. Financial crises – Prevention. I. Bikker, Jacob A., 1952–
II. Leuvensteijn, Michiel van.
HG1601.N497 2014
332.1-dc23 2014007678

ISBN: 978-0-415-87040-5 (hbk)
ISBN: 978-0-203-71108-8 (ebk)

Typeset in Times New Roman
by HWA Text and Data Management, London

To Ingeborg and Jacolijne;
Natalia, Naomi, Gabrielle and Rafael

Contents

List of figures xiii
List of tables xiv
List of contributors xvi
Foreword xviii
Preface xix

1 Introduction 1
JACOB A. BIKKER AND MICHIEL VAN LEUVENSTEIJN

2 Potential obstacles for competition in the financial sector 8
JACOB A. BIKKER AND MICHIEL VAN LEUVENSTEIJN

3 The efficiency of firms: what difference does competition make? 25
DONALD A. HAY AND GUY S. LIU

4 A new way to measure competition 48
JAN BOONE

5 Measuring performance of banks as an assessment of competition 73
JACOB A. BIKKER

6 Identifying different regimes of competition 96
CLEMENS KOOL AND MICHIEL VAN LEUVENSTEIJN

7 A new approach to measuring competition in the loan markets of the euro area 118
JACOB A. BIKKER, MICHIEL VAN LEUVENSTEIJN, ADRIAN VAN RIXTEL AND CHRISTOFFER KOK

8 Impact of bank competition on the interest rate pass-through in the euro area 140

JACOB A. BIKKER, MICHIEL VAN LEUVENSTEIJN, CHRISTOFFER KOK AND ADRIAN VAN RIXTEL

9 Competition in the life insurance industry 169

JACOB A. BIKKER AND MICHIEL VAN LEUVENSTEIJN

Index 202

Figures

4.1 Entry costs $\gamma(n)$ and profits $\pi(n,\{n_{w0}^{i},n_{w1}^{i}\}_{i=1}^{2},\theta)$ as a function of efficiency n, with $n_{w0}^{1}=n_a, n_{w1}^{1}=n_b, n_{w0}^{2}=n_c$, and $n_{w1}^{2}=n_d$ 54

4.2 Firm n's normalized profits $\dfrac{\pi(n,\theta)-\pi(\underline{n},\theta)}{\pi(\overline{n},\theta)-\pi(\underline{n},\theta)}$ as a function of n's normalized efficiency $\dfrac{n-\underline{n}}{\overline{n}-\underline{n}}$ 60

5.1 Positive effect of competition on innovation, financial health and accessibility of the banking industry and on financial stability 74

5.2. Countries examined by category 75

5.3 Relations between market structure, competition, profitability and efficiency 77

5.4 Frequency distribution of correlation coefficients between indicators 79

5.5 Frequency distribution of correlations between indicators and index 88

6.1 Profit-proxy compared with earnings from operations 105

6.2 ASRC's elasticity-adjusted Lerner index 110

6.3 ASRC's PCS indicator over time 113

7.1 Indicators of the countries with no significant change in competition over time 131

7.2 Indicators of the countries with significant change in competition over time 131

9.1 Effect of average variable costs and (adjusted) marginal costs on profits 191

9.2 Effect of average variable costs and (adjusted) marginal costs on market shares 194

Tables

2.1	Determinants of imperfect competition on financial markets	10
3.1	Frontier production functions	32
3.2	Estimates of the relationship between firm inefficiency and market share	38
3.3	Gross investment and the long-run efficiency of firms	40
3.4	The determinants of changes in short-run efficiency	42
4.1	Increasing competition in Example 2 by making goods closer substitutes	66
4.2	Increasing competition in Example 2 by reducing entry costs	66
5.1	Indirect performance indicators for financial institutions	76
5.2	Competition models	78
5.3	Correlation coefficients between indicators and the index	80
5.4	Factor loadings for the first five principal components	82
5.5	Competitiveness ranking of EU countries	83
5.6	Distribution of X-efficiency, costs and profitability across countries	86
5.7	Correlations between the indicators and the index	87
5.8	Explanation of bank competition in 76 countries	89
5.9	Effect of competition on spreads between bank and market lending rates	90
5.10	Competition among banks, insurers and pension funds	91
6.1	The US competition regimes during 1887–1914	101
6.2	Descriptive statistics	103
6.3	Instrumental variable-estimation results for the demand for refined sugar	109
6.4	Wald tests of the elasticity-adjusted Lerner index	110
6.5	Empirical results of the PCS indicator based on profits	111
6.6	Testing hypotheses on the PCS indicator	113
6.A	Descriptive statistics for calculating the elasticity-adjusted Lerner index	115
7.1	Number of banks by country and by type in 2002	126
7.2	Mean values of key variables by countries for the 1992–2004 period	127
7.3	Summary statistics of the PCS indicator for several countries	128

7.4 Development of the PCS indicator over time for various countries 129
7.A.1 Estimates of the translog cost function for Germany 134
7.A.2 Marginal cost estimates of loans across countries and over time 136
8.1 Total number of banks by country and by type 145
8.2 Mean values of key variables for various countries 145
8.3 PCS indicator estimates over time and across eight euro-area countries 146
8.4 Availability of four bank interest rates and corresponding market rates with equivalent fixation periods 152
8.5 Summary statistics of four bank interest rates 153
8.6 Summary statistics of three market rates 154
8.7 Summary statistics of four bank rate spreads 155
8.8 Panel unit root tests on model variables applied to all countries 156
8.9 Pedroni co-integration tests on the six long-run bank interest rate models 156
8.10 Effect of competition on the spreads between bank and market lending rates 158
8.11 Estimates of the long-run models for the six bank interest rates 160
8.12 The short-term ECM model of six bank interest rates 162
9.1 HHI concentration indices based on gross premiums 174
9.2 Description of the data on Dutch insurance firms 182
9.3 Estimation results of the translog cost function 184
9.4 Average cost X-efficiency in 1995–2003 187
9.5 Average cost X-efficiency over size classes 187
9.6 Average profit margins of life insurance firms in various countries 188
9.7 Fixed effects estimates of the PCS model for profits 190
9.8 Fixed effects estimates of the model for market shares 193
9.A.1 Estimation results of the cost and profit X-efficiency models for insurance firms 197

Contributors

Jacob A. Bikker is Professor in Banking and Financial Regulation at the Utrecht University School of Economics and Senior Researcher at the Strategy Department, Supervisory Policy Division, De Nederlandsche Bank (DNB). Previously he was Unit Head Research at the European Monetary Institute (the predecessor of the European Central Bank) in Frankfurt am Main. He graduated from the VU University Amsterdam in 1977 and received his PhD in Economics at the VU in 1983. His research interests are on banking, insurance and pensions, financial conglomerates, competition and efficiency, risk management, procyclicality and regulation and the gravity model. He has written two books on competition in the banking industry (*Competition and efficiency in a unified European banking market*, 2004; with J.W.B. Bos, *Bank performance: A theoretical and empirical framework for the analysis of profitability, competition and efficiency*, 2008) and many journal articles in this and other fields (e.g. Bikker, Shaffer, and Spierdijk, 2012, Assessing competition with the Panzar-Rosse model: the role of scale, costs, and equilibrium, *Review of Economics and Statistics*) Email: j.a.bikker@dnb.nl. Personal page: www.dnb.nl/en/onderzoek-2/onderzoekers/overzicht-persoonlijke-paginas/dnb150116.jsp.

Michiel van Leuvensteijn graduated from the VU University Amsterdam in 1991 and received his PhD in Economics at Utrecht University in 2009. Before joining CPB Netherlands Bureau for Economic Policy Analysis in 2000 as Senior Economist, he was affiliated with the Ministry of Social Affairs and Employment in the Netherlands. Since 2006, he has been engaged in research on the nature of competition in EU insurance and banking markets as Expert at the European Central Bank. Currently, he is Senior Policy Advisor at APG, Department Group Strategy and Policy, where he cooperates with the OECD on the topics of long-term investment and pensions. Email: michiel.van.leuvensteijn@apg.nl. Personal page: http://ideas.repec.org/e/pva105.html.

Jan Boone is Professor in Industrial Organization at the Department of Economics, Tilburg University, the Netherlands.

Donald A. Hay is Emeritus Fellow of Jesus College at the University of Oxford, Oxford, Great Britain.

Christoffer Kok is Principal Financial Stability Expert at the Financial Stability Assessment Division at the European Central Bank, Frankfurt am Main, Germany.

Clemens Kool is Professor in Finance and Financial Markets at the Utrecht School of Economics, Utrecht University, the Netherlands.

Guy S. Liu is Professor in Economics and Finance at the Brunel University, Uxbridge, Great Britain.

Adrian van Rixtel is Senior Economist in the Financial Markets Unit of the Monetary and Economic Department, Bank for International Settlements, Basel, Switzerland.

Foreword

This book provides an analysis of performance of banks and insurance firms, expressed in terms of competition and efficiency. Bank performance has for many years been a topic of major interest both in Europe and elsewhere, notably in the US. For good reason: banks play a pivotal role in providing credit to enterprises. Competition and efficiency in the financial sector are therefore important for social welfare since they promote low lending interest rates, high saving rates and low insurance premiums, high quality and innovation, and give both consumers and enterprises ready access to financial resources. Moreover, competition adds to the speed and strength of monetary policy transmission. Competition and efficiency are difficult if not impossible to observe directly, since comparative data on individual banks' output prices (or credit rates) are rare and figures on the cost of individual banking products are generally unavailable. The literature has tried to measure these elusive concepts with many different methods, none of which, however, has been conclusive or unchallenged. Apart from theoretical shortcomings, a practical problem is that different methods yield different estimates. This book provides a welcome extension to this literature by presenting a rather novel measure of competition, not often applied in the financial sector. Furthermore, it offers a collection of empirical results for this new measurement approach. It aims at opening the theoretical literature, which is less accessible to practitioners in the field, by providing empirical studies as well as a survey on performance measurement. This presents evidence to commercial and central bankers, policy makers and supervisors on what we know and do not know about competition in the financial sector. The topic of this book is of interest to academics, bankers and policy makers, but is also important for supervisors and central banks. Supervisors need to be well informed about the financial institutions under their responsibility and about the markets they operate in. Well-functioning banking markets are a prerequisite for sound and solvent banks and contribute to financial stability, one of the major concerns of central banks. For this reason I recommend this book, edited by two authors who have made their marks in these areas. I trust that this book will contribute to the important field of banking performance studies.

Professor Klaas Knot
President of De Nederlandsche Bank

Preface

In the spring of 2013 we started working on this book with the aim of bringing together the array of theory and, particularly, empirical applications of what we call the performance-conduct-structure (PCS) indicator (introduced by Hay and Liu, 1995, 1997; and Boone, 2001, 2008) on banking and insurance. This approach is based on the efficiency hypothesis that, in competitive markets, more efficient banks may gain a larger market share and earn more profit. It is thereby an opponent of the well-known structure-conduct-performance (SCP) model, which inspired us to come up with our name: performance-conduct-structure model.

Bikker and Bos (2008) introduce a general framework to describe a profit maximizing bank and demonstrate how widely used types of competition measurement models can be fitted into this framework. In particular, the framework sets out the assumptions which are implicit in various competition and efficiency measurement approaches. This in part explains the theorctical shortcomings of thc various methods and the great diversity in the empirical outcomes, which cause many debates on all existing approaches. Where measuring competition is difficult, applying various approaches may present more information than single-approach studies. Our motivation is to expand the literature on measurement of competition in the financial sector by applying this new approach, which has a number of important characteristics; it has a strong theoretical basis, is intuitively plausible, requires only a few data series, is easy to use, and – in a panel dataset – allows estimating developments in competition over time.

We are confident that the mixture of theory and empirics we provide, and the broad area of application, make this book valuable for a large target group of readers. Among them are (i) academics worldwide in the field of competition, but particularly focused on competition in the financial sector and related areas; (ii) government and central bank experts, worldwide, including from ministries of finance, national and international competition agencies, central banks, financial supervisors and stability agencies; and (iii) financial and non-financial institutions and their consultants world-wide, such as banks, insurance firms, and mutual funds, but also all other firms. Finally, our book is also a sound recipe for students taking banking and finance courses. Acquiring textbook knowledge about bank competition, scale economies and the like is a first step in understanding the trade-off between competition and financial stability and its implications for the transmission of monetary policy. All chapters are stand-alone analyses, which can be read in isolation although they fit into a larger set of interrelated papers.

We owe a debt of gratitude to the *Journal of Applied Business and Economics* and *Applied Economics* (three articles), for their permission to base chapters of this book on articles these journals have published. Also, we would like to thank our co-authors for articles that have left their footprint on this book, in chronological order: Donald Hay (University of Oxford) and Guy Liu (Brunel University), Jan Boone (Tilburg University), Clemens Kool (Utrecht University), Christoffer Kok (European Central Bank) and Adrian van Rixtel (Bank of International Settlements). Further, we thank De Nederlandsche Bank and Utrecht University for giving us the opportunity to prepare this book, to De Nederlandsche Bank for the use of Bankscope and Isis (during the research periods), and to Jack Bekooij for outstanding statistical assistance. We thank David Genesove and Wallace P. Mullin for generously providing their data on the American sugar industry and Katrina L. Stierholz of the Federal Reserve Bank of St. Louis for her perseverance in collecting data on the American sugar industry 1890–1914. We are appreciative of Anke de Boer and René Kurpershoek for helping us with their excellent language and editorial skills. Furthermore, we are grateful for all comments from colleagues, conference participants and (unknown) referees. Of course, all remaining errors are ours. All views in this book are personal and do not necessary reflect the views of APG, DNB, BIS, or ECB.

Jacob A. Bikker and Michiel van Leuvensteijn
19 February 2014

References

Bikker, J.A. and Bos, J.W.B. (2008) *Bank Performance: A theoretical and empirical framework for the analysis of profitability, competition and efficiency*, Routledge International Studies in Money and Banking, Routledge, London and New York.

Boone, J. (2001) Intensity of competition and the incentive to innovate, *International Journal of Industrial Organization* 19, 705–726.

Boone, J. (2008) A new way to measure competition, *Economic Journal* 118, 1245–1261.

Hay, D.A., and Liu, G.S. (1995). The efficiency of firms: what difference does competition make? Economics Department Working Paper, Oxford University.

Hay, D.A., and Liu, G.S. (1997). The efficiency of firms: what difference does competition make? *The Economic Journal* 107, 597–617.

1 Introduction

Jacob A. Bikker and Michiel van Leuvensteijn

The competition and efficiency of financial institutions have been investigated exhaustively in the economic literature, because of their important role in smoothing consumption of households over time and providing capital to enterprises. In principle, competition is expected to (i) enhance efficiency, and thus to lower prices; (ii) stimulate new innovations; and (iii) open up new financial markets. However, the financial crisis of 2007–2008 has also revealed to policymakers worldwide that the relationship between competition and financial stability is of major importance. On the one hand, competition may enhance financial stability by pushing unstable banks out of the market. On the other, competition is regarded as one of the possible drivers of risk-taking behaviour of banks. Competition may encourage banks to take more risks in order to be more profitable. To be able to assess the impact of competition on banks' risk-taking behaviour, a good measure of competition is needed. This book aims to contribute precisely to that.

In the aftermath of the collapse of Lehman Brothers, many banks worldwide have been rescued by their national authorities. Some were supported with capital injections, for instance Bank of America, Citigroup and Morgan Stanley in the US, Royal Bank of Scotland (RBS) in the UK, ING in the Netherlands and IKB in Germany. Others were nationalized, including ABN AMRO in the Netherlands, HypoVereinBank in Germany and Northern Rock and Bradford & Bingley in the UK. Furthermore, government guarantees were used to facilitate the funding of banks (OECD, 2011). These interventions have tilted the playing field and distorted competition among banks. Banks receiving state support can attract savings and deposits against lower interest rates and may grant loans against lower lending rates or become involved in riskier projects (because they have an implicit guarantee), compared with banks without government assistance. Bank bail-outs in the US have led to higher profit margins of the banks after the bail-out of all surviving banks and competitive distortions (Koetter and Noth, 2012). In response to possible competitive distortions, the European Commission has 'punished' banks in the European Union (EU) that needed state support with a view to avoiding competitive disadvantages for banks surviving without support. State aid prevents strong banks from being able to acquire a large market share, which they would have been able to acquire in the absence of state support. Punitive measures include requirements to split up banks and financial conglomerates (as in the case of ING) and prohibition of aggressive price setting for banks with state support. Although conducive to competition in the long run, the latter measure may impair competition in the short run. Furthermore, the current crisis has shown that large banks are more likely to be rescued than small banks. This implicit state guarantee may provide large banks with an incentive to take on more risk than otherwise and compared with smaller banks. As a response to this 'too big to fail' moral hazard problem, the EU has developed a bail-in policy, shifting the possible burden of bank defaults not only to the bank's shareholders but also to junior debt holders and large deposit holders (and maybe even to senior debt holders). Finally, during the crisis we have also seen that banks reduced their foreign activities in favour of serving their domestic market. As a consequence, cross-border competition has often run dry. Now the immediate crisis is over and the banking sector is restabilizing, it is time to reconsider the trade-off between financial stability and competition. In a depressed economy, competition in the banking sector is crucial as an engine for accelerating economic growth. All in all, the crisis and its aftermath have shown that the need to measure banking competition, as a basis of anti-trust policy, is larger than ever.

It is difficult, if not impossible, to observe competition and efficiency of banks and other financial institutions directly, since precise information on both input and output is rare and public data on the costs of *separate* bank and insurance products are unavailable. This impairs the calculation of price-cost margins of separate products. The literature has tried to measure competition by means of many different methods, none of which, however, has been entirely conclusive or unchallenged. One stream of literature focuses on the structure of the market, particularly at the level of market concentration; examples are the so-termed Hirschman–Herfindahl index (HHI), the market share of the five largest banks (C_5), and the structure-cost-performance (SCP) model. A second strand of literature estimates competition by focusing on market conduct. Examples of these approaches include the Cournot model, as used in the new empirical industrial organization (NEIO) measurements, the elasticity-adjusted Lerner index, the H-statistic of Panzar and Rosse, regarding the pass-through behaviour of input price increases to revenues, and the conjectural variation parameter λ of the Bresnahan or Lau model, which describes responsiveness on reactions of rival firms.

Apart from the many theoretical shortcomings of competition measures as discussed in the literature, a practical problem is that different methods yield diverging estimates. Evaluating a broad field of research, Bikker and Bos (2008) introduce a general framework to describe a profit-maximizing bank and demonstrate how widely-used types of competition measurement models as listed above can be fitted into this framework. In particular, the framework sets out the assumptions which are implicit in various competition and efficiency measurement approaches. More precisely, the Bikker and Bos model indicates three factors determining competition: market share, price elasticity of demand and conjectural variation. Many approaches contain a partial analysis and focus on a single factor only, or on a combination of two factors. This in part explains the theoretical shortcomings of the various methods and the great diversity in the empirical outcomes. The PCS framework adds a new element to this theoretical analysis by considering how differences in efficiency across banks have impact on either market shares or profits, or both. The stronger this impact is, the heavier is the competition in the respective market. Furthermore, it may introduce dynamics over time; changes in market shares may improve scale economies, so that further market share gains are possible. In order to take endogeneity into account, we need to estimate with instrumental variables.

The structure of this book is as follows. Chapter 2 discusses why competition in the financial sector is of crucial importance and sets out the major structural problems undermining competition on financial markets. It also addresses the ambiguous relationship between competition and financial stability. Chapters 3 and 4 present the seminal introductions of the PCS indicator by Hay and Liu (1995) and Boone (2004), respectively. The foundations for this indicator were laid by Hay and Liu, who provide both its theoretical underpinning under Cournot oligopoly and its first application. They focus on the relationship between efficiency and performance as an indicator of the level of competition, where performance is either profitability or gaining a larger market share. Boone (2004) shows theoretically that the impact of efficiency on profits is a robust measure of competition, using a fairly general model that include the possibilities that firms play Bertrand or Cournot competition. He calls the PCS measure the relative profit differences (RPD) and shows that under the conditions of homogenous goods and equal profits for firms that are equally efficient, the RPD measures competition correctly and does not suffer from the deficiencies of the (elasticity-adjusted) Lerner index, or price-cost margin (PCM). When competition increases, production reallocation may be expected from less efficient banks to more efficient banks, so that the average PCM may rise (Boone et al., 2007). Boone emphasizes the importance of profit elasticity with regard to marginal costs and does not investigate the impact of efficiency on market shares. At the same time, his models provide a theoretical basis for the relationship between market shares and efficiency (as also shown in Chapters 7 and 8). However, using market shares instead of profits may make the indicator theoretically less robust, because there is no relationship when efficiency gains are not translated into lower output prices, in which case market shares remain unchanged, but only in higher profits. Until early 2012, we referred in our papers to the PCS indicator as the Boone indicator, being unaware of the founding work of Hay and Liu (1995, 1997). In this book we introduce a new, more neutral name, reflecting that this approach is based on the efficiency hypothesis; in competitive markets, more efficient banks are expected to gain a larger market share and earn more profit. It is thereby an opposite view to the well-known structure-conduct-performance (SCP) model, which inspired us to come up with our name: the performance-conduct-structure (PCS) indicator.

Many different approaches to measure competition provide disappointingly divergent outcomes. Chapter 5 applies the many approaches from the literature, including the PCS indicator, to one specific dataset and searches for an explanation of the diversity in the results, which cannot be attributed to different datasets. Varying approaches appear to focus on different aspects of competition. Correlations between different approaches are fairly low (which is disappointing), but where they are significant, they all have the correct sign (which is encouraging). These proxies of competition also function quite well, that is, in line with expectations, as explanatory variables; apparently they make sense (which is encouraging too). This chapter develops an index of competition which appears to function better than the underlying components.

Chapter 6 provides an empirical underpinning to the PCS indicator, particularly examining whether this indicator is able to distinguish differences between regimes of competition over time with respect to the American Sugar Refining Company (ASRC). This analysis is based on testimonies at the Congressional hearing on the American sugar industry and data on the ASRC during the period 1890–1914. These old data were used because there was no regulation which hampered competition, ASRC's marginal costs were known and different regimes of competitions can be verified on the basis of testimonies given during the Congressional hearings. This chapter shows that the PCS indicator can indeed properly identify different regimes of competition, like cartels and price wars, at least in the sugar industry case in that period. Furthermore, in this case, the PCS indicator works equally as well as the elasticity-adjusted Lerner index in identifying the different regimes of competition.

Chapters 7 and 8 present empirical studies on the measurement of banking competition in the major economies. In the euro area, banks are the main suppliers of external funds for companies, particularly small and medium-sized enterprises and, hence, play a more important role in this sense than capital markets. For consumers, the mortgage markets are crucial. Chapter 7 concentrates on the measurement of competition in the loan markets of the euro area and the US, the UK and Japan. Our findings indicate that in the period 1994–2004 the US had the most competitive loan market, whereas overall loan markets in Germany and Spain were among the most competitive in the EU. The Netherlands occupied an intermediate position, whereas in Italy competition declined significantly over time. The French, Japanese and UK loan markets were generally less competitive. Chapter 8 uses these results to investigate the role of competition in the functioning of financial markets from a monetary policy perspective across eight euro area countries. The European Central Bank (ECB) has defined an objective of price stability and sets its policy rate to achieve this aim. The effectiveness of the monetary policy instruments in reaching the ECB's objective relies on the degree to which policy rate changes are translated into bank lending rates. We investigate four loan markets and two deposit markets separately. The analysis shows that the strength of monetary transmission depends significantly on the level of competition in loan product markets, particularly mortgage loans, consumer loans and short-term loans to enterprises. Furthermore, banks act as price makers in the deposit market and as price takers in the loan market. Stronger competition causes both lower bank interest rates and a stronger pass-through of market rate changes into bank rates.

Life insurance companies offer, among other things, insurance against old age by providing an annuity, and improve the possibilities to save throughout the life cycle. Chapter 9 investigates the competition in this market, by estimating scale economies, X-efficiency (indication of management shortcomings) and the PCS indicator. In general, given that information on profits is not always available, it is important for the PCS indicator method to have a reliable alternative in 'market shares'. Both scale economies and X-inefficiencies are high, suggesting limited competition; indeed, stronger competition would force insurers to become more cost efficient. We show for the PCS indicator that analyses based on profits and analyses based on market shares produce comparable outcomes. Both point to rather limited competition on the life insurance market, compared with PCS values for other sectors. We use marginal cost derived from estimated translog cost models. A simpler alternative is the use of average costs (defined as operational cost divided by premiums), but it is less accurate because average costs incorrectly include fixed costs. We observe that the marginal cost and average cost results have a fairly similar pattern. Marginal costs refer to inefficiency caused by either economies of scale or X-inefficiencies (or managerial inability). In this chapter, we also derive marginal costs adjusted for scale economies to see the impact of pure X-inefficiencies on market shares. The results show that each type of inefficiency contributes separately to the dynamics in the life insurance market shares and that variation in X-inefficiency is the main source of variation in the PCS indicator over time.

In addition to the chapters in this book, we have recently applied the PCS model to the Chinese loan markets (Xu et al., 2013), an analysis of the effects of securitization on the relationship between competition and bank risk (Altunbas et al., 2013), life insurance (Bikker, 2012) and non-life insurance (Bikker and Popescu, 2014). Although these papers are not yet published in edited journals, they are valuable for further reading. Furthermore, a line of publications is emerging in which the PCS indicator is applied to regional loan markets in the US (Schaeck and Cihák, 2010), the dissolution of cartels (Schiers and Schmidt-Ehmcke, 2011) and the relationship between banking market competition and risk-taking in Latin America (Tabak et al. 2012).

Our experience with the PCS as reflected in this book and in the papers mentioned yields the following lists of strong and weak features.

Favourable characteristics of the PCS indicator include:

- The PCS method has a strong theoretical foundation and its economic rationale is intuitive and plausible (Chapters 3 and 4).
- The PCS indicator requires relatively moderate amounts of data, i.e. time series or cross-sections of either market shares or profits and marginal cost. Marginal costs must be estimated by means of e.g. a translog cost model, but the simple alternative of average cost also functions well (Chapter 9, Bikker and Popescu, 2014).
- The estimation approach is simple: the method of instrumental variables (IV), expanded – in case of panel datasets – with fixed effects.

- In a panel dataset, the PCS allows annual estimates of competitive pressure.
- The PCS approach has the advantage of being able to measure competition on a more disaggregated level (for instance of bank market segments, such as the various loan and deposit markets), whereas many well-known measures of competition, such as the Panzar–Rosse method, consider only the entire banking market, due to lack of data (Chapters 7 and 8).

Critical remarks with respect to the PCS approach include:

- Although the theoretical foundation is strong, it is – as for all approaches – based on certain assumptions (Chapters 3 and 4).
- Efficient banks may choose to translate lower costs either into higher profits (which would qualify the profit model) or into lower output prices in order to gain market shares (which would qualify the market share model). We assume that the behaviour of banks is in between these two extremes, in that they generally pass on at least part of their efficiency gains to their clients (which would qualify both models). More specifically, we assume that the passing-on behaviour does not diverge too strongly across the banks.
- The PCS approach measures one major feature of competition (impact of efficiency, e.g. marginal costs, on market shares or profits) but does not incorporate all multidimensional aspects of it. It has this characteristic in common with all other proxies of competition and model-based measures. At any rate, the PCS approach adds significantly to the existing stock of approaches. As with forecasts, improvement may be achieved by combining the various measurement systems (Chapter 5).
- The PCS indicator ignores differences in terms of bank product quality and design as well as attractiveness of innovations. We assume that banks are eventually forced to provide quality levels that are more or less similar. By the same token, we presume that banks cannot but follow the innovations of their peers.

All in all, the PCS complements other competition indicators and provides additional information on the conduct of firms by taking into account the production reallocation effect within the market due to competition.

References

Altunbas, Y., M. van Leuvensteijn and D. Marques-Ibanez (2013) Competition and bank risk: the role of securitization and bank capital, Working Papers 13005, Bangor Business School, Prifysgol Bangor University, Wales.

Bikker, J.A. (2012) Performance of the life insurance industry under pressure: efficiency, competition and consolidation, DNB Working Paper No. 357, De Nederlandsche Bank, Amsterdam.

Bikker, J.A. and J.W.B. Bos (2008) *Bank performance: a theoretical and empirical framework for the analysis of profitability, competition and efficiency*, Routledge International Studies in Money and Banking, Routledge, London and New York.

Bikker, J.A., and A. Popescu (2014) Efficiency and competition in the Dutch non-life insurance industry: effects of the 2006 health care reform, DNB Working Paper, De Nederlandsche Bank, Amsterdam (forthcoming).

Boone, J. (2004) A new way to measure competition, TILEC Discussion paper 2004-004.

Boone, J., J.C. van Ours and H. van der Wiel (2007) How (not) to measure competition, TILEC Discussion Paper No. 2007-014.

Hay, D.A., and G.S. Liu (1995) The efficiency of firms: what difference does competition make? Economics Department Working Paper, Oxford University, Oxford.

Hay, D.A., and G.S. Liu (1997) The efficiency of firms: what difference does competition make? *The Economic Journal* 107, 597–617.

Koetter, M. and F. Noth (2012) Competitive distortions of bank bailouts, Working paper Frankfurt School of Finance and Management, Frankfurt am Main, http://papers.ssrn.com/sol3/papers.cfm?abstract_id=2190902.

OECD (2011) *Competition and Financial Stability*, OECD Publishing, Paris, http://www.oecd.org/daf/fin/financial-markets/48501035.pdf.

Schaeck, K. and M. Cihák (2010) Competition, efficiency, and soundness in banking: an industrial organization perspective. Discussion Paper 2010-68S, Center for Economic Research, Tilburg University, Tilburg.

Schiers, A. and J. Schmidt-Ehmcke (2011) Is the Boone-indicator applicable? Evidence from a combined data set of German manufacturing enterprises, *Jahrbücher für Nationalökonomie und Statistik* 231 (3), 336–357.

Tabak, B., D.M. Fazio and D.O. Cajueiro (2012) The relationship between banking market competition and risk-taking: do size and capitalization matter? *Journal of Banking & Finance* 36, 3366–3381.

Xu, B., A. van Rixtel and M. van Leuvensteijn (2013) Measuring bank competition in China: a comparison of new versus conventional approaches applied to loan markets, BIS Working Papers 422, Bank for International Settlements, Basel.

2 Potential obstacles for competition in the financial sector

Jacob A. Bikker and Michiel van Leuvensteijn

This chapter discusses structural problems that undermine competition on financial markets, using a diagnostic framework which considers demand and supply side characteristics. Potential impediments to competition are concentration, entry barriers, lack of transparency, product complexity, switching and search costs, financial illiteracy, lack of consumer power and weak intermediaries. In response to such financial market failures, we suggest a number of possible policy measures. Further, the ambiguous relationship between competition and financial stability is addressed.

2.1. Introduction

This chapter discusses structural characteristics of the financial markets, explains why competition in the financial sector is important and describes potential obstacles that may hinder competition. First, in line with Claessens (2009), we discuss the determinants of competition. Then, following CPB (2003), we present an overview of the structural features of financial markets which may impair competition, focusing especially on underlying microeconomic market failures. We use a diagnostic framework to investigate the typical structure of the financial sector, distinguishing between supply and demand characteristics. Weaknesses on the supply side are formal and informal entry barriers (e.g. large-scale economies and brand names), heterogeneity and complexity of bank products, the sometimes limited numbers of suppliers, and cross-ownership and bank productions' network properties. Possible obstacles on the demand side are high search and switching costs, the opaque nature of pricing and quality of financial products, and financial illiteracy of consumers. A further problem is the weakly functioning markets of intermediaries. Given the potential weaknesses of the financial market structure, we suggest a number of possible policy reactions to these market failures.

We also describe the complex relationship between bank competition and financial stability. On the one hand, more market power (or less competition) may result in more financial stability when higher banking profits lead to larger capital buffers. This negative impact of competition on financial stability also occurs when heavier competition ends up in more risk taking behaviour by banks. On the other hand, more competition may also result in more instead of less financial stability, when fragile banks are pushed out of the market. This view is endorsed by the observation that fewer banking crises happen in more competitive banking markets.

The setup of this chapter is as follows. Section 2.2 describes structural problems of competition on financial markets, while Section 2.3 discusses possible policy reactions to financial market failures. Section 2.4 elaborates on the relationship between competition and financial stability.

2.2. Structural problems of competition on financial markets

We apply the general diagnostic framework developed in CPB (2003) to assess whether financial markets harbour impediments to competition. As a starting point, CPB (2003) uses the structure-conduct-performance (SCP) paradigm, which states that the structure of the financial market determines the conduct of its participants and affects its performance in terms of social efficiency. 'Structure of the financial market' means the concentration in supply and demand, the degree of product differentiation and market entry barriers. These are phenomena which are quite stable over time and affect the conduct of market participants. 'Conduct' refers to the strategic behaviour of firms in terms of investment and price behaviour, degree of innovation, advertisement, collusion, etc. Finally, 'performance' refers to the efficiency and profitability of firms. This relates to price margin, production and allocation efficiency, product quality, etc. The advantage of the SCP paradigm is that it provides a very clear analytical framework.

The more structural supply side elements promote the occurrence of supernormal profits during a substantial period of time, in comparison to more competitive market structures. 'Supernormal' refers to profits that exceed a market-conforming rate of risk-adjusted return on capital, while 'substantial period of time' typically reflects several years. We apply this framework to the financial markets. Note that structure itself does not impair competition. It is the conduct of financial institutions and intermediaries that determines competitive behaviour. But structure may create the temptation which incites exploitation of market power.

Coordinated and unilateral demand-side factors also affect the intensity of competition. The elasticity of demand determines how attractive it is for a firm to unilaterally change its prices. High search and switching costs contribute to low firm-level demand elasticity. Stable, predictable demand makes it easier for firms to collude in order to keep prices high, as in that case breaking explicit or tacit collusion of keeping prices high by one or more firms will be detected more easily than when demand fluctuates. These demand and supply side elements that determine imperfect competition are summarized in Table 2.1.

2.2.1. Supply side factors

The diagnostic framework contains a list of coordinated and unilateral factors that increase the probability of a tight oligopoly, see Table 2.1. Coordinated

Table 2.1 Determinants of imperfect competition on financial markets

	Coordinated factors	*Unilateral factors*
Supply side factors		
– Essential	Few financial institutions	Few financial institutions
	High entry and exit barriers	High entry barriers
	Frequent interaction	Heterogeneous products
– Important	Transparency	Structural links
	Symmetry	Adverse selection
Demand side factors		
	Low firm-level elasticity of demand (incl. switching costs and lock-in effects)	Ditto
	Stable demand	Imperfect financial advice

factors refer to explicit or tacit collusion, while unilateral factors refer to actions undertaken by individual financial institutions without any form of coordination with other financial institutions.

High concentration is conducive to the realization of supernormal profits, according to the traditional economic theory. A more recent and dynamic view considers that high concentration may also be the result of heavy competition forcing the market to consolidate and that it is therefore difficult to draw clear conclusions from concentration in the financial industry.

High entry barriers have long been recognized as an obstacle to competition. Although many formal barriers in financial markets have been removed over time in many countries, informal entry barriers are quite common. The existence of large-scale economies in many financial industries, due to relatively large fixed costs, is a hindrance for new entries. Due to developments in informational technologies, increases in regulatory, accounting and legal requirements (e.g. IFRS, Basel III, Solvency II), the high costs of developing new products and so on, the optimal size of financial institutions is ever increasing (e.g. Bikker and Gorter, 2011). The importance of brand names, supporting confidence in the respective financial institutions, has a similar result. For banks, a large scale is also necessary for the supply of certain specific services to large, international firms, such as merger and take-over advice, equity and bond issuance management, and the construction of complex investment products.

Frequent interaction, transparency (with respect to competitors) and *symmetry* (in terms of equal cost structures) are beneficial to a tight oligopoly, since they make it easier for financial institutions to coordinate their actions and to detect and punish deviations from the explicitly or tacitly pre-agreed behaviour. Although frequent interaction is common and sometimes unavoidable (e.g. in the case of efficient payment systems), cost structures of financial markets are quite opaque.

Heterogeneous products make it easier for financial institutions to raise prices independently of competitors, as clients are less likely to choose, or switch to, other financial institutions in response to price differences. Here we observe another severe weakness of financial markets. Most financial products are quite complicated in practice and carry high switching costs. Payment accounts easily become more complex owing to varying tariff structures and services, while savings and deposits accounts may carry diverging withdrawal conditions. Mortgage loans are complicated by redemption rules and the frequency and timing of interest payments. The sophistication of mortgages increases when they are combined with life insurance policies or where redemption is based on investment portfolios. Life insurance, pension and mutual investment products are generally far more complicated than basic banking products. Bank services for wholesale clients usually show an even higher level of sophistication, although, of course, those clients are also more professional. Financial institutions offer a wide range of heterogeneous products, most probably in response to market demands, but in addition, they may well have purposely raised product complexity to be able to exploit monopolistic competition. An incentive to offer more transparent products seems absent. This potential weakness of financial markets is aggravated by the behaviour of the clients of financial institutions, as discussed below.

Structural links between financial institutions such as cross-ownership would give them a stake in each other's performance, thus softening competition. Such links between financial institutions are quite common in European countries, but less so in the US. Information about risks (and the lack of it) plays a crucial role in markets for financial products. Asymmetric information plays a major role in lending. Particularly in lending to small and medium-sized enterprises (SMEs), some local banks are far better informed than others due to long-lasting and close relationships with clients and the benefit of local presence. This severely limits banking competition, but may have gains in terms of access to external financing.[1] In the case of life insurance, adverse selection may play a role when consumers have more information regarding their life expectancy than insurance companies. Adverse selection may lead to higher price-cost margins.

Its *network property* makes the payment market special. Banks need to cooperate in developing technical standards for automatic processing, which adds substantially to market efficiency. Of course, competition may be limited under such an arrangement, due to the trade-off against efficiency, though not absent (NMa, 2006). This is also observed in other financial markets with network properties. Drawbacks of standardization may be increase of entry barriers, risks of illegitimate coordination and a disincentive for innovation.

All in all, we observe a number of supply conditions that may contribute to explicit or tacit collusion and make oligopoly on financial markets more likely than perfect competition. Such dubious conditions are potential market distortions and regulation may be needed to reduce their disruption of competition.

2.2.2. Demand side factors[2]

Demand side factors also affect the intensity of competition (see Table 2.1). As above, we distinguish coordinated and unilateral factors. The elasticity of residual demand determines how attractive it is for a firm to change its prices unilaterally. The firm may relinquish a price agreement, if only demand responds sufficiently strongly to price changes. In the absence of coordination among financial institutions, low elasticity of demand will also help to keep prices above competitive levels, as in that case the loss of sales caused by a price increase will be small. High search and switching costs contribute to low firm-level demand elasticity. Stable, predictable demand makes it easier for financial institutions to collude in order to keep prices high, since cheating by one or more of them will be easier to detect than in the case of volatile demand.

The elasticity of residual demand for financial services is limited, in practice, as substitutes are rare. Bank savings, investment funds and life insurance policies (such as annuities) are, in principle, substitutes for each other, but only in a limited way since their characteristics differ substantially in terms of risk, liquidity and tax treatment. For other financial services, substitutes are absent. Foreign competition may help to alleviate this problem. However, in practice, cross-border competition is often limited, particularly since consumers seldom seek services of foreign banks. Entry by foreign banks may help but in practice remains limited in many markets and segments, probably due to differences in legal, regulatory and institutional structures, consumer preferences, national habits, etc.

High switching costs are typical for many financial products such as mortgage loans, life insurance policies and pension arrangements, since contracts are often of a long-term nature and early termination of contracts involves costs. These high switching costs are prohibitive, so consumers are locked in. Incidentally, this also holds for financial institutions. Switching costs are also high for payment accounts (in terms of the effort required), where automatic payment and collection services are linked to a unique account number. Here, however, the switching costs are not prohibitively high.

Search costs for financial products are high as these products are often complicated or seen as such. The financial market is opaque in the sense that prices and quality are often difficult to observe or assess. Search costs could be alleviated if searching could be entrusted to specialist agents. However, the drawback to this extra link in the supply chain is that is goes with additional costs. Advice would help consumers (and producers) to avoid errors in their product and brand choice. Moreover, it would make the market more competitive by increasing the elasticity of demand. Thus, it is very desirable to have a well-functioning market for financial advice. However, financial advice markets often function improperly. In particular, under less efficient incentive structures in these markets (notably commissions) and with inexperienced consumers, insurance agents may give advice that is not in the consumers' best interest.[3]

Consumer power weakens as a market becomes less transparent. Strong brand names are indicators of non-transparency, as confidence in a well-known brand may replace price comparisons or personal judgement.[4] The power of consumers also depends on their financial literacy. On average, financial literacy is rather low, also among the highly educated. This has been documented particularly for pension services (Van Rooij et al., 2007). Financial illiteracy increases the dependency of consumers on the weak intermediation sector. Another indicator is the degree to which buyers organize themselves, for instance to be informed and to reduce the opaque nature of the market. Consumer organizations, Internet sites and financial magazines compare prices and inform consumers continuously on financial product conditions and prices to enable them to make comparisons and well-founded choices. Although consumer and commercial organizations reduce market opacity, they are unable to overcome all problems because products are inherently complicated and come with a wide range of different properties. Besides, many consumers are not able or not willing to make the effort to search for the best offer. A third indicator is the degree to which consumers can take out financial products collectively. Collective contracts are usually based on thorough comparisons of conditions and prices by experts, are often negotiated via the employer and contribute substantially to consumer power.[5] There are examples in the US of how 401(k) plans offered by large employers carry lower costs. Of course, many people are unable to add to their consumer power this way; for banking products in particular, such collective contracts are rare.

Abundant examples exist of poorly functioning consumer markets. We name a few current examples: interest rates on simple saving accounts are far below market rates. Retail saving accounts go with costs that explain at least part of the difference with the capital market rate, but consumers' loyalty, ignorance or apathy, and banks' smart strategies[6] also play a role. For the same reasons, large spreads exist in prices of annuities and life insurances[7] and cost margins (of around 40 per cent) in life insurance types of saving products are high (see Bikker, 2012). Similarly, regarding failing international competition, we observe large differences in interest rates on deposits across countries, annual costs of payment accounts at one point in time across the EU varying from €34 to €252 (Cap Gemini, 2005), and so on.

Most problems faced by consumers are also affecting SMEs. However, their position may be even more unfavourable, as they usually depend on a few local banks only, due to information asymmetries. Incidentally, dependency on local banks can also have benefits.[8] Boot (2007) recommends introducing legislation and regulations to support the existence of credit registers with fine-grained information about SME clients to make them more attractive to a potential new bank. The position of wholesale firms is more difficult to assess. Of course, for traditional banking products, they are well equipped to assess the prices and quality of banking services. However, we observe a continuous shift over time from traditional intermediation to new, more sophisticated and complex products whose prices and quality are more difficult to assess. Examples are merger and take-over services, equity and bond issuance management, and the construction of complex investment products such as SPVs and SIVs. Furthermore, the price and quality of many wholesale banking services are subject to tailor-made contracts and therefore less public. Consequently, price competition in these new banking service markets is presumably more limited than in traditional intermediation.

Thus on the supply side, we observe a certain degree of supplier power, due in particular to the existence of informal entry barriers and strong product differentiation, where in the case of limited numbers of suppliers the risk of explicit or tacit collusion may increase. On the demand side we find factors such as high search and switching costs, few substitution possibilities, limited consumer power due to the opaque nature of financial products and financial illiteracy of consumers. Furthermore, the booming markets of complex, tailor-made wholesale banking services are also opaque.

All in all, we observe a number of conditions that make some kind of oligopoly or monopolistic competition on financial markets more likely than perfect competition. It should be kept in mind that, given existing trade-offs with stability, impediments to perfect competition may simply result from innovations and access to financial services. Regulation by competition authorities may be needed to improve these conditions and reduce their possible adverse effects on competition, thereby aiming at heavier competition, not necessarily at perfect competition.

To conclude, we are aware that the SCP paradigm taken as a starting point in the CPB general diagnostic framework of this section also has its shortcomings. The framework is static and does not take account of the feedback loop between market power and market structure. For instance, in the SCP paradigm, the structure of markets is presumed to be given exogenously. This may be so in the short term, but in the long term the structure of the market concentration is determined by the market power of banks and insurance companies and thus is endogenous. Furthermore, in markets where innovation plays a key role in the survival of firms, high concentration and market power may be necessary attributes to acquire the rents of the innovation. Also, in the SCP paradigm the current degree of entry or exit is relevant for competition and the threat of entry plays a limited role. The degree of contestability of markets is relevant but ignored in the SCP paradigm (Baumol et al., 1982). Thus, in principle, even a single-firm market may show competitive behaviour. While contestability can be an important determinant of the behaviour of financial market participants, other issues such as information asymmetries, investment in relationships, the role of technology and networks can matter as well in determining the effective degree of competition (see Bikker and Spierdijk, 2010).

2.3. Possible policy reactions to financial market failures

The analysis above points to many factors contributing to financial market failures. Claessens (2009) points to entry and exit barriers as the major impediments to competition. In that spirit, Boot (2007) advises regulators and governments to ensure that costs of minimum capital requirements, regulatory reporting, and essential memberships (such as payment systems, credit bureaus and banking associations) are proportionate to the size of new institutions. Here, we briefly discuss some possibilities to remove other obstacles to competition.

Competition is generally seen as crucial in order to obtain low prices, high quality, efficiency, innovation, easy access for all potential clients, effective monetary policy,[9] financial stability, and so on. Nevertheless, there may be submarkets where, given the underlying market conditions, strong (let alone full) competition cannot produce welfare gains. An example is the market for pensions. The Netherlands has an extensive capital-based collective pension system, which is mandatory for nearly all employees. The employer and the labour unions select a company-specific or industry-wide pension fund,[10] an insurer or a so-termed general pension institution to administer the agreed pension scheme. There is a certain degree of competition as employers can choose from several pension funds and insurers, but competition is limited in the sense that individual employees have no choice at all. The alternative is a free market for pension provisions, where we need to distinguish between freedom with respect to savings (free versus mandatory) and freedom with respect to the way the savings are managed (fund's choice versus employee's own choice). In countries where mandatory savings are likely to be absent, as in the UK and the US, consumers frequently appear unable to save adequately for their old age. Chile and the Netherlands have some mandatory savings components, but management in Chile takes place on a competitive, individual basis, whereas in the Netherlands it is collective. However, 'commercial' pension funds and insurers are compelled to incur high costs to acquire clients and face the possibility of adverse selection and expenses to reduce its unfavourable effects. In addition, insurers need to make a profit.[11] In the Netherlands, the operational costs of free-market voluntary pension provisions for individuals, the only tax-friendly option open to the self-employed, are estimated to be seven times those of compulsory employee pension funds (Bikker and De Dreu, 2007).[12] The operational costs of Dutch pension funds are among the lowest worldwide (Bikker and De Dreu, 2009). Most Dutch employers appear to be quite happy about not having to choose (Van Rooij et al., 2007). Of course, this is a very specific situation, where many issues may raise further discussion. More generally, in the presence of information asymmetries, agency issues and so forth, competition is likely to be imperfect and may lead to perverse results. Hence, for some particular financial submarkets, we should not aim at competition but only at efficiency.

Using our diagnostic framework, we observed that financial illiteracy is one of the major causes of weak consumer power. Providing financial education may relieve the problem and enhance competition. A range of academic articles evaluate the results and indicate what kind of programmes are effective (e.g. Bernheim and Garrett, 1996; Braunstein and Welch, 2002; Mooslechner et al., 2003; Lusardi, 2004; Lusardi and Mitchell, 2011). Programmes should particularly focus on knowledge and information, sense of urgency and self-confidence. It seems likely that only a part of the population is susceptible to such efforts. Further development of price comparison websites may also be very helpful but, again, such sites only serve part of the population, albeit a gradually increasing part.[13]

Heterogeneity is another structural weakness that can be addressed. A possible step forward is to promote more homogeneous or standardized products. A good example was set by the FSA in the UK, which a number of years ago provided a detailed definition of a normalized private pension plan. It also launched and maintains a website listing prices of the financial institutions offering such prescribed pension products. These products are included only after a thorough examination to check whether they meet the standards. This approach helps to solve the heterogeneity problem and to avoid the exploitation of semi-monopolistic power. Similarly, the Netherlands introduced a defined (thus standardized) basic health insurance package, which is a precondition for government support (NMa, 2006).[14] This standardized product enables competition, also where health insurance policies are complicated and many consumers are poorly informed or unwilling to investigate the various offers.

Payment systems typically face serious network property problems. National cooperation has significantly increased efficiency, but at the cost of impairing competition. In the EU, the Single European Payment Area (SEPA) framework aims at introducing several competing, cross-border payment systems, which may benefit from the large, euro area-wide scale (NMa, 2006; Boot, 2007). Two new SEPA instruments were already introduced in 2008 (SEPA credit transfer) and 2009 (SEPA direct debit). EU Regulation No 260/2012 establishes the technical and business requirements for credit transfers and direct debits in euro. The deadline for implementation of SEPA in the euro area is 1 August 2014; non-euro area Member States have until 31 October 2016. As of these dates, the existing national euro credit transfer and direct debit schemes will be replaced. The problem of high costs involved in switching payment accounts to other banks can be solved by allowing bank clients to transfer their unique payment account number, including the linked automatic payment and collection services, to any other bank. Of course, this would entail large IT investments for banks.

Price competition on new tailor-made and complex wholesale banking services is likely to be more limited than in traditional intermediation. The prices and quality of such services are much more opaque than those of standardized consumer services. This problem creates a major challenge for, among others, competition authorities, particularly as these new products increasingly dominate the income of – especially large – banks.

In the banking market, the regulatory regime of the Basel Committee on Banking Supervision (Basel I, II and III) aims at creating an international level playing field by establishing minimum capital requirements, which are identical for internationally operating banks across all joining countries, enabling fair cross-border competition. Similarly, international supervisory regimes for the insurance industries and pension funds would greatly encourage cross-border competition in those sectors. In the EU, Solvency II will be introduced for insurance firms, still leaving room for a worldwide regime. Furthermore, functionally equivalent products should be governed by similar regulations that are as similar as possible, in order to enhance competition between banks and other financial institutions.[15]

In many consumer markets, intermediary agencies play an important role in providing support to financially illiterate clients. To avoid conflicts of interest such agencies need to be independent from financial institutions and their fee structure needs to be transparent to their clients. Such independence is best served by a fixed hourly rate to be paid by the client. In practice, however, consumers are generally less rational and dislike paying for such independent advice. They prefer receiving 'free' advice from financial institutions or intermediaries where, of course, similar costs are hidden in product prices while the advice may be less in line with their own preferences. Such irrational behaviour hampers disciplinary power on the demand side, which is a sound condition for competition. The Netherlands recently introduced an intermediation model for insurance and mortgage products, where clients directly pay for advice. Gorter (2012) proves that intermediaries linked to financial institutions may still provide less than optimal advice.

Although many financial market failures are difficult to solve, the discussion above explains that there are many – general and specific – possible steps in the right direction, which would help to foster competition on financial markets.

2.4. The relationship between competition and financial stability

Healthy competition may also be important as far as it affects financial stability. For that reason, this section investigates the relationship between competition and financial stability. Banks are opaque financial entities; their health and inherent risks are difficult to foresee. Risks may be underestimated by the markets for years. Banks are special; their impact on the real economy is strong, so that shocks from the financial sector may be amplified and propagated. As a country's financial sector is typically closely interconnected with other parts of the world through interbank lending and capital markets, there is a risk of contagion. A banking crisis in, for instance, the US or Asia will therefore be felt throughout the rest of the world.

Financial stability in other financial institutions like insurance companies and pension funds is generally regarded as less important (e.g. Cummins and Weiss, 2013a, b, 2014; Chen et al., 2013a and b). The key issue here is that bank-run risk is fairly absent. If a Dutch life insurance firm becomes insolvent, consumers are to some extent protected by the so-termed safety net regulation for life insurers.[16] Pension funds also have limited systemic risk, because when their funding ratio drops below 105 per cent, they either raise the contributions or reduce the benefits. Pension funds and insurance companies may create some systemic risk by selling shares at the same time. The potential systemic risk is of a different order than for banks because there is no risk of contagion, or amplifying mechanism due to leveraging (Lemmen, 2003).

Two opposing theories exist in the literature on the relationship between banking competition and financial stability (Beck et al., 2006; Schaeck et al., 2009; Wagner, 2010). The traditional view states that market power may go hand in hand with lower competition and more stability. According to this view, more concentrated markets, which (according to Baumol, Panzar, and Willig, 1982) go hand in hand with lower competition, have more large banks that are able to diversify better and therefore contribute to more stability, hence linking less competition to more stability (Diamond, 1984; Ramakrishnan and Thakor, 1984; Boyd and Prescott, 1986; Williamson, 1986; Allen, 1990). Furthermore, a more concentrated banking system implies a smaller number of banks; such a market reduces the supervisory burden and thus may enhance overall banking system stability (Allen and Gale, 2000).

A second strand of literature states that competition enhances financial stability. Here, reference is made to the fact that crises occur less frequently in competitive banking systems. Beck et al. (2006) find that fewer regulatory restrictions on banking activities and lower barriers to bank entry reduce banking system fragility, because competition pushes the more fragile banks out of the market. Furthermore, their findings show that countries with national institutions that facilitate competition in general have a lower likelihood of suffering a systemic banking crisis. This may indicate that malfunctioning banks leave the market at an early stage, before they can infect other banks. In their seminal paper, Boyd and De Nicoló (2005) point out that the standard argument in the traditional view described above ignores the potential negative impact of banks' market power on their borrowers' behaviour. When banks are able to raise their interest rate on lending, the borrowing firms are forced to get involved in projects with both more risks and higher returns to be able to pay these rates. Hence, low competition and the use of market power may impair stability.

If market power in the loan market results in riskier loan portfolios, supporting the traditional competition-fragility paradigm, the overall risks of banks need not necessarily increase. Banks may enjoy higher franchise value derived from this market power, the owners of the bank have an incentive to protect this franchise value from the higher risk of the loan portfolio and are willing to increase equity capital or take other risk-mitigating measures (Berger, Klapper and Turk-Ariss, 2009). Furthermore, banks in concentrated systems receive implicit subsidies through 'too big' or 'too important to fail' policies that may intensify risk-taking incentives and hence increase banking system fragility (e.g. Mishkin, 1999). Having larger banks in a concentrated banking system could also increase the risk of contagion, resulting in a positive impact of concentration (and thus less competition) on systemic fragility.

Allen et al. (2011) develop a theory where inducements to hold capital can come from the asset side of the balance sheet of banks and which explains why banks hold capital in excess of the regulatory required capital. They show that in perfectly competitive markets, banks may be more inclined to hold more costly capital and monitor more strictly than to raise loan interest rates. Lower interest rates contribute to higher profits for the borrowing firms. Given that monitoring is costly and banks have limited liability, banks are subject to a moral hazard problem in the underlying choice of monitoring effort. One way to create greater incentives for monitoring is the use of more equity capital. This forces banks to internalize the costs of their default, thus ameliorating the limited liability problem banks face due to their extensive reliance on deposit-based financing. A second instrument to improve banks' incentives is embodied in the loan rate. Although monitoring is meant to retrieve the loan, a marginal increase in the loan rate gives banks an extra incentive to monitor in order to receive the higher pay-off if the project succeeds and the loan is repaid. Thus, capital and loan rates are alternative ways to improve banks' monitoring incentives, but entail different costs for different parties because to hold capital implies a direct private cost for the banks, whereas higher loan rates have a negative impact only on borrowing firms in terms of a lower return on investment.

Further, there is literature that focuses on the impact of competition on the banks' charter value and thus on risky behaviour (Herring and Vankundre, 1987; Keeley, 1990; Demsetz et al., 1996; Hellmann et al., 2000). Keeley (1990) tests the hypothesis that fiercer competition impairs bank charter value, reducing the market value of the bank relative to its book value. With valuable charters as assets, banks have an incentive not to risk bankruptcy, since their owners cannot sell the charter once the bank is declared insolvent. A bank whose market value exceeds its book value that is insolvent on a book value basis only still has a valuable charter left. So when its market value falls below the book value due to reduced market power, it has less incentive to avoid default at any price. Keeley's empirical results support this hypothesis. Banks with more market power have a larger market-to-book assets ratio, hold more capital relative to assets and have a lower default risk. The latter is reflected in lower risk premiums in their interest rates on uninsured deposits, that is, not covered by a deposit guarantee system. In other words, if the bank's franchise value increases due to higher market power, its management and shareholders will reduce its risk exposure to preserve that value. Similarly, Hellmann, Murdock, and Stiglitz (2000) argue that for instance the removal of interest ceilings on deposits in the US in the 1980s and the removal of regulation eroded franchise value and encouraged moral hazard behaviour by banks. When the market values of banks fall, they become less risk averse and undertake riskier projects. Jimenez, Lopez, and Saurina (2007) find that more competition is correlated with a higher-risk loan portfolio measured using nonperforming loans in Spain, consistent with the view discussed above.

Finally, Ahn and Breton (2011) show a theoretical model on bank behaviour in which banks start with collecting information from potential borrowers in the loan market before the loan contract is signed. An increase in securitization operates as a signalling device that banks will reduce the collection of information (monitoring) after the loan contract is signed. Thus securitization adversely affects loan market efficiency due to less monitoring afterwards. This reduced cost of monitoring increases profitability in the short term. Securitization also lowers competition for other banks' clients after a loan contract is signed, because banks are not making a profit from exploiting information asymmetries once the relationship is established. Instead they sell off the risk in the second period. Securitization also increases the risk profile of the loan portfolio due to fewer incentives to monitor the loan portfolio.

Using data from Latin America, Tabak et al. (2012) show that an inverted U-shape relationship exists between competition and risk taking. Markets with both very low and very high competition have the lowest levels of risk taking. Banks in markets with low competition do not have incentives to take risk and banks in markets with high competition will pay the high price of being taken over or pushed out of the market when they take too much risk. They also find that concentration in the market leads to fragility and not to stability, in line with the findings of Berger et al. (2009) for the banking sector of thirty developed economies. Banks with higher capital ratios are more cautious, whereas banks with more liquidity are less cautious.

2.5. Conclusions

This chapter started by investigating the financial market's structure. We observe quite a number of potential market failures, on both the supply and the demand side, which may tempt financial institutions to exploit market power. Opaqueness hinders the correct perception of pricing and quality of complex financial services and acts as a major obstacle to fierce competition. As the share of traditional bank intermediation in total banking activities over time declined in favour of more complex and tailor-made non-intermediation services, we expect a reduction of competition over time. Other market failures found are informal entry barriers, strong product differentiation, cross-ownership, bank productions' network properties, high search and switching costs, lack of substitution possibilities, insufficient consumer power, weak-functioning intermediaries and consumers' financial illiteracy. Many of these structural weaknesses that harm competition are not unique for financial markets, but also occur in many service industries.

We provide a number of solutions to make it harder for financial institutions to exploit these market failures, including financial education, standardization of financial products, implementation of the right incentive structures for intermediaries, consumer empowerment, etc. Specific issues are likely to require tailor-made measures. While many of these actions will help, they will not suffice to remedy the market weaknesses fully, let alone permanently. Some market failures may be impossible to eliminate or even relieve. In some markets, failures are better solved by structures without full competition.

Further, this chapter discusses the complex interactions between competition and financial stability. Many complex relationships exist and incorporate opposite effects of competition on financial stability. Some theories claim that competition enhances financial stability, while others see a reduction of financial stability under fiercer competition. The empirical literature suggests that the relationship between competition and risk taking has an inverted U shape; both high to very high and low to very low competitive markets could be more stable and may provide the environment for reduced risk taking.

Since the start of the 2007/2008 crisis, governments and regulators have taken many regulatory measures to increase the financial stability of the financial system. The G20 launched a reform agenda that covers a broad range of themes, ranging from strongly increasing level and quality of capital and liquidity standards of banks and mitigating their procyclical impact (Basel Committee on Banking Supervision's Basel III), to 'broadening the scope of regulation of hedge funds', see Bijlsma et al. (2010). Other international standard-setting bodies and international financial organizations like the IMF and the FSB have also played an important role in developing new initiatives for financial stability.

Most of these measures have negative effects on the level of competition in the banking sector. It is understandable that measures for financial stability had priority in the crisis years. Now that victory can be proclaimed over the immediate crisis (see Summers, 2013) and we appear to be entering a phase of low growth and low inflation, it is also the time to find a new balance between financial stability and competition and reconsider financial regulation and their negative side effects on competition. After all, increases in competition in financial markets when enhanced appropriately could drive real economic growth. The first step in changing the balance between financial stability and competition in financial markets is measuring the level and development of competition over time. The latter topic is what this book is all about.

Notes

1 The stronger banking competition is, the less banks are inclined to invest in lasting relationships, as their clients may be snatched by competitors before they have re-earned their investment (Petersen and Rajan, 1995).
2 This section draws on Bikker and Spierdijk (2010).
3 Research in the Netherlands shows that the effect of advice may turn out to be negative; clients who had bought a policy through an insurance advisor received, on average, a significantly lower pay-out than respondents who had bought a policy directly from an insurer. Further, intermediaries appeared to have a detrimental effect on the initial choice of consumers with respect to risk taking, probably because commissions are highest for high risk products, so that their added value is negative (CPB, 2005, Chapter 5). With effect from early 2013, intermediaries are obliged to charge for their services, while commission or income from financial institutions is forbidden.
4 Strong effects of brands names may also reflect a properly functioning reputation mechanism. However, we observe that banks 'use' their brand names, for instance, by offering low deposit rates.
5 In the Netherlands, health insurance arrangements are often offered by employers or social organizations. Of course, the employee pension plan is the best example of a collectively offered financial product.
6 For instance the regular introduction of new account types, while lowering the interest rates on older accounts of mainly immobile clients (referred to as roof tile construction).
7 In the Netherlands, the guaranteed pay-out of a life insurance policy with the same premium may vary across insurers by a factor of 1.5 (CPB, 2005, Chapter 5).
8 Benefits from having local banks could come from relationship lending, where banks are more willing to acquire information on the borrower.
9 More competition lowers bank interest rate spreads on policy and market rates and increases the speed of adjustment after changes in the latter rates (Chapter 8).
10 In the Netherlands, unless an industry-wide pension fund is mandatory under the sector's collective labour agreement.
11 Many of these arguments also apply to many non-financial markets. Stimulation of pension savings may be the primary reason for the authorities to act more paternalistically on the pension market.
12 Different institutional conditions and regulatory regimes across types of providers of voluntary pension schemes also play a role.
13 A further problem is that it remains difficult to compare complex conditions of financial products.

14 Around 50 per cent of the cost is covered by a particular income-dependent tax, levied by the government. Insurers may also offer supplementary packages.
15 This is far from simple in practice. For instance, a long-term mortgage may increase the interest rate risk of a bank (having a low duration), while it generally reduces the interest rate risk of an insurance firm (having a high duration).
16 This regulation stipulates that the central bank can force insolvent life insurers to reinsure or hand over their portfolio to the so-termed safety net. Other life insurers are under a legal obligation to contribute a maximum of €200 million to this fund. Moreover, the amount used to protect the policyholders of a single firm may not exceed €100 million (CPB, 2005).

References

Ahn, J.-H. and R. Breton (2011) Securitization, competition and incentive to monitor, working paper, http://economix.fr/docs/106/ahn_breton_securitization_competition.pdf.

Allen, F. (1990) The market for information and the origin of financial intermediation, *Journal of Financial Intermediation* 1, 3–30.

Allen, F. and D. Gale (2000) *Comparing financial systems*. Cambridge, MA: MIT Press.

Allen, F., E. Carletti, and R. Marquez (2011) Credit market competition and capital regulation, *Review of Financial Studies* 24 (4), 983–1018.

Baumol, W.J., J.C. Panzar, and R.D. Willig (1982) Contestable markets and the theory of industry structure. San Diego, CA: Harcourt Brace Jovanovich.

Beck, T., A. Demirguc-Kunt, and R. Levine (2006) Bank concentration, competition, and crises: First results, *Journal of Banking & Finance* 30, 1581–1603.

Berger, A.N., L. Klapper and R. Turk-Ariss (2009) Bank Competition and Financial Stability, *Journal of Financial Services Research* 35, 99–118.

Bernheim, B.D. and D.M. Garrett (1996) The determinants and consequences of financial education in the workplace: Evidence from a survey of households. Stanford Working Paper nr. 96-007/NBER Working Papers no. 5667, National Bureau of Economic Research.

Bijlsma, M., W. Elzenburg and M. van Leuvensteijn (2010) Four futures for finance; A scenario study, CPB Document 211, CPB Netherlands Bureau for Economic Policy Analysis.

Bikker, J.A. (2012) Performance of the life insurance industry under pressure: efficiency, competition and consolidation, DNB Working Paper No. 357, De Nederlandsche Bank, Amsterdam.

Bikker, J.A. and J. de Dreu (2007) Operating costs of pension schemes. In: O. Steenbeek and S.G. van der Lecq (eds), *Costs and Benefits of Collective Pension Systems*. Springer: Berlin, Heidelberg, New York, 51–74.

Bikker, J.A. and J. de Dreu (2009) Operating costs of pension funds: the impact of scale, governance and plan design, *Journal of Pension Economics and Finance* 8, 63–89.

Bikker, J.A. and J. Gorter (2011) Performance of the Dutch non-life insurance industry: competition, efficiency and focus, *Journal of Risk and Insurance* 78, 163–194.

Bikker, J.A. and L. Spierdijk (2010) Measuring and explaining competition in the financial sector, *Journal of Applied Business and Economics* 11, 11–42.

Boot, A.W.A. (2007) Review of competition in the Dutch retail banking sector. Working Party No. 2 on Competition and Regulation, OECD, Paris.

Boyd, J.H., and G. De Nicoló (2005), The theory of bank risk-taking and competition revisited, *Journal of Finance* 60, 1329–1343.

Boyd, J.H., and E.C. Prescott (1986) Financial intermediary-coalitions, *Journal of Economic Theory* 38, 211–232.

Braunstein, S. and C. Welch (2002). Financial literacy: An overview of practice, research and policy. *Federal Reserve Bulletin* 88 (11), 445–457.

Cap Gemini (2005). *World Retail Banking Report.* Capgemini, http://www.hr-rapportenservice.nl/world-retail-banking-report-2005.5680.lynkx?RapportPointer=9-218-3838-30529

Chen, H., J.D. Cummins, K. Viswanathan, and M.A. Weiss (2013a) Systemic risk and the inter-connectedness between banks and insurers: an econometric analysis, *Journal of Risk and Insurance,* forthcoming, DOI: 10.1111/j.1539-6975.2012.01503.x.

Chen, H., J.D. Cummins, K. Viswanathan, and M.A. Weiss (2013b) Systemic risk measures in the insurance industry: A copula approach, Working paper, Temple University, Philadelphia.

Claessens, S. (2009). Competition in the financial sector: Overview of competition policies. IMF Working Paper WP/09/45, International Monetary Fund.

CPB (2003). Tight oligopolies. CPB Document no. 29, CPB Netherlands Bureau for Economic Policy Analysis, The Hague.

CPB (2005). Competition in markets for life insurance. CPB Document no. 96, CPB Netherlands Bureau for Economic Policy Analysis, The Hague.

Cummins, J. David and Mary A. Weiss (2013a) Systemic risk and the regulation of the US insurance industry, Working Paper, Temple University, Philadelphia.

Cummins, J. David and Mary A. Weiss (2013b) Systemic risk and the insurance industry, in: Georges Dionne (ed.), *Handbook of Insurance*, 2nd edn, New York: Springer.

Cummins, J. David and Mary A. Weiss (2014) Systemic risk and the US insurance sector, *Journal of Risk and Insurance* (forthcoming) DOI: 10.1111/jori.12039.

Demsetz, R., M. Saidenberg and P. Strahan (1996) Banks with something to lose: The disciplinary role of franchise value, *FRBNY Economic Policy Review* October. 1–14.

Diamond, D.W. (1984), Financial Intermediation and Delegated Monitoring, *Review of Economic Studies* 51, 393–414.

Gorter, J. (2012) Commission bans and the source and quality of financial advice, DNB Working Papers no. 350, De Nederlandsche Bank, Amsterdam.

Hellmann, Th.F., K.C. Murdock and J. Stiglitz, (2000), Liberalization, moral hazard in banking and prudential regulation: Are capital requirements enough?, *American Economic Review* 90(1), 147–165.

Herring, R.J., and P. Vankundre (1987) Growth opportunities and risk-taking by financial intermediaries, *Journal of Finance* 42, 583–599.

Jimenez, G., J.A. Lopez and J. Saurina (2007), How does competition impact bank risk taking?, Federal Reserve Bank of San Francisco Working paper 2007-23.

Keeley, M.C. (1990) Deposit insurance, risk and market power in banking, *American Economic Review* 80, 1183–1200.

Lemmen, J.J.G. (2003), Systeemrisico's van Nederlandse pensioenfondsen (Systemic risks of Dutch pension funds), CPB Research Memorandum 60.

Lusardi, A. (2004). Saving and the effectiveness of financial education, in: O.S. Mitchell and S.P. Utkus (eds), *Pension Design and Structure: New Lessons from Behavioural Finance*, Oxford and New York: Oxford University Press, 157–184.

Lusardi, A. and O. Mitchell (2011), Financial literacy around the world: An overview, NBER Working paper 17107.

Mishkin, F.S. (1999) Financial consolidation: Dangers and opportunities, *Journal of Banking & Finance* 23, 675–691.

Mooslechner, P., M. Schürz and B. Weber (2003) Transparency as a mechanism of governance in financial systems. Paper presented at the conference Transformation of Statehood, Austrian Academy of Sciences, Vienna, 23–25 January 2003.

NMa (2006). *Financial Sector Monitor 2006.* The Hague: NMa (Dutch competition authority).

Petersen, M.A. and R. Rajan (1995) The effect of credit market competition on lending relationships. *Quarterly Journal of Economics*, 110, 407–443.

Ramakrishnan, R., and A.V. Thakor (1984), Information reliability and a theory of financial intermediation, *Review of Economic Studies* 51, 415–432.

Schaeck, K., M. Cihák and S. Wolfe (2009) Are competitive banking systems more stable?, *Journal of Money, Credit and Banking* 41, 711–734.

Summers, L. (2013) Larry Summers at IMF Economic Forum, 8 November 2013, http://www.youtube.com/watch?v=KYpVzBbQIX0.

Tabak, B., D. Fazio and D. Cajueiro (2012) The relationship between banking market competition and risk-taking: Do size and capitalization matter? *Journal of Banking and Finance* 36 (12), 3366–3381.

Van Rooij, M.C.J., C.J.M. Kool and H.M. Prast (2007) Risk-return preferences in the pension domain: are people able to choose? *Journal of Public Economics* 91, 701–722.

Wagner, W. (2010) Diversification at financial institutions and systemic crises, *Journal of Financial Intermediation* 19, 373–386.

Williamson, S.D. (1986) Costly monitoring, loan contracts and equilibrium credit rationing, *Quarterly Journal of Economics* 102, 135–146.

3 The efficiency of firms

What difference does competition make?

Donald A. Hay and Guy S. Liu[1]

In Cournot oligopoly the efficiency of a firm relative to others determines its market share; this relationship gives an incentive to improve efficiency. The incentives are greater in markets where firm behaviour is more competitive. Components of firm efficiency are identified empirically by frontier production function techniques in 19 UK manufacturing sectors: technical change, average efficiency of each firm relative to the frontier, and the efficiency of each firm relative to its own 'best practice' in each period. Short-run declines in market shares and profits induce the firm to improve efficiency relative to its 'best practice'. Long-run differences in efficiency are correlated with differences in gross investment. This approach is suitable for all kind of firms, including banking and other financial institutions.

3.1. Introduction

Almost 40 years have elapsed since Demsetz (1974) posed his famous question to applied industrial organization economists: are dominant firms profitable because they are able to monopolize their markets, or are they simply more efficient than their rivals and hence grow larger and generate higher returns? In one respect, this chapter is no more than yet another attempt to answer this question, although it differs markedly from others in the literature (Clarke et al., 1984; Schmalensee, 1987) in its focus on measuring firms' efficiencies and market shares rather than on profitability measured by price-cost margins or return on capital. In another respect, it addresses a wider agenda. The papers in the Demsetz tradition take the cost levels of particular firms as predetermined, and then explore the implications for profitability. In this chapter we explicitly address the determinants of firms' cost, and examine the possibility that the state of competition within the market may affect the incentives for firms to improve their efficiency.

This latter aspect of the problem has also been addressed by Vickers (1995a, b) and Nickell (1996). They point to two ways in which competition may impinge on the behaviour of firms. The first, and most direct, effect is described by Vickers as 'discovery and selection': in a model of entry into a homogeneous good market with Nash–Cournot competition, the post-entry equilibrium reveals the ranking of the entrant in terms of relative costs. A low cost entrant will generate a substantial 'disturbance' to the market equilibrium, and may drive out some high cost incumbent(s). At the very least, the distribution of market shares and the profitability of firms will be affected as output shifts from high cost firms to low cost firms. A model along these lines, but addressing the specific concerns of this chapter, is set out in Section 3.2.

The second effect of competition is to sharpen incentives for managers. One strand in the literature appeals to explicit incentive schemes, where an increase in the number of players in the market enhances the possibilities of comparisons between the performances of managers (Holmstrom, 1982; Nalebuff and Stiglitz, 1983). A second strand (Hart, 1983; Scharfstein, 1988; Hermalin, 1994; Nickell, 1996) focuses on implicit incentives. The idea is that the market is unable to observe either the effort or the ability of the manager; it can only observe output which is additionally affected by productivity shocks. If, however, there are a number of firms, and productivity shocks are correlated across firms more than the underlying managerial ability, then performance over time can be used to distinguish superior managerial ability. A third approach, due to Willig (1987), outlines the conditions under which competition in product markets makes profits more sensitive to the efforts of managers. The owners then have an incentive to relate managerial remuneration to profits, so as to keep managerial effort high.

For the purposes of this chapter, we presume that a mechanism of this third type (i.e. the Willig mechanism) is at work, and link it to the model of product market competition. To put it simply, in the model of Section 3.2, for a given degree of competition in the market (defined in terms of *behaviour* rather than the number of players), a firm with lower relative costs will enjoy a higher market share and a higher price cost margin, and hence, *ceteris paribus*, higher profit than its rivals. If managerial remuneration is in any way linked to performance, then the managers will have incentives to get costs down. (The fact that competition will also enable greater precision in provision of incentives for managerial ability is an additional benefit to the owners, though it is not considered in our analysis below.) Further, the more competitive is the behaviour of the firm, the stronger is the relationship between efficiency and performance and hence the greater the incentives for managers to pursue efficiency.

These considerations set the agenda for the chapter. Section 3.2 models the theoretical relationship between firm market share, firm costs and competitive behaviour, and notes that firms' costs may be endogenous, affected by the state of competition. The next two sections explore this relationship empirically with a sample of firms in 19 UK manufacturing sectors in the period 1970–89 (see appendices for details). In Section 3.3, frontier production function techniques are employed to identify the efficiency of each firm in the short run and the long run. In Section 3.4, these efficiency measures are utilized to test for the relationship between efficiency and market share. The relationship is also interpreted as an index of the degree of competition in a sector. This discussion leads naturally into the analysis of Section 3.5, where firm efficiency is no longer taken to be exogenous, but rather an outcome of the activities of the management, responding to competitive pressures in product markets. Section 3.6 concludes the chapter.

3.2. Firm efficiency, competition and market structure

The simplest model of the relation of market share to firm costs is a Cournot model of homogeneous good oligopoly (see Clarke and Davies, 1982). The interesting feature of such models is that the share of the market accruing to a particular firm is determined by its own cost level relative to the simple average of the cost levels of all firms in the industry.

Consider an industry with an inverse demand curve given by $p = f\ (Q)$, where $Q = \sum_i q_i$, the market output, is the sum of the outputs of the firms. Each firm has a cost function with constant variable cost, c_i, and fixed cost F_i. The profit function for firm i is given by $\pi_i = [f\ (Q) - c_i]q_i - F_i$ which the firm maximizes by choice of q_i. The first order condition for a maximum is

$$\partial\pi_i / \partial q_i = (p - c_i) + q_i(dp / dQ)(\partial Q / \partial q_i) = 0 \tag{3.1}$$

Varieties of competitive behaviour can be introduced by setting $\partial Q / \partial q_i = 1 + \lambda_i$, where λ_i is the expectation of firm i of the extent to which its own output initiatives will trigger changes in the outputs of its rivals (the so-called 'conjectural variation').[2] Thus $\lambda_i > 0$ can be interpreted as collusive behaviour (all firms tend to increase outputs together): $\lambda_i = -(1-s_i)/s_i$, where s_i is the market share of firm i, indicates full collusion with all firms changing outputs so as to preserve market shares. The Nash–Cournot case (zero conjectural variations) has $\lambda_i = 0$. By contrast $\lambda_i < 0$ is competitive: firm i anticipates that other firms will 'make room' for its additional output by cutting back on their own outputs. A conventional lower bound of $\lambda_i = -1$ is assumed.

Equation (3.1) can be rearranged to give an expression for the price-cost margin (where E is the demand elasticity)

$$(p - c_i) / p = (s_i / E)(1 + \lambda_i) \tag{3.2}$$

or

$$s_i = (1 - c_i / p)E / (1 + \lambda_i) \tag{3.3}$$

The interpretation of Equation (3.3) is that a higher market share, s_i, for firm i is associated with a lower cost, c_i However, the price level, p, is endogenous, and should be eliminated before attempting a detailed interpretation. The expression in Equation (3.2) can be summed across all firms $j = 1,\ldots,n$ (including firm i) to give

$$n - \sum c_j / p = (1 + \sum s_j\lambda_j) / E,\ p = \overline{c} / ((1 - (1 + \sum s_j\lambda_j)) / nE), \tag{3.4}$$

where $\overline{c} \equiv \sum c_j / n$ is the simple average of the costs of the different firms. Substituting for p back into Equation (3.3) gives

$$S_i = (E / (1 + \lambda_i))(1 - (1 - (1 + \sum s_j\lambda_j) / nE)(c_i / \overline{c})) \tag{3.5}$$

Note that the expression in parentheses is also the denominator of the expression for the market price in Equation (3.4). More precisely, it determines the mark-up of price over the average costs of the firms, and can therefore be interpreted as an index of the degree of competition in the market. A smaller value indicates a less competitive market.

Equation (3.5) is a system of simultaneous equations for $i = 1,\ldots,n$, which can be solved to give: [3]

$$s_i = \frac{E}{1+\lambda_i} - \frac{c_i}{\bar{c}}\frac{(nE-1)}{n(1+\lambda_i)} + \frac{1}{(1-\mu)}\frac{c_i}{\bar{c}}\frac{1}{n(1+\lambda_i)}\sum_{j=1}^{n}\frac{\lambda_j}{1+\lambda_j}[E - \frac{c_j}{n\bar{c}}(nE-1)] \quad (3.6)$$

where $\mu \equiv \sum_{j=1}^{n} c_j\lambda_j / (n\bar{c}(1+\lambda_j))$. The relationship between s_i and $c_i / \bar{c}$ in Equation (3.6) is highly nonlinear, and the sign of $\partial s_i / \partial(c_i / \bar{c})$ cannot be evaluated. However, for certain values of the λ_s, we can work informally with Equation (3.5). If the λ_s are the same across all firms, then the s_j drop out of the right-hand side of Equation (3.5) to give:

$$S_i = E / (1+\lambda)(1-(1-(1+\lambda)/nE)(c_i / \bar{c})) \quad (3.5')$$

For $-1 < \lambda < 0$ (competitive conjectures), the coefficient on $c_i / \bar{c}$ is negative. For $\lambda = 0$ (Nash–Cournot), the coefficient remains negative but has a smaller absolute value. With full collusion, $\lambda_j = (1-s_j)/s_j$, so $\sum \lambda_j s_j = (n-1)$. Substituting in Equation (3.5) yields $-(E-1)/(1+\lambda_j) < 0$ as the coefficient on $(c_i / \bar{c})$. These three cases are consistent with the intuition that firms with low relative costs will have higher market shares than firms with high relative costs. (It is also evident that they will have higher gross profits.)

The effects of the conjectural variation terms on market share are given, in principle, by evaluating $\frac{\partial s_i}{\partial \lambda_i}$ and $\frac{\partial s_i}{\partial \lambda_j}$ in Equation (3.6). While it can be shown that $\frac{\partial s_i}{\partial \lambda_j} > 0$ for $\lambda_j, \lambda_i > -1$, it is not possible to sign $\frac{\partial s_i}{\partial \lambda_i}$ unequivocally. Further analysis requires the simplifying assumption that all firms have the same costs, in which Equation (3.6) reduces to

$$s_i = 1 / (n(1+\lambda_i)(1-\mu)) \quad (3.7)$$

where $\mu \equiv \sum_{j=1}^{n} c_j\lambda_j / (n(1+\lambda_i)(1-\mu)) = \sum_{j=1}^{n} \lambda_j / (n(1+\lambda_i))$ for $c_j = \bar{c}$.

The derivatives of Equation (3.7) are

$$\partial s_i / \partial \lambda_i = (1 - n(1-\mu)(1+\lambda_i)) / (n^2(1+\lambda_i)^3(1-\mu)^2)$$

(note that for $n \geq 2$ and for $0 \leq \lambda_j \leq (1-s_j)/s_j$, the numerator is negative, so $\partial s_i / \partial \lambda_i < 0$)[4] and $\partial s_i / \partial \lambda_i = 1/(n^2(1+\lambda_i)(1+\lambda_j)^2(1-\mu)^2)$ (which is positive for $\lambda_i > -1$). To conclude, the market share of the firm decreases as it behaves more cooperatively, and increases as its rivals behave more cooperatively.

Holding the number of firms, *n*, constant, we may consider the implications of Equation (3.4) for a market price. A general increase in the λ_i (more cooperative behaviour) increases the market price. The same is true if only some firms behave more cooperatively, and the effect is greater, the larger their market shares, though it should be noted that they will also lose market share to their rivals, since the s_i are endogenous. More competitive behaviour, in contrast, will both reduce the equilibrium market price *and* increase the market share of the firm that initiates it.

Finally, we consider the process which generates the c_i. Two approaches are possible. The first is that cost levels are outside the control of the firms, being random samples from some prior distribution of costs. Whether a firm with a high cost is able to survive will then depend on the state of competition in the market, and the costs of its competitors. More competitive markets will weed out high cost firms.

The second approach is that low costs are the result of good investment and R&D decisions, and the degree of managerial effort in keeping costs down (Hermalin, 1992). Responsibility for the performance of the firms in terms of market share and profits is naturally assigned to the management. So there is a strong incentive for the manager to ensure that the firm's costs do not get out of line with those of its rivals, especially where the competitive environment is aggressive. This second approach is the one which we adopt for our empirical work. We distinguish between the highest feasible efficiency attainable by the firm in a particular period, and the degree to which the firm deviates from that efficiency. In the short run, greater managerial effort probably can increase efficiency, but only within the constraints of the physical plant and technology currently available to the firm. In the long run, by investment in innovation and capacity, the firm establishes its position in the ranking of long-run efficiencies of firms in the industry.

In the empirical work, we distinguish the following components of c_i: the frontier of the sector to which firm i belongs, which will shift over time due to technical progress and innovation; the average efficiency of firm i relative to that frontier, which we identify empirically as a time-invariant element; and the degree to which the firm achieves its own 'best practice' efficiency in a particular time period. The theoretical relationship between firm efficiency and market share is then examined empirically. Next the analysis seeks to identify the determinants of the firm-specific efficiency components. In particular, we focus on the gross investment rate, which is taken to incorporate new technologies, as a determinant (or simply a correlate) of the efficiency of the firm relative to the frontier; and on competition affecting the incentives for firms to improve their short-run efficiency.

3.3. Specification of the firm production function

To explore the efficiency of the firms in our sample we adapt the stochastic frontier production function model of Aigner et al. (1977), the ALS model:[5]

$$y_{it} = f(x_{it}) + v_{it} - u_{it}, \tag{3.8}$$

where y_{it} is the natural log output of firm i in year t, $f(x_{it})$ is a conventional production function, v_{it} are production shocks with distribution $N(0,\sigma_v^2)$, and u_{it} are firm specific inefficiencies, on which more will be said below.

Following Nickell (1996), $f(x_{it})$ is specified as a Cobb–Douglas function with lagged adjustment of output to inputs:

$$f(x_{it}) = a_i + b_t + \alpha(1-\theta)l_{it} + \beta(1-\theta)k_{it} + \theta y_{it-1} + \gamma h_t, \tag{3.9}$$

where l_{it} and k_{it} are labour and capital in natural logs. The null hypothesis is that there are constant returns to scale in production (i.e. $\alpha + \beta = 1$). The θ coefficient reflects lags in adjustment of output to inputs. h_t is an indicator of cyclical conditions (demand, capacity utilization) in the sector to which firm i belongs. The coefficients b_t are time-specific efficiency effects, picking up shifts in the production frontier over time. The change in b_t between periods is a measure of the rate of technical change. a_i is a firm-specific time-invariant efficiency effect; in a cross-section of firms the a_i pick up the efficiencies of firms. The possible reasons for differing a_i across firms are various. The most obvious variation is likely to be the differing quality of management due to innate abilities and business experience. But firms may also differ in access to high quality factors of production, in location, in ability to utilize the latest technologies (i.e. lack of expertise within the firm and/or exclusion by patent protection), and in inherited capital stock and technologies.

In addition to the a_i, Equation (3.8) includes firm-specific but time-variant inefficiency effects, u_{it}, which are assumed to be distributed either as truncated normal or half normal distributions, or as an exponential distribution. The u_{it} reflect the shortfall of the firms relative to their own 'best practice' in each period, where best practice for the firm is determined by the time-invariant a_i efficiency coefficient. Changes in the u_{it} indicate the extent to which the firm makes an effort in a particular period to improve its relative efficiency, or alternatively allows its efficiency to drift.

The inclusion of two firm-specific effects, a_i and u_{it}, is a departure from the existing literature on frontier production functions. In their original article on frontier production functions with panel data, Schmidt and Sickles (1984) argued for the inclusion of only the time-invariant firm-specific effect, a_i. The advantage of this procedure was that it was no longer necessary to make assumptions about the distribution of firm-specific effects. Subsequently, this was acknowledged to be too restrictive, and Cornwell et al. (1990) proposed that the a_i should be modelled as a quadratic function of time. But it is hard to see any economic justification for such a formulation. Including a_i and u_{it} has the advantage of an obvious economic interpretation, distinguishing long-run average efficiency for the firm (arising from quality of management, technologies and plant available to the firm) from short-run efficiency (arising from the efforts of management to use the given resources of the firm productively). It seems entirely reasonable to allow the latter to vary over time, as the management raises its effort in response to performance and competitive pressures. The disadvantage is that it is necessary to pre-specify the distribution of the u_{it}; however this is a drawback mainly in the econometric application, it will be necessary to try a number of alternative distributions of the u_{it} and to compare their performance.

The empirical equation is obtained by substituting (3.9) into (3.8). For estimation purposes, the equation is rewritten with output per unit of capital $(y_{it} - k_{it})$ or output per worker $(y_{it} - l_{it})$ as the dependent variable. This removes potential problems of heteroscedasticity and multicollinearity.

The econometric specification of the time- and firm-specific effects needs careful consideration. For estimation, one time period dummy (b_0) and one firm dummy (a_j) have to be dropped; the sum of these two elements is estimated as the constant in the equation. The estimated coefficients on dummies for other firms and other time periods are therefore identifying deviation from a_i plus b_0. In particular, the most efficient firm (relatively) in each industry is chosen to be firm j, the dummy of which is dropped from the estimation.[6] The implication is that the estimated coefficients on the firm dummies (denoted $a_i^{'}$) are all less than or equal to zero, since by definition all the other firms are less efficient than the 'frontier' firm, j. The reason for proceeding in this way is to provide parallel treatment for both time-invariant efficiency $(a_i^{'})$ and time-variant efficiency (u_{it}) both are being identified as (negative) deviations from the frontier.

The problems of simultaneity between outputs and inputs, and of correlation between the lagged dependent variable and the error term, are addressed by extensive instrumenting of the repressors. As each industry regression was performed separately, slightly different sets of instruments were found to be appropriate in each case. In general, lagged values up to $t-3$ were used.

Estimation procedures for frontier production functions have been very fully surveyed by Greene (1993). Here we note a practical problem of implementation. When the frontier production function has been fitted, the residuals $\hat{v}_{it}$ should be normally distributed. If they turn out to be skewed, the problem may be either extreme data points that are biasing the results, or that the assumption about the distribution of the u_{it} is inappropriate. Estimation had to proceed by a judicious elimination of outliers in the data (see notes to Table 3.1), and by switching to an exponential distribution of the u_{it} when a truncated normal or half normal proved not to fit the data.[7]

The detailed production function results for 19 industries are given in Table 3.1. The following features of the results should be noted: (i) In all but two sectors (Small Tools, and Confectionery) the firm-specific time-invariant efficiency effects (the $a_i^{'}$) are significant as a group. The implication is that there are efficiency differences between firms which persist over time. Our results are consistent with the findings of Baily et al. (1992) who also find persistent differences in the productivity of US manufacturing plants. (ii) In fifteen out of the nineteen sectors, there is also significant time-variant firm inefficiency u_{it} that is appropriately modelled by one of the distributions that have been suggested by frontier production function analysis (see the section headed ALS-DV, and note 6). (iii) The null hypothesis of constant returns to scale (CRS) can be rejected in only two sectors (Newspapers, with diminishing returns, and Pharmaceuticals, with strongly increasing returns). Given that our samples are restricted to fairly large companies in each sector, the prevalence of constant returns is not perhaps surprising. (iv) The movement of the sectoral production frontier over time varies a good deal between sectors.

Table 3.1 Frontier production functions

Industry	Estimation method	*Part 1: Estimation of Variables* Constant	1977–9	1980–2	1983–5	1986–8	Market demand h_t	Capital	Labour	Lagged output
1. Bricks	LSDV	0.796	–0.209*	–0.318*	0.052	-	0.683 (2.1)	CRS	0.408 (4.5)	0.010 (0.1)
	ALS-DV	1.345*	–0.280*	–0.364*	0.017	-	0.742 (2.1)	CRS	0.448 (5.0)	0.020 (0.2)
2. Cement	LSDV	2.9868*	–0.0567	0.136*	0.105	0.219*	0.109 (0.8)	CRS	0.442 (2.5)	0.024 (0.1)
	ALS-DV	3.0236*	–0.0589	0.138*	0.105	0.224*	0.107 (0.7)	CRS	0.443 (2.8)	0.012 (0.1)
5. Pumps valves	LSDV	5.032*	–0.067	–0.036	0.116	0.134	0.108 (1.6)	CRS	0.883 (1.9)	–0.576 (0.7)
	ALS-DV	5.173*	–0.017	–0.046	0.115*	0.151*	0.042 (0.5)	CRS	0.646 (2.0)	–0.368 (0.6)
6. Machinery for chemical industry	LSDV	6.605*	0.085	0.080	0.164	0.109	–0.231 (0.8)	CRS	0.748 (7.3)	0.038 (0.3)
	ALS-DV	6.712*	0.072	0.085	0.162	0.096	–0.283 (1.1)	CRS	0.745 (7.0)	-
7. Small tools	LSDV	3.154*	–0.018	–0.137*	0.535	0.352	0.259 (1.5)	0.126 (2.1)	CRS	0.446 (4.8)
	ALS-DV	3.253*	–0.020	–0.092*	0.318	0.486	0.284 (1.5)	0.094 (1.6)	CRS	0.478 (6.1)
8. Basic electric equipment	LSDV	5.985*	0.226*	0.318*	0.585*	0.538*	0.755 (1.9)	CRS	0.839 (6.0)	-
	ALS-DV	4.697*	0.166*	0.284*	0.501*	0.551*	0.508 (1.5)	CRS	0.684 (6.8)	-
9. Wires and cables	LSDV	2.403*	–0.086	–0.196*	–0.143*	0.057	0.094 (0.4)	CRS	0.362 (3.2)	0.209 (1.9)
	ALS-DV	2.431*	–0.074	–0.144*	–0.099*	0.076	0.125 (0.5)	CRS	0.357 (4.8)	0.232 (2.3)
10. Electrical goods	LSDV	1.804*	0.042	0.054	0.123*	0.162*	-	0.082 (1.6)	CRS	0.679 (6.5)
	ALS-DV	2.795*	0.022	0.091	0.139*	0.176*	-	0.041 (0.9)	CRS	0.645 (7.7)
11. Carpets	LSDV	7.153*	0.027	–0.047	0.137*	0.296*	1.363 (2.4)	CRS	1.001 (6.4)	–0.023 (0.2)
	ALS-DV	3.058*	–0.010	–0.030	0.031	0.198*	1.756 (3.6)	CRS	0.705 (6.2)	-
12. Wool	LSDV	7.196*	0.186*	0.056	0.067	0.296*	0.657 (2.1)	CRS	0.803 (2.6)	–0.033 (0.4)
	ALS-DV	7.873*	0.186*	0.114	0.147	0.348*	0.739 (2.9)	CRS	0.718 (2.8)	–0.012 (0.1)
13. Furniture	LSDV	3.803*	–0.009	–0.166	–0.066	0.067	0.313 (0.8)	CRS	0.473 (1.8)	0.313 (0.8)
	ALS-DV	3.665*	–0.011	–0.104	–0.065	0.149*	0.576 (1.5)	CRS	0.468 (2.6)	–0.219 (0.8)

14. Brewing	LSDV	0.072	0.040	0.085*	0.107*	0.176*	0.490 (2.7)	0.213 (1.9)	CRS	0.647 (13.6)
	ALS-DV	–0.348	0.065*	0.110*	0.114*	0.165*	0.493 (2.9)	0.128 (1.7)	CRS	0.812 (21.8)
15. Confectionery	LSDV	1.149	–0.020	–0.128	–0.023	–0.014	–0.252 (0.6)	0.439 (2.3)	CRS	0.414 (3.0)
	ALS-DV	1.314	–0.005	0.009	0.045	0.023	–0.050 (0.1)	0.367 (2.8)	CRS	0.454 (5.0)
16. Cereals	LSDV	4.347	–0.135	–0.187	–0.259	–0.259	-	–0.080 (0.2)	CRS	0.638 (3.5)
	ALS-DV	4.578	-	-	-	-	-	–0.143 (0.5)	CRS	0.704 (6.7)
17. Newspaper	LSDV	0.983	0.142*	0.141*	0.367*	0.538*	–0.179 (0.4)	0.188 (1.8)	0.382 (2.4)	0.317 (3.4)
	ALS-DV	1.209	–0.154*	0.153*	0.377*	0.538*	0.123 (0.2)	0.184 (2.3)	0.364 (2.2)	0.319 (4.4)
18. Tobacco	LSDV	9.564*	–0.169	–0.253	–0.153	0.260	0.012 (0.1)	–0.044 (0.1)	CRS	0.012 (0.1)
	ALS-DV	4.473*	–0.232*	–0.200*	–0.104	0.035	-	0.399 (2.6)	CRS	0.155 (0.7)
19. Tyres	LSDV	1.612	0.136	0.084*	0.187	0.272*	0.817 (1.2)	CRS	0.322 (1.3)	0.575 (2.5)
	ALS-DV	2.503	0.059	–0.003	0.066	0.250*	0.435 (0.6)	CRS	0.423 (1.6)	0.453 (1.7)
20. Pharmaceuticals	LSDV	6.416*	0.136*	0.139*	0.072	0.343*	–0.323 (0.5)	0.526 (6.6)	0.289 (2.0)	0.769 (6.9)
	ALS-DV	7.201*	0.138*	0.192*	0.331*	0.609*	0.772 (1.1)	0.566 (7.5)	0.208 (1.5)	0.823 (7.5)
21. General chemicals	LSDV	1.366	0.171*	0.055	0.269*	0.289*	0.287 (1.7)	CRS	0.290 1.6)	0.388 (4.1)
	ALS-DV	1.846	0.099	–0.038	0.233*	0.291*	0.202 (1.3)	CRS	0.297 (1.6)	0.432 (3.8)

Notes: LSDV are least squares dummy variables estimators, with dummies for time periods (b_t) and firm effects (a_i'). ALS-DV are Aigner, Lovell and Schmidt maximum likelihood estimators, also with time period and firm fixed effects dummies. No dummy is included for the period 1974–6, which is subsumed in the constant. * Indicates that time dummies are significant at at least 5per cent level. Values in parentheses ( ) are t-statistics. Likelihood ratio statistics (χ^2): the values in square brackets are the associated probabilities. Market demand is measured by annual changes in total industry scales to account for changes in capacity utilization. CRS indicates constant returns to scale: where the relevant χ^2 test indicated that CRS could not be rejected in a sector, estimation proceeded on the assumption that long-run coefficients on capital and labour summed to unity. The Breusch–Pagan test is for heteroscedasticity. ALS-DV statistics: for the half normal (H) distribution of the u_{it} the relevant statistics are λ and $\left(\sigma_v^2+\sigma_u^2\right)$; for the truncated normal (T), λ, i, and μ/σ_v and for the exponential (E) distribution, μ/σ_v and θ If the appropriate λ, $\left(\sigma_v^2+\sigma_u^2\right)$ and θ_s ar e not significant, then the null hypothesis of the u_{it} being zero (no time-variant inefficiency) is not rejected. See Greene (1993) for further discussion of the techniques. The number of observations is after removing missing values and outliers. The procedure for eliminating observations is best explained by an example. In industry 14 three outliers were eliminated: one had a studentized residual value of 5.74, a second had a missing studentized value, and a third had a recorded output growth of 219per cent per annum. Data points with high studentized residual values are omitted because they tend to have an undue influence on the ALS estimates

continued…

Table 3.1 Frontier production functions (continued)

Industry	Estimation method	*Part 2: Statistics of Estimation*											
		LSDV						*ALS-DV*					
		CRS χ^2	*Firm effects* (χ^2)	*Breusch-Pagan* (χ^2)	*AR[2]* $\hat{\rho}_{t-2}$	$\hat{\sigma}$	R^2	*Lambda* $\sigma_v - \sigma_u$	*Sigma* $\sqrt{\sigma_v^2+\sigma_u^2}$	μ/σ_u $(\hat{\sigma})^o$	*Theta*	*Distribution of* u_i	*Observation (number of firms)*
1. Bricks	LSDV	0.547	80.94	59.87	-0.240	0.148	0.96	2.501	0.283	-	-	H	72
	ALS-DV	[0.400]	[0.001]	[0.0623]	(1.3)			(1.6)	(5.8)				(7)
2. Cement	LSDV	2.304	2.03	41.86	0.444	0.113	0.96	-	-	0.090	26.99	E	42
	ALS-DV	[0.130]	[0.005]	[0.433]	(1.1)					(1.8)	(0.3)		(4)
5. Pumps valves	LSDV	1.074	64.56	71.34	-0.115	0.183	0.54	-	-	7.408	0.061	E	107
	ALS-DV	[0.280]	[0.001]	[0.661]	(1.0)					(9.5)	(4.1)		(8)
6. Machinery for chemical industry	LSDV	2.962	14.76	56.47	0.096	0.165	0.91	1.356	0.197	-	-	H	86
	ALS-DV	[0.094]	[0.048]	[0.818]	(0.5)			(1.2)	(4.8)				(7)
7. Small tools	LSDV	1.157	13.058	49.83	-0.167	0.112	0.72	1.886	0.157	0.589	-	T	98
	ALS-DV	[0.600]	[0.110]	[0.983]	(-1.1)			(2.2)	(1.4)	(0.1)			(8)
8. Basic electric equipment	LSDV	1.024	12.01	36.02	-0.138	0.166	0.93	-	-	0.079	7.724	E	62
	ALS-DV	[0.620]	[0.080]	[0.798]	(-0.7)					(3.3)	(3.9)		(6)
9. Wires and cables	LSDV	0.745	34.89	49.76	-0.063	0.119	0.89	-	-	0.113	7.819	E	73
	ALS-DV	[0.700]	[0.001]	[0.798]	(-0.2)					(5.1)	(5.2)		(6)
10. Electrical goods	LSDV	0.406	15.07	41.88	-0.156	0.138	0.92	-	-	0.640	9.226	E	93
	ALS-DV	[0.500]	[0.005]	[0.964]	(-0.8)					(4.1)	(6.2)		(8)
11. Carpets	LSDV	2.686	31.04	77.55	-0.022	0.213	0.95	154.95	1.147	5.069	-	T	114
	ALS-DV	[0.120]	[0.001]	[0.731]	(-0.1)			(0.3)	(0.7)	(0.3)			(10)
12. Wool	LSDV	0.122	163.41	77.72	-0.085	0.230	0.95	-	-	0.888	5.075	E	122
	ALS-DV	[0.600]	[0.001]	[0.838]	(-0.7)					(4.1)	(7.0)		-10

13. Furniture	LSDV	0.138	70.49	90.35	-0.278	0.190	0.96	-	-	0.091	6.312	E	92
	ALS-DV	[0.680]	[0.001]	[0.440]	(-1.5)					(3.6)	(4.6)		(8)
14. Brewing	LSDV	2.00	25.49	74.56	0.107	0.138	0.91	-	-	0.064	11.14	E	233
	ALS-DV	[0.175]	[0.001]	[0.651]	(1.0)					(11.5)	(14.2)		(18)
15. Confectionery	LSDV	1.100	9.38	48.15	-0.040	0.180	0.87	-	-	0.037	7.575	E	78
	ALS-DV	[0.780]	[0.120]	[0.952]	(-0.2)					(2.4)	(9.7)		(7)
16. Cereals	LSDV	0.375	5.437	28.30	-0.389	0.240	0.86	93.63	1.052	5.146	-	T	31
	ALS-DV	[0.520]	[0.080]	[0.449]	(-0.9)			(0.2)	(0.4)	(0.2)			(3)
17. Newspaper	LSDV	5.89	22.20	74.29	-0.027	0.172	0.77	3.174	0.290	0.985	-	T	98
	ALS-DV	[0.002]	[0.001]	[0.851]	(-0.3)			(3.4)	(2.8)	(0.5)			(8)
18. Tobacco	LSDV	1.37	8.05	37.52	-0.007	0.263	0.75	74.47	1.039	5.807	-	T	38
	ALS-DV	[0.210]	[0.025]	[0.445]	(0.1)			(0.2)	(0.5)	(0.2)			(3)
19. Tyres	LSDV	0.264	11.45	39.66	-0.303	0.145	0.58	-	-	0.086	8.512	E	45
	ALS-DV	[0.880]	[0.001]	[0.574]	(-1.6)					(2.4)	(2.8)		(4)
20. PharmaceuticAls	LSDV	42.88	332.0	139.27	0.092	0.294	0.96	44.88	1.545	4.080	-	T	160
	ALS-DV	[0.000]	[0.00]	[0.294]	(0.5)			(0.5)	(0.6)	(0.2)			(15)
21. General chemicals	LSDV	0.561	19.03	56.25	-0.126	0.216	0.96	-	-	0.116	6.603	E	80
	ALS-DV	[0.400]	[0.00]	[0.744]	(0.8)					(3.4)	(4.3)		(6)

The time dummies are for three-year intervals (too few degrees of freedom to use annual dummies) for 1974–6, 1977–9, 1980–2, 1983–5, 1986–9. In a few sectors, the frontier apparently regressed in the period 1977–82, possibly due to the shocks induced by the oil price rise in 1979 and by the high exchange rate in 1981–2. However, in the later periods most sectors show an upward shift in their production frontier. (v) The market demand variable (annual changes in industry sales), intended to proxy the effects on efficiency of changes in capacity utilization, is significant in four sectors. It is difficult to distinguish these effects from the movements in the frontier just reported.

In the following sections, we explore the effects of efficiency on market share, and the determinants of the components of firm efficiency identified in (i) and (ii) in the notes to Table 3.1.

3.4. The relationship between efficiency and market share: identifying the state of competition in a sector

The discussion in Section 3.2 indicated the role of competition in the market in stimulating firms to improve their efficiency. The empirical difficulty is that competition in the behavioural sense cannot be directly measured. We certainly should not succumb to the temptation to use some measure of concentration as a proxy variable, for two reasons. The first is that it is not evident that concentration maps into behaviour in any precise way. The second is that concentration (market shares) is the outcome of the interaction of competitive behaviour, and the relative efficiencies of the firms, so at best it would be a noisy signal of the former.

One approach (compare Clarke et al. 1984) might be to exploit the linear equilibrium relationship between market shares and firms' costs given in Equation (3.5′) in Section 3.2, where we make the assumption that $\lambda_j = \lambda$ for all firms including i:

$$S_i = E/(1+\lambda)(1-(1-(1+\lambda)/nE)(c_i/\overline{c})) \qquad (3.5')$$

The effect of the degree of competition on the relationship between market share and firm costs is easily discerned in Equation (3.5′). An increase in cooperative behaviour (λ), or a decrease in the number of firms (n), reduces the absolute value of the (negative) coefficient on $c_i/\overline{c}$. In this linear case it is appropriate to identify the coefficient as an index of the degree of competition in the market.

In the general case, things are not quite so clear cut, since the relationship is highly nonlinear (see Equation (3.6) in Section 3.2). However it can be shown that an increase in cooperation or a decrease in the number of rivals does make market share less responsive to firms' costs, at the same time increasing the nonlinearity of the relationship. There is an additional reason for thinking that the relationship may be nonlinear. Dominant firms may behave less competitively than smaller firms. In which case more efficient (and hence dominant) firms will have smaller market shares, and less efficient (and hence smaller) firms will have larger market shares, than would be the case where their competitive stance was identical. These arguments suggest that it is appropriate to specify a nonlinear relationship in the empirical work which follows. A log-linear relationship gives acceptable empirical results, though we present tests for an alternative linear formulation.

The results for seventeen[8] industries in our sample are given in Table 3.2. The dependent variable is firm market share, denoted by MKS_{it}, measured by the reported value of total sales of a firm divided by the total sales of the industry, including both exports and domestic sales. The repressors are firm relative inefficiency, the lagged dependent variable, and firm and time fixed effects. Firm relative inefficiency is defined as follows. The expression $(a_i^{'} - u_{it})$ is the relative efficiency of firm i, where the $a_i^{'}$ are defined as (negative) deviations from the most efficient firm. So $\exp(a_i^{'} - u_{it}) \leq 1$ is the ratio of actual output to potential output, $(1 - \exp(a_i^{'} - u_{it}))$ is a measure of relative inefficiency. Evidently, market share is expected to be negatively related to this measure.

In three of the sectors (15, Confectionery; 17, Newspapers and 18, Tobacco) Box–Cox tests did not reject the hypothesis of a linear relationship as in (3.5′). In the other sectors there was clear evidence of a nonlinear relationship which we captured by the log-linear specification. Obviously the latter is at best an approximation to the general relationship derived in Equation (3.6). The relationship is overall negative in all sectors except 17, Newspapers, where the coefficient is positive and insignificant. Thirteen out of the sixteen negative coefficients are statistically significant.

In twelve sectors there were significant time effects; these indicate shifts in market share between the larger firms included in the sample and the rest of the industry. In all the sectors except 8, Basic Electrical Equipment, the regressions gave significant firm effects, picking up variables other than efficiency which affect firm market shares, presumably product quality and product differentiation.

Lagged market share was a significant variable in each of the industry regressions, indicating that the long-run impact of cost inefficiency on market share was greater than the short-run adjustment by factors that ranged from 1.1 to about 11. This suggests that the speed at which competition erodes the market share of firms which become inefficient varies substantially between sectors. There is a pattern in these results related to the types of sectors. Sectors making ‘commodity’ goods such as 1, Bricks; 2, Cement; 19, Tyres and 21, Chemicals exhibit the fastest adjustment. The slowest adjustment is in consumer goods, especially 13, Furniture, 11, Carpets and 18, Tobacco, although it should be noted that the first two have the highest short-run elasticities of shares with respect to relative inefficiency among the seventeen sectors.

The coefficients on relative inefficiency and lagged market share can be combined in the usual manner to derive the long-run elasticity of market share with respect to relative inefficiency. High elasticities are derived for 11, Carpets, 13, Furniture, 18, Tobacco and 8, Basic Electrical Equipment; low elasticities result for 1, Bricks, 5, Pumps and Valves, 19, Tyres and 20, Pharmaceuticals. No simple categorization in terms of type of product or ‘market structure’ is sufficient to explain this pattern. As noted above, a less competitive sector (fewer firms or more cooperative behaviour) is predicted to give a lower elasticity. Moreover, though this is not incorporated in our formal analysis, differentiation

Table 3.2 Estimates of the relationship between firm inefficiency and market share

	Model specification				*Model estimation*			*Statistical tests*					
Industry	*Linearity (Box–Cox test)*	*Exogeneity of inefficiency*	*Time effects*	*Firm effects*	*Constant*	*Relative inefficiency*	*Lagged market share*	*Heteroscedasticity* (χ^2)	*AR[2]* $\hat{\rho}_{t-2}$	$\hat{\sigma}$	R^2	*Sargan* (χ^2)	*Observations*
1. Bricks	No	Yes	Yes	Yes	−2.636	−0.217	0.203	44.35	−0.355	0.136	0.99	9.189	59
	(2.1)	(0.2)	[34.6/3]	[62.1/9]	(−7.5)	(−2.3)	(1.8)	[0.499]	(−1.3)			[0.102]	
2. Cement	No	Yes	Yes	Yes	−1.728	−0.429	0.279	26.96	−0.01	0.095	0.99	15.078	30
	(2.5)	(1.2)	[37.4/3]	[20.7/3]	(−6.1)	(−3.9)	(2.6)	[0.520]	(0.1)			[0.129]	
5. Pumps, valves	No	Yes	Yes	Yes	−1.232	−0.110	0.558	43.59	−0.356	0.098	0.96	15.952	78
	(3.0)	(0.2)	[7.9/3]	[37.2/7]	(−7.3)	(−3.5)	(8.2)	[0.759]	(1.6)			[0.101]	
6. Machinery for chemical industry	No	Yes	Yes	Yes	−2.312	−0.226	0.457	40.51	−0.289	0.154	0.96	6.463	63
	(4.0)	(1.2)	[14.4/3]	[22.7/6]	(−4.4)	(−2.2)	(3.4)	[0.662]	(−1.2)			[0.091]	
7. Small tools	No	Yes	Yes	Yes	−1.714	−0.156	0.605	51.94	−0.202	0.151	0.97	5.965	75
	(5.0)	(0.9)	[13.3/3]	[18.9/7]	(−4.1)	(−1.9)	(6.1)	[0.360]	(−1.0)			[0.818]	
8. Basic electric equipment	No	Yes	Yes	Yes	−1.538	−0.495	0.732	14.94	−0.139	0.146	0.98	8.408	45
	(3.9)	(1.4)	[8.97/3]	[11.0/5]	(−5.2)	(−5.1)	(14.1)	[0.382]	(−0.5)			[0.135]	
9. Wires and cables	No	Yes	Yes	Yes	−1.265	−0.215	0.642	31.40	−0.006	0.237	0.96	12.019	54
	(2.8)	(1.1)	[2.36/3]	[22.59/5]	(−3.0)	(−1.9)	(5.0)	[0.801]	(−0.1)			[0.100]	
11. Carpets	No	Yes	Yes	Yes	−0.756	−0.886	0.874	36.13	−0.265	0.140	0.97	14.113	70
	(3.9)	(0.8)	[6.32/3]	[18.74/8]	(−1.1)	(−5.6)	(4.5)	[0.920]	(−1.1)			[0.293]	
12. Wool	No	Yes	Yes	Yes	−0.767	−0.151	0.793	56.96	0.015	0.158	0.97	8.366	98
	(2.2)	(0.9)	[3.52/3]	[16.7/9]	(−1.5)	(−2.2)	(6.4)	[0.720]	(0.1)			[0.301]	
13. Furniture	No	Yes	Yes	Yes	0.274	−1.419	0.910	43.61	0.091	0.087	0.98	10.144	74
	(5.3)	(0.8)	[6.20/3]	[43.0/8]	(−0.7)	(−10.4)	(10.5)	[0.817]	(0.5)			[0.181]	
14. Brewing	No	Yes	Yes	Yes	−1.081	−0.144	0.777	84.43	0.024	0.115	0.99	21.382	171
	(2.6)	(0.4)	[6.89/3]	[32.0/16]	(−2.5)	(−1.2)	(8.7)	[0.882]	(0.3)			[0.164]	

15. Confectionery	Yes	Yes	No	Yes	−0.660	−0.120	0.753	40.32	−0.408	0.138	0.99	3.635	57
	(1.02)	(1.2)	[1.19/3]	[63.0/6]	(−2.0)	(−1.6)	(6.6)	[0.630]	(−0.4)			[0.723]	
17. Newspapers	Yes	No	No	Yes	−0.451	0.156	0.756	42.03	−0.064	0.229	0.93	48.801	73
	(0.64)	(1.7)	[1.93/3]	[28.43/6]	(−0.7)	(0.6)	(4.3)	[0.781]	(−0.4)			[0.022]	
18. Tobacco	Yes	Yes	No	Yes	−0.616	−0.354	0.893	21.30	−0.456	0.172	0.93	10.446	27
	(1.0)	(0.6)	[0.43/3]	[5.02/2]	(−1.5)	(−1.8)	(5.7)	[0.621]	(−1.3)			[0.107]	
19. Tyres	No	Yes	Yes	Yes	−2.786	−0.015	0.104	25.73	−0.068	0.066	0.98	14.591	33
	(3.3)	(0.1)	[65.2/3]	[11.2/3]	(−18.0)	(−0.4)	(1.6)	[0.533]	(−0.2)			[0.102]	
20. Pharmaceu-ticals	No	Yes	Yes	Yes	1.352	−0.070	0.555	73.23	−0.067	0.106	0.99		119
	(2.4)	(0.1)	[26.2/3]	[79.3/4]	(−7.2)	(−2.2)	(9.0)	[0.769]	(−0.5)				
21. General chemicals	No	Yes	Yes	Yes	−3.105	−0.259	0.382	38.90	0.066	0.155	0.98	6.293	61
	(2.9)	(0.2)	[17.0/3]	[10.4/5]	(−3.3)	(−2.6)	(1.9)	[0.649]	(0.2)			[0.506]	

Notes: Values in parentheses are t-statistics. The Box–Cox statistic is applied to test for linear versus log-linear specification (see Column 1):

linear $MKS_{it} = Z'\beta + \varepsilon_{it}$, (i)

log-linear $mks_{it} = z'\beta + \varepsilon_{it}$, (ii)

$$MKS_{it} = Z'\beta + \alpha\left[\overline{mks_{it}} - \ln(\overline{MKS_{it}})\right] + \varepsilon_{2it}, \quad \text{(iii)}$$

where *MKS* is market share, *Z* is a vector of independent variables, a bar indicates a fitted value of the dependent variables from Equation (i) or Equation (ii), and lower case indicates logs. The criterion for using the log-linear specification is a computed t-statistic for a, greater than or equal to 1.6. On this basis the log-linear specification was preferred in all but three sectors: 15, Confectionary; 17, Newspapers; 18, Tobacco. To facilitate comparisons between sectors, all the estimates in the table are for the log-linear specification. In principle, the causality between market share and firm inefficiency could run in either direction. We report Wu–Hausman tests for the exogeneity of our measure of inefficiency (see Column 2). The Log-likelihood Ratio Statistic is applied to test firm-fixed effects and time effects, respectively; the figures in square brackets are the values of χ^2, and degrees of freedom. Firm fixed effects are present in all sectors except for 8, Basic Electrical Equipment. In sector 11, Carpets, all observations relating to one firm, which is very efficient but has a very small market share, were dropped. The firm, Brintons Ltd, produces very high quality carpets, and is not competing with other producers for the mass market. The Breusch–Pagan statistic tests for the presence of heteroscedasticity; figures in square brackets are the probability of critical values greater than the computed χ^2. Outliers, defined as the value of studentized residuals greater than or equal to 3.0, were excluded from the estimation.The presence of autocorrelation is examined on the basis of u_{it} where $\hat{e}_{it}$ are the residuals from the regression. The estimate ρ_{t-2} is reported in the table. The lagged dependent variable is instrumented. The instruments include mks_{it-2}~mks_{it-12}, u_{it-3}~u_{it-12}, Δmks_{it-3}~ Δmks_{it-12} and Δu_{it-3}~ Δu_{it-8} the precise set of instruments varies between sectors. An exception is 20, Pharmaceuticals, where the Sargan test for instrument validity was not accepted.

Table 3.3 Gross investment and the long-run efficiency of firms (dependent variable: firm long-run efficiency)

Independent variables	*Coefficient*	*t-value*
Constant	1.72	11.4
Investment rate	0.939	2.0
Investment rate squared	–0.275	–3.2
Industry dummies (χ^2)	315.09 (14 DF)	
R^2	0.98	
F-test	246.5	
Number of observations	75	

Notes: The dependent variable is exp (constant + $a_i^{'}$) where $a_i^{'}$ is the estimated coefficient of *i*th firm dummy and the constant is the estimated constant in the two-factor ALS frontier production function. A higher value implies more efficient production; recall that $a_i^{'} \leq 0$. The investment rate is the average rate of investment by the firm defined by the ratio of gross investment to capital stock in each period. The estimation method is OLS.

of the products will reduce the cross-elasticity of demand, and might be expected to lower the elasticity.[9] How these factors add up is specific to each sector; for example, the high elasticities for 11, Carpets and 13, Furniture, reflect the intense competition that characterized these sectors in the period under analysis, despite the differentiation of the products; by contrast, 20, Pharmaceuticals has a low elasticity reflecting a high degree of differentiation; and at the other extreme, the low elasticities for 1, Bricks and 19, Tyres presumably reflect the absence of competitive behaviour. The results are a warning against attempts to categorize the state of competition in a market *a priori*, on the basis of market structure and degree of product differentiation.

3.5. Determinants of the efficiency of firms

3.5.1. The determinants of relative efficiency in the long run

The results of Section 3.3 have shown that in the long run firms operate at different levels of efficiency. In analysing the determinants of the $a_i^{'}$, data limitations mean that we have limited options. We focus on the proposal of Scott (1991) that the appropriate contribution of capital accumulation to the growth of an economy (or a firm) should be measured by gross investment. His reasoning is that gross investment incorporates new techniques, and therefore does more for output than merely replacing old capital. Indeed old capital stock may be scrapped, not because it is 'worn out' in some sense, but because it is technically obsolete. In the context of the current analysis, the suggestion is that a firm's position in the ranking of efficiencies within a sector will be correlated with its investment rate.

In Table 3.3 the long-run efficiency of the firm, derived from the frontier production functions, is related to the average gross investment rate of the firm over the period. Once industry effects are controlled for, the long-run efficiency of the firm is positively related to the gross investment rate, but as indicated by the negative coefficient on the quadratic term, the relationship is subject to diminishing returns. This leaves open the question of exactly how additional investment relates to greater efficiency; one possibility, which cannot be addressed with the data available, is that higher investment reflects previous investment in R&D, with product and process innovations requiring additional or replacement plant.

3.5.2. The determinants of relative efficiency in the short run

u_{it} is an indicator of the failure of the firm to achieve its own best efficiency in period t. The empirical approach reported in this section is an application of the idea that a firm which is performing badly, in particular losing market share or facing falling profits, will generally have an incentive to improve its short-run efficiency. The dependent variable is $\Delta u_{it} = -(u_{it} - u_{it-1})$. A positive value indicates that the firm is becoming more efficient; a negative value that the firm is allowing its short-run efficiency to slip. Note that Δu_{it} is implicitly a first difference of log values; it is therefore appropriate to express all repressors as first differences in logs. The explanatory variables are of three kinds, reflecting the different types of competition that the firm may face (Vickers, 1995a). The first type is competition by comparison; if rival firms in the sector are becoming more efficient then there is more pressure on the firm to improve its own efficiency. This comparative efficiency aspect is addressed by introducing the change in efficiency of all other firms in the sector, Δu_{jt}. The coefficient is expected to be positive; the more efficient the rivals, the more efficient the firm. The second type of competition is in the product market: given the results of the previous section it is evident that inefficiency, in the long run, reduces a firm's market share. Here we introduce lagged changes in market share (Δs_{it-1} and Δs_{it-2}) to capture incentive effects; a falling market share should stimulate the firm to take action to improve its relative position, so a negative coefficient is expected. We also introduce the change in gross profits lagged one period $(\Delta \pi_{it-1})$. The idea is that deteriorating profits might spur the firm to improve efficiency by, for example, laying off staff, whereas an improving cash flow would allow the firm to relax its efforts. So a negative coefficient is expected. The third type of competition is in the market for corporate control; even if the threat of an actual takeover is weak, the firm will be concerned about changes in its market value (Δv_{it-1}). A falling market value may stimulate the firm to greater efficiency; a negative coefficient on lagged change in market value would be consistent with this interpretation. The empirical equation is completed by introducing firm and year fixed effects. We would not expect firm dummies to be significant given that the equation is in first differences. Year dummies should pick up any cyclical effects, though it should be noted that the estimating equations for the u_{it} in Section 3.3 have already controlled for these effects with both time-period dummies and a variable for sectoral demand changes, designed to proxy the effects of capacity utilization. The rate of technical progress in the sector, rtp_t, measured by the change in b_t (the shift of the frontier over time) in Equation (3.9), was also included in the equation; the idea is that where technical change is occurring rapidly firms may not give much attention to short-run efficiency gains.

Table 3.4 The determinants of changes in short-run efficiency (dependent variable: $\Delta u_{it} = -(u_{it} - u_{it-1})$

Explanatory variables (first differences)		*Coefficients*	*t-statistics*
Lagged short-run efficiency	Δu_{it-1}	0.1867	–2.6
	Δu_{it-2}	–0.1219	(–1.7)
Lagged market share	Δs_{it-1}	–0.0433	(–1.5)
	Δs_{it-2}	–0.0647	(–2.1)
Lagged gross profits	$\Delta \pi_{it-1}$	0.1344	–5.7
Lagged market value	Δv_{it-1}	–0.0206	(–0.7)
Rival firms efficiency	Δu_{jt}	0.3974	–9.1
Technical progress	Δrtp_t	–0.1431	(–1.1)
Firm fixed effects (χ^2)		No [34.5, 52]	
Year fixed effects (χ^2)		No [20.2, 14]	
Breusch–Pagan statistic (χ^2)		156.6 [0.929]	
Autocorrelation			
AR[2]	ρ_{t-2}	–0.0876	(–1.3)
AR[3]	ρ_{t-3}	–0.0067	–0.1
$\overline{R}^2$		0.13	
σ^2		0.011	
Number of observations		813	

Notes: The log-likelihood ratio test statistic (χ^2) is used to test firm and time-fixed effects; figures in square brackets are χ^2 values and degrees of freedom. Heteroscedasticity is tested by the Breusch–Pagan statistic; the figure in square brackets is the probability of the critical value greater than the computed χ^2. High order autocorrelation is detected by $\hat{e}_{it} = \rho_{t-2}\hat{e}_{it-2} + \rho_{t-3}\hat{e}_{it-3} + \varepsilon_{it}$, $\varepsilon_{it} \sim N(0, \sigma^2)$ where $\hat{e}_{it}$ are the residuals from the regression. Lagged dependent variables are instrumented; for Δu_{it-1} the instruments are Δu_{it-1}, Δu_{jt-2}, u_{jt-3}; and for Δu_{it-2} they are Δu_{it-3} and Δu_{jt-3}. The data are unbalanced due to missing values and elimination of some outliers. Outliers are deleted on the basis of (i) the value of studentized residuals greater than or equal to 4.0, (ii) the annual growth rate of regressors greater than 100 per cent (but for the growth of market value, greater than 120 per cent). The total number of outliers deleted was 40 observations, less than 5 per cent of the sample observations. Dropping the insignificant independent variables made no substantive difference to the coefficients on other variables. The equation was rerun with the assumption that Δu_{jt} was endogenous, with lagged values as instruments. The Hausman test indicated that the exogeneity of Δu_{jt} could not be rejected.

This empirical equation encounters two econometric problems. The first is that the dependent variable, Δu_{it} is itself an estimate derived from the analysis reported in Section 3.2. One consequence is that there may be serial correlation. The approach adopted here is to include Δu_{it-1} and Δu_{it-2}, appropriately instrumented, among the regressors, and to test for second and higher order serial correlation. The second issue is that we need to be sure that the equation is identified. The analysis in Section 3.4 explored a negative relationship in levels between market share (s_i) and firm inefficiency $\left(1-exp\left(a_i^{'}-u_{it}\right)\right)$. Here the focus is on the reverse causation, from changes in market share to changes in efficiency. How can we be sure that we have identified the relationships appropriately? First, the results in Table 3.2 include Wu–Hausman tests for the exogeneity of the inefficiency measure, which are accepted in every sector. Secondly, the repressors in the current analysis are lagged, rather than contemporaneous, changes in market share. Thirdly, we introduce rival firms' efficiency as a repressor, which is clearly not endogenous (and turns out to be highly significant). These repressors should suffice to identify the equation.

The regression results are given in Table 3.4, and are much as expected. Lagged declines in market share lead to improvements in current efficiency though the coefficients are not large. Contemporaneous efficiency improvements by rivals have a strong positive effect on efficiency.[10] Other explanatory variables, with one exception, have the expected signs, although they are not significant. The exception is lagged profits; unexpectedly this comes up with a positive and significant coefficient. One explanation is that the higher profitability facilitates investments for efficiency improvement. A two-period lagged profit, Δu_{it-2}, was also tried, but was not significant. Finally, as anticipated, neither firm nor year fixed effects are significant. The absence of year fixed effects suggests that the frontier production function estimations have successfully distinguished the Δu_{it} cyclical effects.

To sum up, there is support for the hypothesis that the short-run efficiency of the firm as measured by the Δu_{it} is affected by competition of two kinds. The first is competition by comparison with rivals, and is identified by the variable Δu_{jt}. The second is competition in the market place; loss of market share stimulates a firm to improve its efficiency.

3.6. Conclusions

In a simple model of homogeneous oligopoly, the relative efficiency of the firm determines its market share and its profitability. There is then an incentive to the firm to improve its relative efficiency, and the incentive is greater in markets where firm behaviour is more competitive. A simple indicator of the degree of competition is the slope of the relationship between market share and relative efficiency. In highly competitive markets (e.g. Bertrand competition with a homogeneous product) only the most efficient firms will survive. In less competitive markets (e.g. more collusive behaviour, differentiated products) less efficient firms may be able to maintain substantial market shares in protected market segments; so the relationship between efficiency and market share will be weaker.

In this chapter, we have attempted to put some empirical flesh on these theoretical structures in a study of efficiency and market shares in 19 UK manufacturing sectors in the 1970s and 1980s. Firm efficiency was analysed using frontier production functions, which enabled us to identify the long-run relative efficiency of each firm, and short-run departures from that efficiency level. These efficiency measures formed the basis for a number of subsequent analyses. We found that the relationship between relative efficiency and market share varies substantially across sectors, indicating different degrees of competition. Long-run efficiency is related to investment by the firm, suggesting that in a more competitive environment the firm has not only a strong incentive to improve its efficiency performance (increased market share and higher profitability), but also the means (investment) to do so. There is evidence of response by firms to short-run declines in market share. Short-run improvements in efficiency resulted, probably the result of greater managerial effort; and these improvements were larger the greater the improvements achieved contemporaneously by rival firms.

Appendix 3.I. The sample

The full sample was 181 firms in 21 three- or four-digit SIC UK manufacturing industries in the period 1970–89. All firms belonging to the selected industries, and appearing in the *Times 1000* list of top UK companies were included. In addition, we included firms which were identified as important players in other sources, e.g. Keynote Reports, and Monopolies and Mergers Commission Reports. The industries, which are listed below, were selected on a number of criteria: (a) they are fairly 'narrowly' defined in terms of products and markets; (b) they represent a range of industries in terms of technology and product type (producer goods, capital goods, consumer goods); and (c) they vary in structure – some are 'fragmented', others have a single dominant firm, others have a dominant group of firms. Two industries (3, Aerospace, 4, Ferrous Foundries) were not included in the analysis reported in this chapter because of data problems.

1 Bricks
2 Cements
3 Aerospace
4 Ferrous Foundries
5 Pumps, Valves
6 Machinery for Chemicals
7 Small Tools
8 Basic Electrical Equipment
9 Wires
10 Electrics
11 Carpets
12 Wool
13 Furniture
14 Brewing
15 Confectionery
16 Cereals
17 Newspapers
18 Tobacco
19 Tyres
20 Pharmaceuticals
21 General Chemical

Appendix 3.II. Data sources

1 *Companies accounts data*: EXSTAT on-line companies accounts data (main source), DATASTREAM on-line companies accounts data, published accounts of individual companies. These include employment data.

2 *Price indices (output and capital goods)*: Central Statistical Office, Reports MM17 (and comparable earlier publications), and *Annual Abstract of Statistics*.
3 *Sectoral data*: Business Statistics Office, Annual Reports on the Census of Production, PA series.
4 *Exports*: Business Statistics Office, Overseas Trade Statistics of the United Kingdom, MA20 series.
5 *Market valuation*: London Business School On-Line London Share Price Databank.

3.II.1. Data matching

The matching procedures for the data involved: (a) matching firms between EXSTAT and DATASTREAM using the name of the firm, and comparisons of sales and investment figures, (b) linking the industrial classification for each firm with the equivalent sectoral price indices, (c) matching the dates of company accounts (item C2 in EXSTAT) with the appropriate quarterly price series.

3.II.2. Data manipulation

1 *Fixed capital investment*: EXSTAT gives figures for gross additions and disposals of capital stock, and for acquisition and disposals of subsidiaries, distinguishing structures and equipment in each case. Disposals of capital stock, and changes in subsidiaries are in historic book values, and were revalued assuming an eight-year average age, and depreciation rates of 0.025 for structures and 0.0819 for equipment (see R. Blundell et al. (1989). 'Investment and Tobin's Q: evidence from panel data.' University College London Working Paper, 89-16, p. 32).
2 *Capital stock*: Capital stock was calculated using the perpetual inventory method. The earliest book value reported for each firm was taken as a starting value, revalued in the same way as the additions and disposals of subsidiaries. Depreciation rates (δ) were as assumed above. Investment (I_t) is the sum of gross additions minus disposals of capital stock, plus acquisitions minus disposals of subsidiaries (all revalued as described above). The formula for capital stock is then $K_t = \left[(1-\delta)K_{t-1} + I_{t-1}\right]P_t^k / P_{t-1}^k$, Note that this is the nominal capital stock at the beginning of each period; revaluation on the basis of sector-specific capital goods price indices $\left(P^k\right)$. The nominal capital stock is calculated separatedly for structures and equipment, and then aggregated.
3 *Profits*: Gross operating profits, excluding income from other sources (investments). Net profit is calculated using the capital stock series and the depreciation rates given above.
4 *Market shares*: Calculated as ratio of firm sales to sectoral sales including exports.

Notes

1 Email addresses: donald.hay@dsl.pipex.com, guy.liu@brunel.ac.uk. This chapter is based on a working paper of the Economics Department of Oxford University (1995), which derived from a project on Dynamic Efficiency and Corporate Performance, financed by the ESRC Functioning of Markets Initiative (project number: WIo2251013). In research for this chapter we have been greatly assisted by I. Ganoulis, who prepared the dataset, and John Roe and Catherine Gwilliam, who showed us how to derive Equation (3.6). Very helpful comments on previous versions were received from Katy Graddy, Steve Nickell, Robin Nuttall, Andrew Oswald, Howard Smith, John Vickers and two unknown referees.

2 Though theoretically imprecise, the concept of conjectural has been defended by Bresnahan (1989) as a useful device for summarizing the behaviour of oligopolists in multiperiod games.

3 All derivations are contained in a mathematical appendix to this chapter available from the authors on request.

4 For $\lambda = 0, \mu = 0$ (Nash–Cournot), so $\frac{\partial s_i}{\partial \lambda_i} < 0$. For $\lambda_j = (1 - s_j)/s_j$ (collusion), $\lambda_j/(1+\lambda_j) = (1 - s_j)$: hence $\mu = \sum_j 1/(n(1-s_j)) = 1 - 1/n$. Substituting in the expression for $\partial s_i / \partial \lambda_i$ shows that $\partial s_i / \partial \lambda_i < 0$. We conjecture that the derivative is negative over the whole range of behaviour from Nash–Cournot to collusion.

5 As our main concern in this chapter is not the specification and econometric estimation of frontier production functions, we make no pretence at a full discussion of the issues. The interested reader should consult Greene (1993) for a comprehensive survey.

6 The most efficient firm, j, was identified by running the regression with an arbitrary firm omitted. The estimated firm fixed effects were then inspected to identify the most efficient firm.

7 Green and Mayes (1991) give a helpful discussion of the choice of distribution for the u_{it}. Details of the comparative performance of different specifications of the distribution of the u_{it} are available from the authors on request.

8 Two sectors, 10, Electrical Goods and 16, Cereals, were dropped from the analysis of this section because of data problems.

9 The intuition may be illustrated as follows. Assume the simplest model of product differentiation, the Hotelling model with two products located on the market line, and with linear transport costs. If one product has lower costs of production, then with price competition it will have a lower price and hence a higher market share as it cuts into its rival's market area. However, this competition effect will be reduced if the linear transport costs are higher (the products are more 'differentiated'): so that market shares will be less responsive to cost differences between the firms. A formal analysis is beyond the scope of this chapter.

10 A referee commented that it is possible that this effect 'indicates a joint determination of improved efficiency for all firms (e.g. through technical developments) rather than competitive pressure'. Against this interpretation we note that the u_{it} are estimated in Section 3.3 in a specification which allows separately for technical change affecting all firms, and for cyclical demand effects on productivity.

References

Aigner, D.J., Lovell, C.A.K. and Schmidt, P. (1977). Formulation and estimation of stochastic frontier production function models. *Journal of Econometrics* 6, 21–37.

Baily, M.N., Julten, C. and Campbell, D. (1992). Productivity dynamics in manufacturing plants. *Brooking Papers on Economic Activity: Microeconomic,* 187–268.

Bresnahan, T.F. (1989). Empirical studies of industries with market power. In: R. Schmalensee and R.D. Willig (eds), *Handbook of Industrial Organization,* Chapter 17. Amsterdam and New York: North Holland.

Clarke, R. and Davies, S. (1982). Market structure and price-cost margins. *Economica* 49, 277–287.

Clarke, R., Davies, S. and Waterson, M. (1984). The profitability-concentration relation: market power or efficiency. *Journal of Industrial Economics* 32 (4), 435–450.

Cornwell, C., Schmidt, P. and Sickles, R.C. (1990). Production frontiers with cross-sectional and time-series variation in efficiency levels. *Journal of Econometrics* 46, 185–200.

Demsetz, H. (1974). Two systems of belief about monopoly. In: H.J. Goldschmid, H.M. Mann and J.F. Weston (eds), *Industrial Concentration: the New Learning* Boston, MA: Little Brown.

Green, A.J. and Mayes, D.G. (1991). Technical efficiency in manufacturing industries. *Economic Journal* 101, (May), 528–538.

Greene, W.H. (1993). The econometric approach to efficiency analysis. In: H.H. Fried, C.A.K. Lovell and S.S. Schmidt (eds), *The Measurement of Productive Efficiency*, 68–119. New York and Oxford: Oxford University Press.

Hart, O.D. (1983). The market mechanism as an incentive scheme. *Bell Journal of Economics* 14 (3), 366–382.

Hermalin, B.E. (1992). The effects of competition on executive behaviour. *Rand Journal of Economics* 23 (3), 350–365.

Hermalin, B.E. (1994). Heterogeneity in organizational form: why otherwise identical firms choose different incentives for their managers. *Rand Journal of Economics* 25 (4), 518–537.

Holmstrom, B. (1982). Moral hazard in teams. *Bell Journal of Economics* 13 (2), 324–340.

Nalebuff, B. and Stiglitz, J.E. (1983). Prizes and incentives: towards a general theory of compensation and competition. *Bell Journal of Economics* 14 (1), 21–43.

Nickell, S.J. (1996). Competition and corporate performance. *Journal of Political Economy* 104 (4), 724–745.

Scharfstein, D. (1988). Product market competition and managerial slack. *Rand Journal of Economics* 19 (1), 399–425.

Schmalensee, R. (1987). Collusion versus differential efficiency: testing alternative hypotheses. *Journal of Industrial Economics* 35 (4), 399–425.

Schmidt, P. and Sickles, R.C. (1984). Production frontiers and panel data. *Journal of Business and Economic Statistics* 2 (2), 367–374.

Scott, M.F.G. (1991). *A New Theory of Economic Growth.* Oxford: Oxford University Press.

Vickers, J.S. (1995a). Concepts of competition. *Oxford Economic Papers* 7 (1), 1–23.

Vickers, J.S. (1995b). Entry and selection under imperfect competition. Mimeo, Oxford: Institute of Economics and Statistics.

Willig, R.D. (1987). Corporate governance and product market structure. In: A. Razin and E. Sadka (eds), *Economic Policy in Theory and Practice*, 481–494. London: Macmillan.

4 A new way to measure competition

Jan Boone[1]

This chapter introduces a new way to measure competition based on firms' profits. Within a general model, we derive conditions under which this measure is monotone in competition, where competition can be intensified both through a fall in entry barriers and through more aggressive interaction between players. The measure is shown to be more robust theoretically than the price cost margin. This allows for an empirical test of the problems associated with the price cost margin as a measure of competition.

4.1. Introduction

A question often asked in both economic policy and research is how the intensity of competition evolves over time in a certain sector. To illustrate, a competition authority may want to monitor an industry so that it can intervene when competition slackens. Alternatively, there may have been a policy change in an industry (e.g. abolishing a minimum price or breaking up a large incumbent firm) with the goal of intensifying competition in the industry. Afterwards policy makers want to check whether the policy change had the desired effect. In economic research, there are empirical papers trying to identify the effect of competition on firms' efficiency (Nickell 1996), on firms' innovative activity (Aghion et al. 2002 and references therein) and the effects of competition on wage levels (Nickell 1999 for an overview) and wage inequality (Guadalupe 2003). The question is how should competition be measured for these purposes.

The price cost margin (PCM) is widely used as a measure of competition for these purposes. However, the theoretical foundations of PCM as a competition measure are not very robust. Theoretical papers like Amir (2002), Bulow and Klemperer (1999), Rosenthal (1980) and Stiglitz (1989) present models where more intense competition leads to higher PCM instead of lower margins. We believe that there are two reasons why PCM is still such a popular empirical measure of competition. First, we do not know how important these theoretical counterexamples are in practice. Is it the case that in 20 per cent of an economy's industries the structure is such that more competition would lead to higher PCM or is this only the case in 1 per cent of the industries? In the former case there would be big problems for the empirical papers mentioned above which use PCM as a measure of competition. In the latter case, the theoretical counterexamples do not seem to pose acute problems for empirical research. As long as there is no evidence that the theoretical counterexamples are important empirically, one would expect that PCM remains a popular competition measure. The second reason for the popularity of PCM is that the data needed to get a reasonable estimate of PCM is available in most data sets.[2]

The idea of this chapter is to develop a competition measure that is both theoretically robust and does not pose more stringent data requirements than PCM. This new measure can then be estimated in the same data sets as where PCM is estimated. This allows a comparison between the new measure and PCM for a number of industries over time together. If in 99 per cent of the industries the two measures indicate the same development in intensity of competition over time, this would indicate that the theoretical counterexamples cited above are not particularly relevant in practice. However, if in 20 per cent of the cases the two measures diverged then one should be more careful in using PCM as a measure of competition in empirical research and policy analysis.

The measure we introduce here is called performance-conduct-structure (PCS) indicator. It is defined as follows. Let $\pi(n)$ denote the variable profit level of a firm with efficiency level $n \in \Re_+$ (more details follow below on how variable profits and efficiency are defined). Consider three firms with different efficiency levels, $n'' > n' > n$, and calculate the following variable $\frac{\pi(n'')-\pi(n)}{\pi(n')-\pi(n)}$. Then more intense competition (brought about by either lower entry costs or more aggressive interaction among existing firms) raises this variable for a broad set of models. More precisely, in any model where a rise in competition reallocates output from less efficient to more efficient firms it is the case that more intense competition raises $\frac{\pi(n'')-\pi(n)}{\pi(n')-\pi(n)}$. Since this output reallocation effect is a general feature of more intense competition, PCS is a rather robust measure of competition from a theoretical point of view. Moreover, we show that the output reallocation effect is a natural necessary condition for PCM to be decreasing in intensity of competition, but it is not sufficient.

The intuition for PCS is related to the relative profits measure ($\pi(n')/\pi(n)$) is increasing in intensity of competition for $n' > n$) introduced by Boone (2000). The intuition for the relative profits measure is that in a more competitive industry, firms are punished more harshly for being inefficient. However, Boone (2000) analyses the relative profits measure in a number of specific examples, not in a general framework as we use here. Next, as explained below, it is harder to derive sufficient conditions for the relative profits measure to be monotone in intensity of competition because of a level effect. This level effect is removed by working with profit differences instead of profit levels.

The intuition why PCS is increasing in intensity of competition can be stated as follows. As the industry becomes more competitive, the most efficient firm n''

gains more relative to a less efficient firm n than firm n' does (with $n'' > n' > n$). Think, for instance, of a homogenous good market where firms produce with constant marginal costs. If these firms compete in quantities (Cournot), one would find (if n is close enough to n'') that $\pi(n'') > \pi(n') > \pi(n) > 0$. If competition is intensified by a switch to Bertrand competition, the profit levels satisfy $\pi(n'') > \pi(n') = \pi(n) = 0$. Hence the rise in competition raises $\pi(n'') - \pi(n)$ relative to $\pi(n') - \pi(n)$.

Recent papers measuring PCM include the following. First, Graddy (1995), Genesove and Mullin (1998) and Wolfram (1999) estimate the elasticity adjusted PCM. This yields the conduct (or conjectural variation) parameter, which can be interpreted as a measure of competition. This approach has been criticized by Corts (1999) who shows that, in general, efficient collusion cannot be distinguished from Cournot competition using the elasticity adjusted PCM. Second, Berry, Levinsohn and Pakes (1995) and Goldberg (1995) estimate both the demand and cost side of the automobile market. Their models can be used to simulate the effects of trade or merger policies on the industry. Using their estimates, one can also derive firms' PCMs. Nevo (2001) uses the same methods to estimate PCMs for firms in the ready-to-eat cereal industry. He does this under three different models of firm conduct and then compares the outcomes with (crude) direct observations of PCM. In this way he is able to identify the conduct model that explains best the observed values of PCM. As we argue below, in these papers one would also have been able to derive PCS, which has a more robust relation with intensity of competition.

This chapter is organized as follows. The next section introduces the model and the way that more intense competition is identified in this general set-up using the (generalized) output reallocation effect. Section 4.3 shows that PCS is increasing in competition and discusses which type of data are needed to estimate PCS in practice. Section 4.4 compares PCS and PCM and argues that both require similar data to be estimated. Further, we show that whereas the output reallocation effect is sufficient for PCS to be monotone in competition, it is only a necessary condition for PCM to be decreasing in competition, which explains the theoretical counterexamples. Finally, Section 4.5 concludes. The proofs of results can be found in Boone (2004).

4.2. The model

The aim of this section is to introduce a fairly general model of firms competing in a market. To keep things general we do not impose either Bertrand or Cournot competition. We simply assume that each firm n chooses a vector of strategic variables $a_n \in \Re^K$. This choice leads to output vector $q(a_n, Q, \theta) \in \Re^L_+$ for firm n where Q aggregates actions chosen by the firms in the industry that affect firm n's output (see below) and θ is a parameter that affects the aggressiveness with which firms interact in the market. For instance, θ could be related to the substitution elasticity between goods from different producers or it could denote whether firms play Cournot or Bertrand competition. Further, the choices of the strategic variables also lead to a vector of prices $p(a_n, P, \theta) \in \Re_+^L$ for firm *n*'s products, where *P* aggregates actions chosen by the firms in the industry that affect *n*'s prices. We assume that *Q* and *P* take the following form

$$Q = \int \zeta(a_n)\, dn$$

$$P = \int \xi(a_n)\, dn$$

for some functions $\zeta(.)$ and $\xi(.)$ where we integrate over all firms in the industry.[3] To illustrate, consider the case where demand is derived from a CES utility function $\left(\int x_n^\theta dn\right)^{\frac{1}{\theta}}$ where each firm *n* produces one product and consumers spend an amount *Y* in this industry. Then firm *n* faces demand of the form $x_n = p_n^{\frac{-1}{1-\theta}} \dfrac{Y}{\int p_j^{\frac{\theta}{1-\theta}} dj}$. In the notation used here, we get $p(a_n, P, \theta) = p_n$ and $q(a_n, Q, \theta) = p_n^{\frac{-1}{1-\theta}} \dfrac{Y}{Q}$ where $Q = \int p_j^{\frac{\theta}{1-\theta}} dj$.

Finally, we specify the costs of production for firm *n* as $C(q(a_n, Q, \theta), n)$. We say that $n \in \Re_+$ measures a firm's efficiency level because of the following assumption.

Assumption 1 For a given output vector $q \in \Re_+^L$ we assume that

$$\frac{\partial C(q,n)}{\partial q_l} > 0$$

$$\frac{\partial C(q,n)}{\partial n} \leq 0$$

$$\frac{\partial \left(\dfrac{\partial C(q,n)}{\partial q_l} \right)}{\partial n} \leq 0$$

for each $l \in \{1, 2, ..., L\}$, where the last inequality is strict for at least one combination of *q* and *l*.

That is, higher production levels lead to higher costs. Further, higher *n* firms produce the same output vector *q* with (weakly) lower costs *C* and (weakly) lower marginal costs for each product *l*. We assume that the efficiency distribution in the industry is given. In particular, we assume that *n* has an atomless distribution on the interval $[n_0, n_1]$ with density function *f*(.) and distribution function *F*(.). Although this distribution is exogenously given, the firms that are active in equilibrium are endogenously determined, as discussed below. The essential assumption here is that efficiency can be captured by a one-dimensional variable *n*. This assumption is not innocuous and will be discussed further below.

Using this set-up, consider the following two-stage game. In the first stage, firms decide simultaneously and independently whether or not to enter. Let's normalize actions a_n in such a way that a firm n that does not enter has $a_n = 0$ (while firms that do enter have $a_n \neq 0$). If a firm of type n enters it pays an entry cost $\gamma(n)$, where γ is a continuous function of efficiency, n. In the second stage firms know which firms entered in the first stage and all firms that entered choose simultaneously and independently their action vectors a_n.[4]

Definition 1 The set of actions $\{\hat{a}_n\}_{n\in[n_0,n_1]}$ denotes a pure strategy equilibrium if the following conditions are satisfied

$$\max_{a_n}\left\{p\left(a_n,\hat{P},\theta\right)^T q\left(a_n,\hat{Q},\theta\right)-C\left(q\left(a_n,\hat{Q},\theta\right),n\right)\right\}-\gamma(n)<0 \text{ implies } \hat{a}_n=0$$

where $p(.)^T$ denotes the transpose of the column vector $p(.)$ and

$$\left\{p\left(\hat{a}_n,\hat{P},\theta\right)^T q\left(\hat{a}_n,\hat{Q},\theta\right)-C\left(q\left(\hat{a}_n,\hat{Q},\theta\right),n\right)\right\}-\gamma(n)\geq 0 \text{ for } \hat{a}_n\neq 0$$

further

$$\hat{a}_n=\arg\max_{a_n}\left\{p\left(a_n,\hat{P},\theta\right)^T q\left(a_n,\hat{Q},\theta\right)-C\left(q\left(a_n,\hat{Q},\theta\right),n\right)\right\}$$

with

$$\hat{Q}=\int_{n_0}^{n_1}\zeta\left(\hat{a}_n\right)f(n)\,dn$$

$$\hat{P}=\int_{n_0}^{n_1}\xi\left(\hat{a}_n\right)f(n)\,dn$$

The following lemma derives an intuitive property of this equilibrium. If two firms n^* and n with $n^* > n$ both enter and producc positive output levels, then n^* produces (weakly) more than n and n^* is (weakly) more profitable.

Lemma 1 Consider two firms n^* and $n < n^*$ that both produce positive output levels in equilibrium (i.e. $\hat{a}_{n^*},\hat{a}_n\neq 0$). Then

$$q\left(\hat{a}_{n^*},\hat{Q},\theta\right)\geq q\left(\hat{a}_n,\hat{Q},\theta\right)$$

and

$$p\left(\hat{a}_{n^*},\hat{P},\theta\right)^T q\left(\hat{a}_{n^*},\hat{Q},\theta\right)-C\left(q\left(\hat{a}_{n^*},\hat{Q},\theta\right),n^*\right)$$

$$\geq p\left(\hat{a}_n, \hat{P}, \theta\right)^T q\left(\hat{a}_n, \hat{Q}, \theta\right) - C\left(q\left(\hat{a}_n, \hat{Q}, \theta\right), n\right)$$

We allow the entry cost γ to vary with a firm's efficiency level, $\gamma(n)$. It may be the case that more efficient firms face lower entry costs, $\gamma'(n) < 0$, because these firms are more efficient in both entry and production. But we also allow for the case where more efficient firms pay a higher entry cost to realize their cost advantage, $\gamma'(n) > 0$. For instance, this could reflect investments in R&D to develop a better production technology, investing more in capital or building a bigger factory to reap advantages of economies of scale. Thus an important distinction between $C(q, n)$ and $\gamma(n)$ is that $C(q, n)$ is weakly decreasing in n (for given q) while the sign of $\gamma'(n)$ is unrestricted.

The case with $\gamma'(n) > 0$ is also interesting as it allows for the *selection effect* of competition. In particular, more aggressive interaction between firms may lead to entry by more efficient firms at the expense of less efficient rivals.

Example 1 Consider an industry with two firms producing perfect substitutes where the demand curve is given by $p = 1 - q_1 - q_2$.[5] Firm i produces with cost function $\frac{q_i}{n_i}$ and faces entry cost γ_i. Assume that $n_1 > n_2$ and $n_2 > \frac{2n_1}{1+n_1}$. If both firms enter in Cournot equilibrium, price, output and profits equal $p^C = \frac{1 + \frac{1}{n_1} + \frac{1}{n_2}}{3}, q_i^C = \frac{1 - \frac{2}{n_i} + \frac{1}{n_{-i}}}{3}, \pi_i^C = \left(\frac{1 - \frac{2}{n_i} + \frac{1}{n_{-i}}}{3}\right)^2$.

Similarly, in Bertrand equilibrium

$$p^B = \frac{1}{n_2}, q_1^B = 1 - \frac{1}{n_2}, q_2^B = 0, \pi_1^B = \left(\frac{1}{n_2} - \frac{1}{n_1}\right)\left(1 - \frac{1}{n_2}\right), \pi_2^B = 0.$$

Consider the case where $n_1 = 100, \gamma_1 = 0.2, n_2 = 3, \gamma_2 = 0$. Then we find that $\pi_1^C = 0.19 < 0.2$ and hence firm 1 does not enter. However, with Bertrand competition $\pi_1^B = 0.22 > 0.2$. Hence more intense competition makes it possible in this case for the more efficient firm to recoup its entry cost. In this sense, the switch from Cournot to Bertrand competition selects the more efficient firms into the industry at the expense of less efficient ones.

Assuming that the second stage equilibrium in Definition 1 is unique, we can write the following reduced form expressions for firm n's equilibrium variable profits and output levels

$$\pi\left(n, \{n_{w0}^i, n_{w1}^i\}_{i=1}^I, \theta\right) \equiv \begin{bmatrix} p(\hat{a}_n, \hat{P}, \theta)^T q(\hat{a}_n, \hat{Q}, \theta) \\ -C(q(\hat{a}_n, \hat{Q}, \theta), n) \end{bmatrix} \tag{4.1}$$

$$q\left(n, \{n_{w0}^i, n_{w1}^i\}_{i=1}^I, \theta\right) \equiv q(\hat{a}_n, \hat{Q}, \theta) \tag{4.2}$$

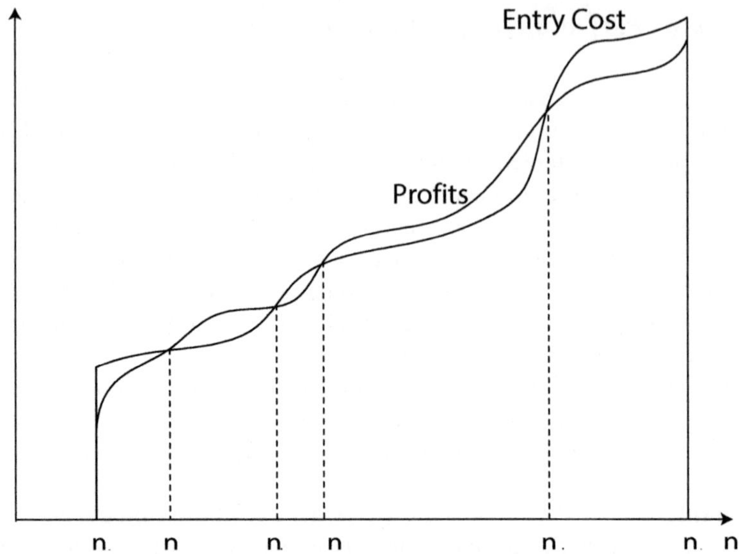

Figure 4.1 Entry costs $\gamma(n)$ and profits $\pi(n,\{n_{w0}^i,n_{w1}^i\}_{i=1}^2,\theta)$ as a function of efficiency n, with $n_{w0}^1 = n_a, n_{w1}^1 = n_b, n_{w0}^2 = n_c$, and $n_{w1}^2 = n_d$

where $\{n_{w0}^i, n_{w1}^i\}_{i=1}^I$ denotes the intervals of firms that enter the market. Since we allow for the possibility that the entry cost γ rises with n we cannot exclude the case where firm n enters while a more efficient firm $n' > n$ stays out of the market as it cannot recoup its entry costs. Hence in equilibrium there are $I \geq 1$ intervals of firms that enter the market. Put differently, we let $\cup_{i=1}^I \left[n_{w0}^i, n_{w1}^i\right]$ denote the set of firms that enter the market in equilibrium. Clearly, the bounds n_{w0}^i and n_{w1}^i depend on the aggressiveness of interaction θ but this is supressed to ease notation. Figure 4.1 gives an illustration of these equilibrium intervals of active firms $\{n_{w0}^i, n_{w1}^i\}_{i=1}^2$.

In this framework we consider two ways in which competition can be intensified. First, an across the board reduction in entry costs $-d\gamma > 0$ (more formally, $d\gamma(n) = d\gamma < 0$ for all types $n \in [n_0, n_1]$) and second more aggressive interaction between players, parameterized as $d\theta > 0$. The key to the analysis is the following way in which more intense competition is identified in this general framework.

Definition 2 The effects of $d\theta$ and $d(-\gamma)$ in the equilibrium above are as follows. The expression

$$\frac{d\ln\left(-\dfrac{\partial C\left(q\left(n,\{n_{w0}^i,n_{w1}^i\}_{i=1}^I,\theta\right),n\right)}{\partial n}\right)}{d\theta} \tag{4.3}$$

is increasing in n, where the effect of θ is partial in the sense that $\{n_{w0}^i, n_{w1}^i\}_{i=1}^I$ is here taken as given. And the expression

$$\frac{d\ln\left(-\frac{\partial C\left(q\left(n,\{n_{w0}^i,n_{w1}^i\}_{i=1}^I,\theta\right),n\right)}{\partial n}\right)}{d(-\gamma)} \tag{4.4}$$

is increasing in n.

Although these conditions do not look intuitive at first sight, we view them as a generalization of the output reallocation effect to the case where $q(., n)$ is a vector.[6] In the case where firms produce homogenous goods, Boone (2000) and Vickers (1995) identify a rise in competition as a parameter change that raises output of a firm relative to a less efficient firm. Put differently, a rise in θ (or fall in γ) raises $\frac{q(n^*)}{q(n)}$ for $n^* > n$. In words, if more intense competition reduces (raises) firms' output levels, the fall (rise) in output is bigger (smaller) for less efficient firms. Alternatively, the *output reallocation effect* can be stated as:

$$\frac{d\ln q(n)}{d\theta} \text{ and } \frac{d\ln q(n)}{d(-\gamma)} \text{ are increasing in } n. \tag{4.5}$$

Note that the output reallocation effect does not assume anything about the output levels of firms (only about relative output). This is important since we know that a change from Cournot to Bertrand competition tends to raise output of efficient firms, while it reduces output for inefficient firms. Thus there is no direct relation between intensity of competition and a firm's output level. Also, entry by new firms (as a result of a reduction in entry barriers) can both reduce every incumbent firm's output level and increase firms' output levels. See Amir and Lambson (2000) for details.

The reason why we look at the partial effect of θ, for given firms $\{n_{w0}^i, n_{w1}^i\}_{i=1}^I$ that participate in the market, is the well-known 'topsy turvy' result. In the case where firms produce differentiated goods, it may be the case that there are twenty firms under Cournot competition while there are sixteen firms under Bertrand competition. The reason is that Bertrand competition leads to lower rents and hence fewer firms enter in equilibrium. To avoid having to resolve this ambiguity (more aggressive interaction but smaller number of players), we consider the change in θ for a given set of firms in the market. It is clear that a switch from Cournot to Bertrand competition with a given number of firms in the market is a rise in competition. Only in this clear-cut case do we require the reallocation effect to hold.

If goods are not perfect substitutes, $\frac{q(n^*)}{q(n)}$ is not well defined ('dividing apples by oranges'). Taking this into account and allowing each firm to produce a number of products, it becomes clear that the reallocation effect has to be expressed in money terms. In principle, there are two ways to do that: costs $C(q, n)$ and revenues $p^T q$. The disadvantage of using revenues is that prices p will be affected by θ as well as output q. To illustrate, intensifying competition by making goods closer substitutes directly affects firms' demand functions and prices irrespective of a change in firms' output levels. Hence costs $C(q, n)$ seem a more natural choice here as it allows for the isolation of the effect of competition θ and γ on output q.

To gain further intuition for definition 2, note that the conditions above can also be stated as follows. Consider two firms n^{**} and $n^* < n^{**}$. Then the reduction in costs due to a small rise in efficiency $dn > 0$ for firm n^{**} relative to n^* is

$$\frac{-\left.\dfrac{\partial C\left(q\left(n,\left\{n_{w0}^i, n_{w1}^i\right\}_{i=1}^I,\theta\right),n\right)}{\partial n}\right|_{n=n^{**}}}{-\left.\dfrac{\partial C\left(q\left(n,\left\{n_{w0}^i, n_{w1}^i\right\}_{i=1}^I,\theta\right),n\right)}{\partial n}\right|_{n=n^{*}}}$$

The conditions above say that a rise in competition raises this ratio. That is, more intense competition leads to a bigger fall in costs (due to the efficiency gain $dn > 0$) for the high efficiency firm n^{**} as compared with the less efficient firm n^*.[7] This makes sense. More intense competition tends to marginalize inefficient firms by reducing their output levels. Therefore their costs become less dependent on their efficiency level. Consider the switch from Cournot to Bertrand competition in Example 1. In that example, we find that $-\dfrac{\partial C(q,n)}{\partial n} = \dfrac{q(n_i)}{n_i^2}$ for $i = 1, 2$. With Bertrand competition, a small change in the efficiency level of the inefficient firm has no effect on its costs. It does not produce anyway and hence $\dfrac{\partial C(q,n)}{\partial n} = 0$. While under Cournot competition, the same change in efficiency of the inefficient firm does affect its cost level. For the efficient firm, the effect of its efficiency level on its costs is bigger under Bertrand competition than under Cournot because its output level is bigger under Bertrand. Hence, the ratio $\dfrac{-\dfrac{\partial C(q,n_i)}{\partial n_i}}{-\dfrac{\partial C(q,n_j)}{\partial n_j}} = \dfrac{q(n_i)}{q(n_j)}\dfrac{n_j^2}{n_i^2}$ (with $n_i > n_j$) goes up with a switch from Cournot to Bertrand competition.

The next two examples illustrate this reallocation effect further.

Example 2 Consider an industry where each firm i produces only one product, faces a demand curve of the form

$$p(q_i, q_{-i}) = a - bq_i - d\sum_{j\neq i} q_j$$

and has constant marginal costs $\frac{1}{n_i}$. Then firm i chooses output q_i which solves

$$\max_{q\geq 0}\{(a - bq - d\sum_{j\neq i} q_j)q - \frac{1}{n_i}q\}$$

where we assume that $a > \frac{1}{n_i} > 0$ and $0 < d \leq b$. Then the first order condition for a Cournot–Nash equilibrium can be written as

$$a - 2bq_i - d\sum_{j\neq i} q_j - \frac{1}{n_i} = 0 \tag{4.6}$$

Assuming N firms produce positive output levels, one can solve the N first order conditions (4.6). This yields

$$q(n_i) = \frac{\left(\frac{2b}{d} - 1\right)a - \left(\frac{2b}{d} + N - 1\right)\frac{1}{n_i} + \sum_{j=1}^{N}\frac{1}{n_j}}{(2b + d(N-1))\left(\frac{2b}{d} - 1\right)} \tag{4.7}$$

Now assume that because of a fall in entry cost γ an additional firm $N + 1$ with constant marginal costs $1/n_{N+1}$ can enter the industry. Then it is routine to verify that

$$\frac{-\frac{\partial C(q, n_i)}{\partial n_i}}{-\frac{\partial C(q, n_j)}{\partial n_j}} = \frac{q(n_i)\, n_j^2}{q(n_j)\, n_i^2}$$

increases after entry for $n_i > n_j (i, j \neq N+1)$.

Example 3 Consider a Hotelling beach of length 1 with consumers distributed uniformly over the beach with density 1. Firm 1 is located on the far left of the beach and firm 2 on the far right. Firm i has constant marginal costs $1/n_i$ $(i = 1, 2)$. A consumer at position $x \in \langle 0, 1\rangle$ who buys a product from firm 1 incurs a linear travel cost tx, and if she buys from firm 2 she incurs travel cost $t(1 - x)$. Assume that each consumer buys one and only one product and that he buys from the firm with the lowest overall cost. Then demand for firm i equals $q_i(p_i, p_j; t) = \frac{1}{2} + \frac{p_j - p_i}{2t}$. As travel costs decrease, consumers are more inclined to buy from the cheapest firm rather than the closest one. So as travel costs decrease, firms' monopoly power is reduced and competition is more intense. Parameterizing competition as $\theta = \frac{1}{t}$, the Nash equilibrium output levels equal respectively

$$q_i = \frac{1}{6}\left(3+\theta\left(\frac{1}{n_j}-\frac{1}{n_i}\right)\right) \tag{4.8}$$

Clearly, we find that an increase in θ raises

$$\frac{-\frac{\partial C(q,n_i)}{\partial n_i}}{-\frac{\partial C(q,n_j)}{\partial n_j}} = \frac{3+\theta\left(\frac{1}{n_j}-\frac{1}{n_i}\right)}{3-\theta\left(\frac{1}{n_j}-\frac{1}{n_i}\right)}\frac{n_j^2}{n_i^2} \text{ for } n_i > n_j .$$

In these simple examples with constant marginal costs, we see that the condition on

$$\frac{d\ln\left(-\frac{\partial C(q,n)}{\partial n}\right)}{d\theta} \text{ and } \frac{d\ln\left(-\frac{\partial C(q,n)}{\partial n}\right)}{d(-\gamma)}$$

actually boils down to the output reallocation effect. That is,

$$\frac{d\ln\left(-\frac{\partial C(q,n)}{\partial n}\right)}{d\theta} \text{ and } \frac{d\ln\left(-\frac{\partial C(q,n)}{\partial n}\right)}{d(-\gamma)}$$

increasing in *n* is equivalent to $\frac{d\ln q(n)}{d\theta}$ and $\frac{d\ln q(n)}{d(-\gamma)}$ increasing in *n*. This is true for more general cost functions as well, as the next lemma illustrates.

Lemma 2 Consider the case where a firm produces only one product, $L = 1$. Assume that the cost function $C(q, n)$ can be written as

$$C(q,n) = \int_n^{+\infty} \omega(t) e^{\int_{q_0}^{q} \frac{\phi(t,x)}{x} dx} dt \tag{4.9}$$

with $q_0, \omega(.), \phi(.,.), \frac{\partial \phi(n,q)}{\partial n}, \frac{\partial \phi(n,q)}{\partial q} \geq 0$. Then the output reallocation effect, that is

$$\frac{d\ln\left[q\left(n,\{n_{w0}^i, n_{w1}^i\}_{i=1}^I, \theta\right)\right]}{d\theta}$$

is increasing in *n*, is sufficient for (4.3) to hold. The same is true for $d(-\gamma)$.

Although the cost function in Equation (4.9) looks nonstandard, it is quite general. It is, for instance, routine to verify that $\omega(n) = \frac{1}{n^2}$ and $\phi(n,q) = \frac{\sum_{m=1}^{M} \gamma_m m q^m}{\sum_{m=0}^{M} \gamma_m q^m}$ lead to a cost function of the form $C(n,q) = \frac{\Gamma}{n}\left(\sum_{m=0}^{M} \gamma_m q^m\right)$ for some constant $\Gamma > 0$ and $M + 1$ scalars γ_m. Indeed, the case considered in the example above with $C(n,q) = \frac{q}{n}$ is a special case of this cost function.

Finally, to get some intuition for the multiproduct case, consider the case where the cost function $C(q, n)$ can be written as $C(q,n) = \omega(n)\phi(q)$ with $\omega : \Re_+ \to \Re_+, \omega'(.) < 0$ and $\phi : \Re_+^L \to \Re_+$ an increasing function of the output vector q. Then it is routine to verify that the following two conditions are sufficient for Definition 2 to hold. The elasticity $\frac{\partial \phi(q)}{\partial q_l}\frac{q_l}{\phi(q)}$ is nondecreasing in q_i and the output reallocation effect ($\frac{d \ln(q_l)}{d\theta}$ and $\frac{d \ln(q_l)}{d(-\gamma)}$ are increasing in n) holds at the product level for each product l.

4.3. New measure of competition

This section introduces relative profits differences as a measure of competition, called PCS indicator, and discusses under which conditions this measure can be estimated using firm-level panel data. Broadly speaking, the better one is able to separate fixed and variable costs in the data, the more robust the competition measure will be that one can estimate.

The innovation of this chapter is to measure intensity of competition in an industry by estimating the following variable

$$\frac{\pi\left(n^{**}, \left\{n_{w0}^{i}, n_{w1}^{i}\right\}_{i=1}^{I}, \theta\right) - \pi\left(n, \left\{n_{w0}^{i}, n_{w1}^{i}\right\}_{i=1}^{I}, \theta\right)}{\pi\left(n^{*}, \left\{n_{w0}^{i}, n_{w1}^{i}\right\}_{i=1}^{I}, \theta\right) - \pi\left(n, \left\{n_{w0}^{i}, n_{w1}^{i}\right\}_{i=1}^{I}, \theta\right)} > 0 \qquad (4.10)$$

for any three firms with $n^{**} > n^{*} > n$, where $\pi(.)$ is defined in Equation (4.1). The following theorem shows why this is a robust measure of competition.

Theorem 1 An increase in competition raises the expression in Equation (4.10) for any three firms with $n^{**} > n^{*} > n$. That is,

$$\frac{d\left(\frac{\pi\left(n^{**}, \left\{n_{w0}^{i}, n_{w1}^{i}\right\}_{i=1}^{I}, \theta\right) - \pi\left(n, \left\{n_{w0}^{i}, n_{w1}^{i}\right\}_{i=1}^{I}, \theta\right)}{\pi\left(n^{*}, \left\{n_{w0}^{i}, n_{w1}^{i}\right\}_{i=1}^{I}, \theta\right) - \pi\left(n, \left\{n_{w0}^{i}, n_{w1}^{i}\right\}_{i=1}^{I}, \theta\right)}\right)}{d\theta} > 0$$

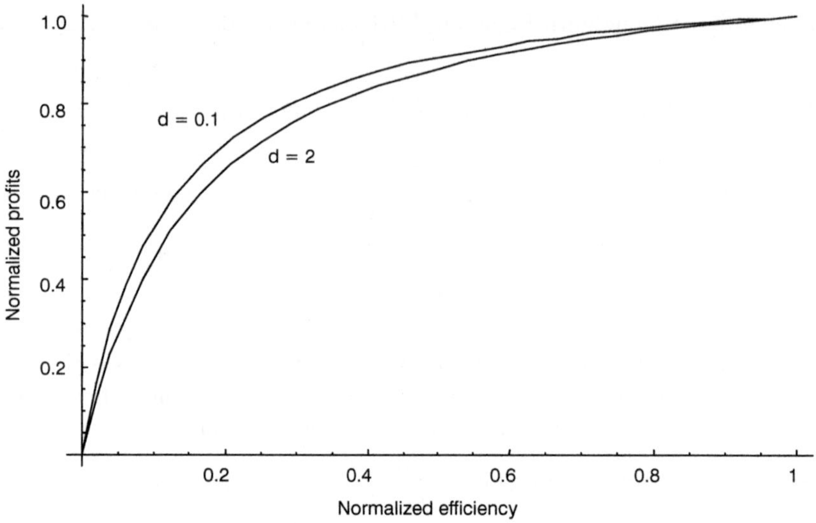

Figure 4.2 Firm n's normalized profits $\frac{\pi(n,\theta)-\pi(\underline{n},\theta)}{\pi(\overline{n},\theta)-\pi(\underline{n},\theta)}$ as a function of n's normalized efficiency $\frac{n-\underline{n}}{\overline{n}-\underline{n}}$

where the effect of θ is partial, i.e. taking $\left\{n_{w0}^i, n_{w1}^i\right\}_{i=1}^I$ as given, and

$$\frac{d\left(\frac{\pi\left(n^{**},\left\{n_{w0}^i,n_{w1}^i\right\}_{i=1}^I,\theta\right)-\pi\left(n,\left\{n_{w0}^i,n_{w1}^i\right\}_{i=1}^I,\theta\right)}{\pi\left(n^{*},\left\{n_{w0}^i,n_{w1}^i\right\}_{i=1}^I,\theta\right)-\pi\left(n,\left\{n_{w0}^i,n_{w1}^i\right\}_{i=1}^I,\theta\right)}\right)}{d(-\gamma)}>0$$

To illustrate this result, consider the example in Figure 4.2. This is based on Example 2 with a = 20, b = 2, N = 20 and firm $i \in \{1,2,...,20\}$ has constant marginal costs equal to $\frac{i}{10}$ (hence efficiency of i equals $n_i = \frac{10}{i}$). Figure 4.2 has $\frac{n-\underline{n}}{\overline{n}-\underline{n}}$ on the horizontal axis and $\frac{\pi(n,\theta)-\pi(\underline{n},\theta)}{\pi(\overline{n},\theta)-\pi(\underline{n},\theta)}$ (note that this is the inverse of the expression in (4.10) to avoid dividing by zero for $n=\underline{n}$) on the vertical axis with $\underline{n} \le n \le \overline{n}$ ($\underline{n}=1, \overline{n}=10$) and where $\pi(n,\theta)$ is used as a shorthand for $\pi\left(n,\left\{n_{w0}^i,n_{w1}^i\right\}_{i=1}^I,\theta\right)$. This relation is increasing (more efficient firms make higher profits π). The more competitive the industry, the more this curve is pulled into the corner at bottom-right. This is illustrated in the graph for the case where competition is intensified by making goods closer substitutes (d increases from 0.1 to 2). Further, with Bertrand competition, homogenous goods and constant marginal costs one finds that the curve is flat and equal to zero for all $n \in [\underline{n}, \overline{n}\rangle$ and equal to 1 at $n = \overline{n}$. This corresponds to perfect competition. Competition can now be measured as the area under this curve. The smaller this area, the more intense competition is (note that because of the normalizations used on the axes, this area under the curve lies between 0 and 1). In particular, in the Bertrand equilibrium just mentioned, the area under the curve equals 0.

Note that one does not need to observe all firms in an industry to make a graph like the one in Figure 4.2. Indeed Figure 4.2 also just uses a subset of the firms ($i \in \{1,...,10\}$). The reason is that the result in Theorem 1 holds for any three firms. This is in contrast to concentration measures which make no sense if not all firms in the industry are observed.

What type of data is needed to estimate the measure in Equation (4.10)? The data we have in mind is firm- or plant-level data that specify per firm total revenues, total wage bill (or preferably wage costs split according to production workers (blue collar) and management (white collar), see below), costs of inputs used, energy etc. Data sets like this are available in more and more countries (usually at a country's statistical offices where this data forms the basis of the national accounts). Examples of papers using such data are Aghion et al. (2002), Klette (1999), Klette and Griliches (1999) and Lindquist (2001). Further, the data should be available at the four- or five-digit level such that the one-dimensional efficiency assumption is a decent approximation. In particular, the more aggregated the data become, say at the two-digit level, the more likely it is that one firm is more efficient in producing one good and another firm more efficient in producing another good within this two-digit category. In that case, efficiency is no longer a one-dimensional variable. As we will argue below, this one-dimensional efficiency assumption is also necessary for the price cost margin as a measure of competition.

Equation (4.1) defining variable profits $\pi(.)$, states that the costs $C(q, n)$ should be included in calculating profits while $\gamma(n)$ should not be included. Hence $\pi(.)$ equals total revenues for a firm minus costs $C(q, n)$.

The following describes how to decide which cost categories in the data should be included in $C(q, n)$ and which in $\gamma(n)$. First, any costs, like materials and energy, that are viewed as variable costs (i.e. varying with small changes in production) should be included in $C(q, n)$. Second, fixed costs that are seen as being positively correlated with a firm's efficiency level should be included in $\gamma(n)$ because only the costs γ are allowed to be increasing in n (see Assumption 1). Examples mentioned above are investments in R&D and capital stocks, where higher investments may lead to lower marginal costs and hence higher efficiency in production. For cost categories in the data that are seen as fixed costs that do not vary with efficiency, it is immaterial whether they are included under $C(q, n)$ or $\gamma(n)$.[8] Finally, with fixed costs that fall with efficiency, one has a choice whether to incorporate them under $C(q, n)$ or $\gamma(n)$. Here the decision should be based on Definition 2 and the equilibrium properties of the model one has in mind to describe the sector.

To illustrate this last point, first consider Example 3 but suppose that firm *i*'s costs are of the form $q/n_i + c_0/n_i$ for $i = 1, 2$. In that case, both

$$\frac{-\frac{\partial\left(\frac{q(n_i)}{n_i}\right)}{\partial n_i}}{-\frac{\partial\left(\frac{q(n_j)}{n_j}\right)}{\partial n_j}} = \frac{3+\theta(\frac{1}{n_j}-\frac{1}{n_i})}{3-\theta(\frac{1}{n_j}-\frac{1}{n_i})}\frac{n_j^2}{n_i^2}$$

and

$$\frac{-\frac{\partial\left(\frac{q(n_i)}{n_i}+\frac{c_0}{n_i}\right)}{\partial n_i}}{-\frac{\partial\left(\frac{q(n_j)}{n_j}+\frac{c_0}{n_j}\right)}{\partial n_j}} = \frac{\frac{3+\theta(\frac{1}{n_j}-\frac{1}{n_i})}{6}+c_0}{\frac{3-\theta(\frac{1}{n_j}-\frac{1}{n_i})}{6}+c_0}\frac{n_j^2}{n_i^2}$$

are increasing in θ for $n_i > n_j$. Thus in this model one is free to choose whether $\frac{c_0}{n_i}$ is part of *C*(*q*, *n*) or γ(*n*). In other models, however, it may be the case that the conditions in Definition 2 only hold when the fixed cost is categorized under γ(*n*). In that case it is essential that these costs are not included in costs *C*(*q*, *n*) nor in profits π(.). It appears to be the case that the conditions in Definition 2 are more easily satisfied the more categories of fixed costs are included under γ(.) and hence the closer *C*(0, *n*) gets to 0. In this sense, *C*(*q*, *n*) should ideally include only variable costs and no fixed costs.

If the data allows the researcher to identify different cost categories, variable costs should be calculated as the sum of labour costs (if possible only the costs of (blue collar) production workers, since (white collar) managers tend to be viewed as fixed costs), material costs, intermediate inputs and energy expenditure. Hence expenditures on or depreciation of R&D, advertisement and capital should not be included in the variable costs nor in profits π(.). Since costs of depreciation that are economically relevant (instead of advantageous from a tax point of view) are usually hard to come by, it is actually an advantage that such costs should not be included in the calculation of π(.).

However, if the data set only specifies total costs per firm, the observable profit level is $\pi(n)-\gamma(n)$. In that case, we need additional assumptions for the PCS measure to work. The following proposition formulates conditions for the measure $\frac{\pi(n^{**})-\gamma(n^{**})-[\pi(n)-\gamma(n)]}{\pi(n^{*})-\gamma(n^{*})-[\pi(n)-\gamma(n)]}$ to be monotone in θ and γ.

Proposition 1 Take three firms with $n^{**} > n^{*} > n$. Then the assumption that

$$\frac{\gamma'(t)}{\left(-\frac{\partial C\left(q\left(t,\{n_{w0}^{i},n_{w1}^{i}\}_{i=1}^{I},\theta\right),t\right)}{\partial t}\right)}$$

is nondecreasing[9] in $t \in \langle n, n^{**}\rangle$ is sufficient for the measure

$$\frac{\pi(n^{**})-\gamma(n^{**})-[\pi(n)-\gamma(n)]}{\pi(n^{*})-\gamma(n^{*})-[\pi(n)-\gamma(n)]}$$

to be monotone in competition ($d\theta > 0$ and $d(-\gamma) > 0$) if either of the following conditions holds for all $t \in \langle n, n^{**}\rangle$:

(i) $$\frac{d\left(-\frac{\partial C\left(q\left(t,\{n_{w0}^{i},n_{w1}^{i}\}_{i=1}^{I},\theta\right),t\right)}{\partial t}\right)}{d\theta} \geq 0$$

and $$\gamma'(t) < -\frac{\partial C\left(q\left(t,\{n_{w0}^{i},n_{w1}^{i}\}_{i=1}^{I},\theta\right),t\right)}{\partial t}$$

(ii) $$\frac{d\left(-\frac{\partial C\left(q\left(t,\{n_{w0}^{i},n_{w1}^{i}\}_{i=1}^{I},\theta\right),t\right)}{\partial t}\right)}{d\theta} \leq 0$$

and $$\gamma'(t) > -\frac{\partial C\left(q\left(t,\{n_{w0}^{i},n_{w1}^{i}\}_{i=1}^{I},\theta\right),t\right)}{\partial t}$$

with similar expressions for $d(-\gamma)$.

In words, the condition prevents the case where $\gamma'(n)$ falls faster than $-\frac{\partial C\left(q\left(n,\{n_{w0}^{i},n_{w1}^{i}\}_{i=1}^{I},\theta\right),n\right)}{\partial n}$ as a function of *n*. The intuition for this is the following. We know from above that a rise in θ raises $\frac{\pi(n^{**})-\pi(n)}{\pi(n^{*})-\pi(n)}$. That is, it raises the difference $\pi(n^{**})-\pi(n)$ more in percentage terms than it raises $\pi(n^{*})-\pi(n)$. If $\gamma'(n)$ falls 'too fast', the difference $\gamma(n)-\gamma(n^{**})$ is going to be big and hence $\pi(n^{**})-\gamma(n^{**})-[\pi(n)-\gamma(n)]$ is going to be big in absolute value. In case (i), the increase (due to $d\theta > 0$) in $\pi(n^{**})-\pi(n)=\int_{n}^{n^{**}} -\frac{\partial C(.,t)}{\partial t}dt$

(see Boone 2004) becomes too small to raise $\pi\left(n^{**}\right)-\gamma\left(n^{**}\right)-\left[\pi\left(n\right)-\gamma\left(n\right)\right]$ more in percentage terms than the rise in θ raises $\pi\left(n^{*}\right)-\gamma\left(n^{*}\right)-\left[\pi\left(n\right)-\gamma\left(n\right)\right]$. So we need to exclude this case to be sure that $\dfrac{\pi\left(n^{**}\right)-\gamma\left(n^{**}\right)-\left[\pi\left(n\right)-\gamma\left(n\right)\right]}{\pi\left(n^{*}\right)-\gamma\left(n^{*}\right)-\left[\pi\left(n\right)-\gamma\left(n\right)\right]}$ is increasing in competition. A similar intuition applies in case (ii).

Above we have focused on the partial effects of θ, taking the firms active in the market as given. As one would expect, if condition (4.3) in Definition 2 holds for the overall effect of θ (i.e. taking the effect on the active firms into account as well), then the overall effect of a rise in θ is indeed to increase the PCS measure in Equation (4.10).

Corollary 1 If the expression

$$\frac{d\ln\left(-\dfrac{\partial C\left(q\left(n,\left\{n_{w0}^{i}\left(\theta\right),n_{w1}^{i}\left(\theta\right)\right\}_{i=1}^{I(\theta)},\theta\right),n\right)}{\partial n}\right)}{d\theta} \tag{4.11}$$

is increasing in n, where the effect of θ on $\left\{n_{w0}^{i}\left(\theta\right),n_{w1}^{i}\left(\theta\right)\right\}_{i=1}^{I(\theta)}$ is taken into account, then the overall effect of an increase in θ on

$$\frac{\pi(n^{**},\{n_{w0}^{i}(\theta),n_{w1}^{i}(\theta)\}_{i=1}^{I(\theta)},\theta)-\pi(n,\{n_{w0}^{i}(\theta),n_{w1}^{i}(\theta)\}_{i=1}^{I(\theta)},\theta)}{\pi(n^{*},\{n_{w0}^{i}(\theta),n_{w1}^{i}(\theta)\}_{i=1}^{I(\theta)},\theta)-\pi(n,\{n_{w0}^{i}(\theta),n_{w1}^{i}(\theta)\}_{i=1}^{I(\theta)},\theta)}$$

for any three active firms with $n^{**}>n^{*}>n$ is positive:

$$\frac{d\left(\dfrac{\pi(n^{**},\{n_{w0}^{i}(\theta),n_{w1}^{i}(\theta)\}_{i=1}^{I(\theta)},\theta)-\pi(n,\{n_{w0}^{i}(\theta),n_{w1}^{i}(\theta)\}_{i=1}^{I(\theta)},\theta)}{\pi(n^{*},\{n_{w0}^{i}(\theta),n_{w1}^{i}(\theta)\}_{i=1}^{I(\theta)},\theta)-\pi(n,\{n_{w0}^{i}(\theta),n_{w1}^{i}(\theta)\}_{i=1}^{I(\theta)},\theta)}\right)}{d\theta}>0$$

$$\frac{d\left(\dfrac{\pi(n^{**},\{n_{w0}^{i}(\theta),n_{w1}^{i}(\theta)\}_{i=1}^{I(\theta)},\theta)-\pi(n,\{n_{w0}^{i}(\theta),n_{w1}^{i}(\theta)\}_{i=1}^{I(\theta)},\theta)}{\pi(n^{*},\{n_{w0}^{i}(\theta),n_{w1}^{i}(\theta)\}_{i=1}^{I(\theta)},\theta)-\pi(n,\{n_{w0}^{i}(\theta),n_{w1}^{i}(\theta)\}_{i=1}^{I(\theta)},0)}\right)}{d\theta}>0$$

4.4. Discussion

This section compares the PCS and PCM measures of competition. We argue that the data requirements to estimate these two measures are the same. Further, although some of the assumptions made above (like one-dimensional efficiency) are not usually mentioned when PCM is used as a measure of competition, we show that these assumptions are needed to interpret a fall in PCM as an increase in competition. Finally, we show that the generalized output reallocation effect in Definition 2 is a natural necessary condition for PCM to be monotone in competition, but it is not sufficient. This explains why PCS is a theoretically robust measure of competition while there are counterexamples where a rise in competition leads to higher PCM.

Broadly speaking, there are two ways in the literature to estimate price cost margins. One is to approximate firm i 's price cost margin by an expression like (see, for instance, Scherer and Ross 1990:418)

$$\frac{revenues_i - variable\ costs_i}{revenues_i} \tag{4.12}$$

Using this to calculate PCM requires similar data as one needs to calculate profits $\pi(.)$ in (4.1) as revenues minus variable costs. An important assumption in the PCM case is that average variable costs can be used as an estimate for marginal costs. This is correct if marginal costs are constant.[10] Note that this assumption is not directly required for estimating π, since $C(q, n)$ is allowed to take any form. However, for the PCS measure we need to rank firms according to their efficiency level. And assuming that marginal costs are constant clearly makes the ranking of firms in terms of efficiency n very simple. In other words, although assuming that marginal costs are constant is, strictly speaking, not needed to estimate PCS, the assumption does make the implementation of PCS a lot simpler.

The other way to estimate price cost margins is to use a structural approach (see Reiss and Wolak 2007 for a survey). In this case, the researcher specifies precisely what the demand function and the cost function $C(q, n)$ look like and what equilibrium is played by the firms. The data are then used to identify the specified demand and cost parameters. From this PCM can be derived.

Note that the PCS measure is a variable that can be estimated in both ways. One can estimate PCS in an analogous way as PCM is estimated in Equation (4.12). But it is also possible to use a structural approach and be more specific about the functional forms of demand and costs $C(q, n)$. To illustrate, Table VIII in Berry, Levinsohn and Pakes (1995) contains all the necessary information (efficiency n and variable profits π) to calculate PCS. This chapter just offers PCS as a complementary competition measure to PCM and does not take a position on how the measures should be estimated in practice.

When PCM is used as a measure of competition, it is not always explicitly assumed that efficiency is one dimensional nor that the efficiency level can be observed. We argue, using two simple examples, that these assumptions are, in fact, implicitly made once the estimated PCM is interpreted as a measure of competition. The first example shows that information about efficiency is needed if one wants to interpret a higher price cost margin as less intense competition.

Example 4 Consider the same, homogenous good, industry in two countries A and B. In both countries, demand in the industry takes the form $X(p) = 1/p$ where $X(p)$ is the quantity demanded at price p. Assume the most efficient firm in country A produces with constant marginal costs equal to $c_1^A = 1$ and in country B with $c_1^B = 3$. Further, assume that the next efficient firm produces with constant marginal costs $c_2^A = 5$ in country A and with $c_2^B = 6$ in country B. If in both countries, the industry is characterized by

Table 4.1 Increasing competition in Example 2 by making goods closer substitutes with $c_1 = 0.1$; $c_2 = 6.5$, $c_3 = 7$, $\gamma_1 = \gamma_2 = \gamma_3 = 0$, $a = 20$, $b = 2$

	d = 1.5	*d = 2.0*
PCM_1	0.99	0.99
PCM_2	0.30	0.23
PCM_3	0.26	0.17
Industry PCM	0.68	0.76
$PCS = \frac{\pi(c_2) - \pi(c_3)}{\pi(c_1) - \pi(c_3)}$	0.04	0.02

Table 4.2 Increasing competition in Example 2 by reducing entry costs ($d\gamma = -0.1$) with $c_1 = c_2 = 0.1$, $c_3 = 3$, $c_4 = c_5 = 6$, $\gamma_1 = \gamma_2 = 16.5$, $\gamma_3 = 5$, $\gamma_4 = \gamma_5 = 0.7$ $a = 20$, $b = 2$, $d = 1.5$

	dγ = 0	*dγ = –0.1*
PCM1	0.99	0.98
PCM2	*	0.98
PCM3	0.60	0.55
PCM4	0.25	0.17
PCM5	0.25	n.a*
Industry PCM	0.66	0.81
$PCS = \frac{\pi(c_2) - \pi(c_3)}{\pi(c_1) - \pi(c_3)}$	0.37	0.34

* Not active in the equilibrium

Bertrand competition, one finds that the equilibrium price cost margins equal $PCM^A = 4/5$ and $PCM^B = 3/6$. Clearly, the industry is more competitive in country *A* but PCM (without information on the marginal cost levels of firms) points in the opposite direction as $PCM^A > PCM^B$.

Indeed, Nevo (2001) compares the PCM generated by his estimated model with a (crude) direct observation of PCM based on accounting cost data to see how the magnitude of PCM should be interpreted in terms of intensity of competition.

The second example shows that in the multiproduct case where efficiency is not one dimensional, more intense competition can be associated with higher PCM.

Example 5 Suppose that a researcher observes two firms, 1 and 2, which both can produce two goods, *a* and *b*. The data contains only information about aggregate sales and costs of both goods at the firm level. Instead of assuming that efficiency is one dimensional, we assume that it is two dimensional. More precisely we assume that firm 1 is more efficient than firm 2 in producing good *a* while firm 2 is more efficient than firm 1 in producing *b*: $n_{1a} = 10, n_{1b} = 2.5, n_{2a} = 2.5$ and $n_{2b} = 10$. The cost function is of the form

$C(q,n) = \frac{q}{n}$ for each firm and product combination. Finally, demand for good *i* (= *a*, *b*) is of the form $p_i = 1 - q_{1i} - q_{2i}$. PCM for firm *f* (= 1, 2) at the aggregate level is defined as total revenue minus total (variable) costs divided by total revenue

$$PCM_f = \frac{\left(p_a - \frac{1}{n_{fa}}\right) q_{1a} + \left(p_b - \frac{1}{n_{fb}}\right) q_{fb}}{p_a q_{fa} + p_b q_{fb}}$$

With Cournot competition on both markets one finds

$$q_{fi}^C = \frac{1 - \frac{2}{n_{fi}} + \frac{1}{n_{-fi}}}{3}, \; p_i^C = \frac{1 + \frac{1}{n_{1i}} + \frac{1}{n_{2i}}}{3}$$

and hence $PCM_1^C = PCM_2^C = 0.68$. Under Bertrand competition each firm only produces the product at which it is most efficient (and hence has the highest PCM) and we find $PCM_1^B = PCM_2^B = \frac{\frac{1}{2.5} - \frac{1}{10}}{\frac{1}{2.5}} = 0.75$. In other words, if at the unit of observation the firms produce more than one product and the researcher wants to use PCM as a measure of competition, he has to assume that efficiency is a one-dimensional variable. Put differently, he has to assume, as we did above, that $\frac{\partial C(q,n)}{\partial n} \leq 0$ and $\frac{\partial \left(\frac{\partial C(q,n)}{\partial q_l} \right)}{\partial n} \leq 0$; the more efficient firm is (weakly) more efficient in the production of all goods. Without this assumption, an increase in competition can lead to higher PCM.

As argued so far, the data requirements and assumptions for PCM and PCS to measure competition are similar. The main advantage of the PCS measure is the robust theoretical foundation for the relation between PCS and the intensity of competition. We will now argue that the generalized output reallocation effect in Definition 2 is a natural candidate for a necessary condition to get that more intense competition leads to lower PCM. However, this condition is not sufficient which explains theoretical counterexamples where more intense competition leads to higher PCM. This is the sense in which PCS is a theoretically more robust measure of competition than PCM.

Writing PCM as

$$PCM(n) = \frac{p(n)^T q(n) - C(q(n),n)}{p(n)^T q(n)} = \frac{\pi(n)}{\pi(n) + C(q(n),n)}$$

one can show the following result on the effect of competition on PCM.

Lemma 3 The effect of θ on PCM can be written as

$$\operatorname{sign}\left(\frac{dPCM(n)}{d\theta}\right)=\operatorname{sign}\left(\frac{-\gamma}{\left[C(q(n,\theta),n)\right]^2}\frac{dC(q(n,\theta),n)}{dq}\frac{dq(n,\theta)}{d\theta}+\int_{n_w}^{n}\frac{d\left[\frac{\left(-\frac{\partial C(q(t,\theta),t)}{\partial t}\right)}{C(q(n,\theta),n)}\right]}{d\theta}dt\right)$$

where the effect of θ is partial (as above). Next, assume for notational simplicity that $\cup_{i=1}^{I}\left[n_{w0}^{i},n_{w1}^{i}\right]=\left[n_w,n_1\right]$. Then the effect of γ on PCM can be written as

$$\operatorname{sign}\left(\frac{dPCM(n)}{d\gamma}\right)$$

$$=\operatorname{sign}\left(\frac{1}{C(q(n),n)}-\frac{\left(-\frac{\partial C(q(t,\theta),t)}{\partial t}\Big|_{t=n_w}\right)}{C(q(n),n)}\frac{dn_w}{d\gamma}-\frac{\gamma}{[C(q(n,\theta),n)]^2}\frac{dC(q(n,\theta),n)}{dq}\frac{dq(n,\theta)}{d\gamma}+\int_{n_w}^{n}\frac{d\left[\frac{\left(-\frac{\partial C(q(t,\theta),t)}{\partial t}\right)}{C(q(n,\theta),n)}\right]}{d\gamma}dt\right)$$

One case for which one wants the result $\frac{dPCM(n)}{d\theta}<0$ to hold, is the case where $\gamma = 0$. Hence a natural requirement is

$$\frac{d\left[\frac{\left(-\frac{\partial C(q(t,\theta),t)}{\partial t}\right)}{C(q(n,\theta),n)}\right]}{d\theta}<0$$

for $n > t$.

For the class of cost functions where $C(q, n) = \omega(n)c(q)$ this condition boils down to the output reallocation effect in Definition 2. However, the condition in Definition 2 is not sufficient to get $\frac{dPCM(n)}{d\theta}<0$ because we cannot exclude the case where more intense competition leads to lower output levels for inefficient firms. Hence $\frac{dq(n,\theta)}{d\theta} < 0$ and $\gamma > 0$ works in the direction of $\frac{dPCM(n)}{d\theta} > 0$ and the output reallocation effect is no longer sufficient.

Similarly, when the entry cost γ is increased one would expect the PCM to go up. A natural condition here is

$$\frac{d\left[\frac{\left(-\frac{(\partial C(q(t,\theta)t)}{\partial t}\right)}{C(q(n,\theta),n)}\right]}{d\gamma} > 0$$

For cost functions of the form $C(q, n) = \omega(n)c(q)$ this again boils down to the reallocation effect in Definition 2. Again the condition is not sufficient here, because the other terms in the expression for $\text{sign}\left(\frac{dPCM(n)}{d\gamma}\right)$ can go either way.

As with PCM, a necessary condition for the relative profits measure $\frac{\pi(n^{**})}{\pi(n^{*})}$ (introduced by Boone 2000) to be monotone in competition is the reallocation effect in Definition 2. As is routine to verify, this reallocation effect is also sufficient for $\frac{\pi(n^{**})}{\pi(n^{*})}$ to be monotone in θ but not for $\frac{\pi(n^{**})}{\pi(n^{*})}$ to be monotone in γ because of a level effect of $d\gamma$.[11] This level effect drops out when considering differences, which explains why PCS needs less stringent sufficient conditions to be monotone in both γ and θ than relative profits.

Lemma 3 considers the PCM of an individual firm. However, the question here concerns the measurement of industry competition. This is usually done by calculating the weighted industry average PCM, where the weight of a firm equals its market share in the industry (see, for instance, Wolfram 1999). Tables 4.1 and 4.2 show simulations to illustrate that industry PCM is not monotone in competition while PCS does pick up what happens to competition in these two cases. Both tables work with the framework introduced in Example 2 with $a = 20$, $b = 2$, $d = 1.5$ and Cournot competition. In Table 4.1 there are three firms with constant marginal costs equal to $c_1 = 0.1$, $c_2 = 6.5$, $c_3 = 7$. Competition is intensified by making goods closer substitutes (raising d to $d = 2$). The PCM for firms 2 and 3 falls, but industry PCM goes up as competition is intensified. The reason is the output reallocation effect; as competition is intensified, output is reallocated from firms 2 and 3 to the most efficient firm 1 which is the firm with the highest PCM.

This increases the weight of firm 1 in the industry average PCM and thus raises the industry PCM. PCS (defined here as $\frac{\pi(c_2)-\pi(c_3)}{\pi(c_1)-\pi(c_3)}$ which is the only point that changes with d in a graph like Figure 4.2)[12] falls with the rise in d indicating correctly that competition becomes more intense. Table 4.2 considers the case of a fall in entry costs $d\gamma = -0.1$ for all firms. In particular, it considers the following costs distributions: $c_1 = c_2 = 0.1$, $c_3 = 3$, $c_4 = c_5 = 6$ and $\gamma_1 = \gamma_2 = 16.5$, $\gamma_3 = 5$, $\gamma_4 = \gamma_5 = 0.7$. Before the fall in γ, there is a Cournot equilibrium where firms 1, 3, 4 and 5 are active. Firm 2 cannot profitably enter in this equilibrium. After the across the board reduction in γ however, this equilibrium is broken and firm 2 can enter at the expense of firm 5. Although PCM falls for each individual firm, the industry average PCM goes up as firm 2 has a higher PCM than firm 5. Again PCS (defined here as $\frac{\pi(c_3) - \pi(c_4)}{\pi(c_1) - \pi(c_4)}$, as above the only relevant point in a graph like Figure 4.2) falls with the fall in entry costs, correctly indicating more intense competition.

4.5. Conclusion

This chapter started off with the observation that PCM is often used as a measure of competition in empirical research. From a theoretical point of view, however, it is not clear what the relation between PCM and competition actually is. There are a number of theoretical papers where more intense competition leads to higher PCM. At the moment we do not know how relevant these theoretical counterexamples are from an empirical point of view.

To answer this question we have developed a new measure of competition, PCS, which has two properties. First, PCS has a robust theoretical foundation as a measure of competition. It is monotone in competition both when competition becomes more intense through more aggressive interaction between firms and when entry barriers are reduced. Second, the data requirements to estimate PCS are the same as the requirements to estimate PCM. That implies that any firm (or plant) level data set which allows a researcher to estimate PCM should also allow for the estimation of PCS. In this way we can see in which percentage of industries both measures point in the same direction. If it turns out that the measures are congruent for more than 95 per cent of the industries, PCM can be used as a measure of competition in empirical research without much concern for the theoretical counterexamples.

Notes

1 This chapter is based on the TILEC Discusion paper 2004-004 ‘A new way to measure competition’. The author would like to thank Michelle Goeree for her comments. Financial support from NWO, KNAW and VSNU through a Vernieuwingsimpuls grant is gratefully acknowledged.

2 Sometimes PCM is defended as measure of competition with reference to its interpretation as a welfare measure (prices closer to marginal costs lead to higher welfare). However, as shown by Amir (2002) there is, in general, no simple relation between PCM and welfare. The same is true for the measure introduced here; there is no simple relation with welfare.

3 We allow $\zeta(.)$and $\xi(.)$to be vectors. In that case the integration is done for each vector element separately to obtain the vectors Q and P.

4 To simplify notation, we assume that all firms with efficiency n choose the same action a_n in equilibrium.

5 Although the theory is developed for a continuum of firms, we use examples with discrete firms for two reasons. First, such examples are often easier to verify. Second, it illustrates that the results derived here do not crucially depend on the choice to model firms as a continuum, although this assumption simplifies the analytical exposition.

6 As we will show below these conditions are also natural candidates for necessary conditions to get the result that more intense competition leads to lower PCM. However, in that case the conditions are not sufficient.

7 In other words, if the model would allow for firms investing in R&D to improve their efficiency n, we would see the following effect. More intense competition raises R&D investments of firms relative to less efficient firms. This is in line with results found by Aghion et al. (2002).

8 To see this, note that fixed costs that do not vary with n have no effect on the expression $-\frac{\partial C(q,n)}{\partial n}$ (in Definition 2) and such fixed costs drop out when considering profit differences $\pi(n^*)-\pi(n)$ (in Equation (4.10)).

9 The case where $\dfrac{\gamma'(t)}{\left(-\dfrac{\partial C\left(q\left(t,\{n^i_{w0},n^i_{w1}\}^I_{i=1},\theta\right),t\right)}{\partial t}\right)}$ is decreasing in $t\in\langle n,n^{**}\rangle$ is considered in Lemma 4 in Boone (2004).

10 To see this, consider the one-dimensional case where q is a scalar. Then $PCM=\dfrac{p-\dfrac{c(q)}{q}}{p}$ only measures the price cost margin if $\dfrac{c(q)}{q}$ is equal to marginal costs. That is, if variable costs are of the form $c(q)=cq$ and marginal costs are constant.

11 More precisely, profits can be written as $\pi(n)=\gamma+\int_{n_w}^{n}\pi'(t)dt$ where n_w is the least efficient firm to enter. When γ changes this has three effects on $\pi(n)$ (which can potentially go in opposite directions): (a) direct effect of γ, (b) effect of γ on n_w and (c) effect of γ on firms' conduct which appears in $\pi'(t)$. Only effect (c) is relevant here and this is the only effect of γ that remains when considering $\pi(n^*)-\pi(n)=\int_n^{n^*}\pi'(t)dt$.

12 That is, with $\dfrac{c_3-c}{c_3-c_1}$ on the horizontal axis the other two points are (0, 0) and (1, 1).

References

Aghion, P., N. Bloom, R. Blundell, R. Griffith and P. Howitt, 2002, *Competition and innovation: an inverted U relationship*, NBER working paper no. 9269.

Amir, R., 2002, Market structure, scale economies and industry performance, mimeo. Technical paper, Université Catholique de Louvain, Center for Operations Research and Econometrics (CORE).

Amir, R. and V. Lambson, 2000, On the effects of entry in Cournot markets, *Review of Economic Studies*, 67 (2): 235–254.

Berry, S., J. Levinsohn and A. Pakes, 1995, Automobile prices in market equilibrium, *Econometrica*, 63, 841–890.

Boone, J., 2000, *Competition*, CEPR Discussion Paper no. 2636.

Boone, J., 2004, *A new way to measure competition*, TILEC Discussion Paper 2004-004.

Bulow, J. and P. Klemperer, 1999, Prices and the winner's curse, *RAND Journal of Economics*, 33 (1), 1–21.

Corts, K., 1999, Conduct parameters and the measurement of market power, *Journal of Econometrics*, 88, 227–250.

Genesove, D. and W. Mullin, 1998, Testing static oligopoly models: conduct and cost in the sugar industry, 1890–1914, *Rand Journal of Economics*, 29 (2), 355–377.

Goldberg, P., 1995, Product differentiation and oligopoly in international markets: the case of the US automobile industry, *Econometrica,* 63 (4), 891–951.

Graddy, K., 1995, Testing for imperfect competition of the Fulton fish market, *RAND Journal of Economics*, 26 (1), 75–92.

Guadalupe, M., 2003, Does product market competition increase wage inequality?, Mimeo LSE.

Klette, T.J., 1999, Market power, scale economies and productivity: estimates from a panel of establishment data, *Journal of Industrial Economics*, 67 (4), 451–476.

Klette, T.J. and Z. Griliches, 1999, *Empirical patterns of firm growth and R&D investment: a quality ladder model interpretation*, Institute for Fiscal Studies Working Paper Series No. W99/25.

Lindquist, K.G., 2001, The response by the Norwegian aluminium industry to changing market structure, *International Journal of Industrial Organization*, 19, 79–98.

Nevo, A., 2001, Measuring market power in the ready-to-eat cereal industry, *Econometrica*, 69 (2), 307–342.

Nickell, S., 1996, Competition and corporate performance, *Journal of Political Economy*, 104, 724–746.

Nickell, S., 1999, Product markets and labour markets, *Labour Economics*, 6, 1–20.

Reiss, P. and F. Wolak, 2007, Structural econometric modeling: rationales and examples from industrial organization, *Handbook of Econometrics*. Amsterdam: Elsevier

Rosenthal, R., 1980, A model in which an increase in the number of sellers leads to a higher price, *Econometrica*, 48 (6), 1575–1579.

Scherer, F.M. and D. Ross, 1990, *Industrial market structure and economic performance*, Houghton Mifflin, Boston, third edition.

Stiglitz, J., 1989, Imperfect information in the product market, In R. Schmalensee and R. Willig, ed, *Handbook of Industrial Organization*, Volume I, Elsevier Science Publishers.

Vickers, J., 1995, Entry and competitive selection, Mimeo Oxford University.

Wolfram, C., 1999, Measuring duopoly power in the British electricity spot market, *American Economic Review,* 89 (4), 805–826.

5 Measuring performance of banks as an assessment of competition[1]

Jacob A. Bikker

Adequate performance of financial institutions is of crucial importance to their customers. Prices and quality of their products are determined by efficiency and competition. Since efficiency and competition cannot be observed directly, various indirect measures in the form of simple indicators or complex models have been devised and used both in theory and in practice. This chapter demonstrates that it is difficult to measure the performance of banks and that indicators differ strongly in terms of quality. It investigates which methods are to be preferred and how by combining certain indicators stronger measures may be developed. Finally, an analysis is made of the predictive validity of these indicators.

5.1. Introduction

This chapter addresses the question how well financial institutions are performing in providing their services to consumers and businesses, and how much we know about that. Various performance aspects cannot be observed directly whereas they are economically important. While shareholders will view performance in terms of profits made on their behalf, whether or not adjusted for risks taken, this chapter focuses on performance in a broader sense, that is, the contribution financial institutions make to common wealth, on behalf of consumers and businesses. These households and firms will be interested mainly in whether financial products are of sufficient quality and not too expensive. This raises the issue of, on the one hand, the efficiency of financial institutions (i.e. whether unnecessary costs are made in bringing a product to market) and, on the other, the level of competition in the relevant markets (i.e. whether profit margins are not unnecessarily high). Since efficiency and competition cannot be observed directly, they have to be measured in an indirect way. If a cut in mortgage rates by one bank, for instance, is promptly copied by all its competitors, then this is a sign of competition – even if it does not enable us to distinguish between a little competition and strong competition. Yet the price and quality of other banking services such as investment consultancy or payment services are much harder to determine, making competition far more difficult to measure. As mentioned in Chapter 2, difficulty in determining prices and quality levels, incidentally, is a widespread phenomenon in financial products markets. A recent example in the Netherlands is the investment-linked insurance policy, popularly known as a 'profiteering policy'. The fact that consumers find it hard to pick such a product on the basis of price and quality (due to opaqueness and risks materializing only over time) takes away their disciplinary influence and weakens competition. This problem is inherent in many of the products of banks and insurers (Bikker and Spierdijk, 2010a).

As also noticed in Chapter 2, there is another kind of performance that works in the interest of consumers, but does so in the long run. It is the reliability of a financial institution in terms of solvency and liquidity or, in other words, whether customers can be sure to get their money back, thus the financial stability of the banking system in the broadest sense of the term. Now that the subprime mortgage and liquidity crisis has engulfed us all, the amount of risk banks take in carrying on their business is a focal point of attention. Although this long-term performance is also affected by competition and efficiency, this chapter concerns itself solely with the more palpable short-term performance exhibited in quality services and affordable prices.

Banks of course play a crucially important role in the economy because of their core products: loans to businesses and mortgage loans. Hence competition and efficiency in banking are also highly important: high quality at low cost boosts welfare. Competition is also important for adequate monetary transmission, which is the speed at which policy interest rates set by central banks pass through to bank interest rates (see Chapter 8).

Competition also affects financial innovations, banks' financial health, financial stability and the accessibility of banking services to customers – with accessibility meaning the extent to which small and medium-sized businesses have access to affordable financing. For all these four factors, the relation to competition is represented by an inverted U-shape as in Figure 5.1 (Van Lamoen, 2011). Promoting competition enhances these factors up to an optimum, whose position is uncertain. Stronger competition beyond the optimum has a counterproductive effect on these factors. To give an example: when competition is very strong and excess profits

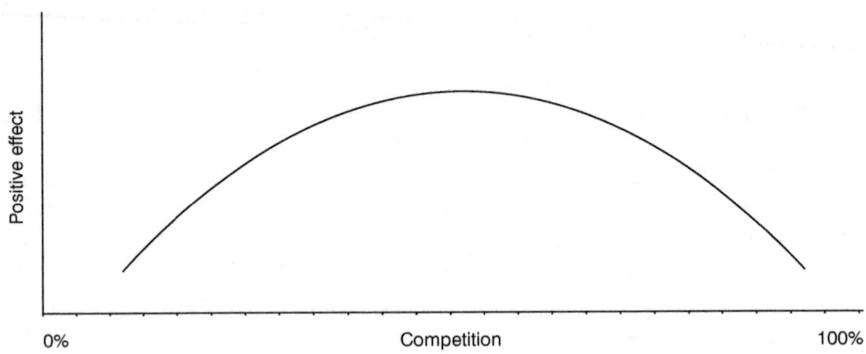

Figure 5.1 Positive effect of competition on innovation, financial health and accessibility of the banking industry and on financial stability

dwindle, banks will find it hard to build extra buffers to protect them from adverse shocks. Healthy competition, in this sense, is better than fierce competition.

So what do banks, scientists and supervisors actually know about important variables such as competition and efficiency in the banking system? This chapter will establish that, perhaps to our surprise or disappointment, we know far less than has often been claimed.

In practice, highly simplified approximations have been used to represent competition or efficiency, such as the concentration index or the cost-to-income ratio. While some indicators have been used without challenge in even the most highly-ranked scientific journals, they are in fact too primitive in nearly every case and not very reliable.

Theoretically founded models that attempt to estimate competition and efficiency for a particular country, are expected to perform better than such simplified proxies.[2] How well have such models been doing in practice? This chapter shows that the consensus between even the best-founded models is surprisingly weak. In other words, different methods lead to sometimes widely different results for the same country and largely the same dataset. This brings us to the central problem addressed by this chapter: how far does the sounding rod of our measuring methods reach? And what can we do to reach just a little further?

5.2. Performance measures for financial institutions

As a first step toward a closer analysis, about 20 methods were used to measure banking competition and efficiency for the most important 46 countries.[3] These countries comprise the old and new EU countries (in Figure 5.2 these are dark grey and light grey, respectively), the other OECD countries (grey) and emerging markets (black). Together, they account for 90 per cent of global GDP.

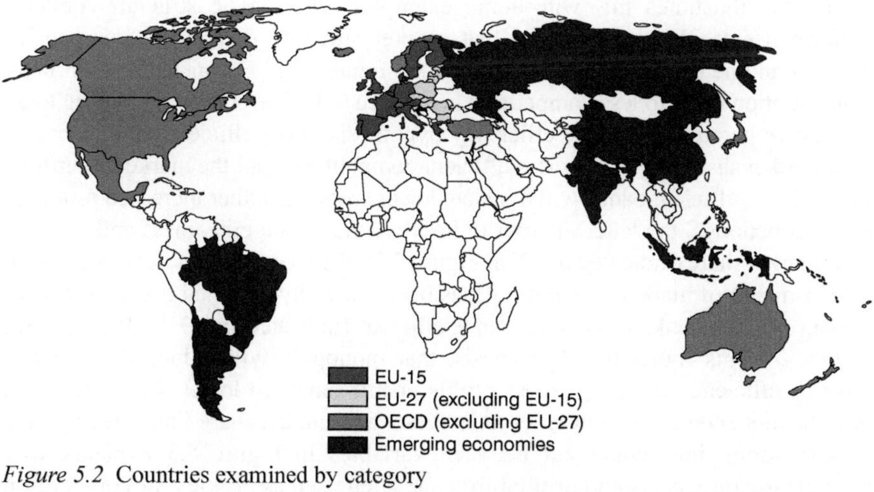

Figure 5.2 Countries examined by category

Table 5.1 Indirect performance indicators for financial institutions

Performance indicators	*Correlation with competition*	*Indicators represented as*
Efficiency	Positive	Cost X-efficiency
		Profit X-efficiency
		Scale economies
		Scope economies
Costs	Negative	Cost-to-income ratio
		Cost margin
		Total costs/total income
Profit	Negative (?)	Return on capital
		Return on assets
		Net interest margin
Market structure		
– number of banks	Positive	Number of banks
		Per capita number of banks
– concentration	Ambivalent	HHI, C_3, C_5, C_{10}

All 20 simple approximations and model estimates of competition will from now on be referred to as indicators. Five types of performance indicators are distinguished (see Table 5.1). Apart from competition and efficiency, these are costs, profit/profit margin and market structure.

5.2.1. Mutual relationships

Various theoretical relationships exist between the several types of performance. Figure 5.3 illustrates this with some examples. The classic structure-conduct-performance (SCP) theory holds that market structure determines competitive conduct and hence profits (referred to by the figure '1').[4] For instance, high bank concentration leads to less competition and hence to higher profits. According to an alternative paradigm, e.g. the efficiency hypothesis, more efficient banks increase their market share by pushing less efficient competitors from the market (Demsetz, 1973). More efficient banks will translate lower costs into either increased profits or price reductions – the latter in order to improve their competitiveness and increase their market share (indicated by '2' in Figure 5.3). Efficiency thus is not an effect but a determinant of market structure.[5] It has been generally assumed that competitive pressure forces banks to become more efficient (indicated by '3'). Hicks (1935) assumes, in his 'quiet life' hypothesis, that monopoly will reduce the pressure towards efficiency. Finally, excess profits enable banks to lower their prices and become more competitive in order to increase their market share (indicated by '4').

The strong intertwinement between variables in Figure 5.3 explains why market structure, costs and profitability are often used as proxies for competition

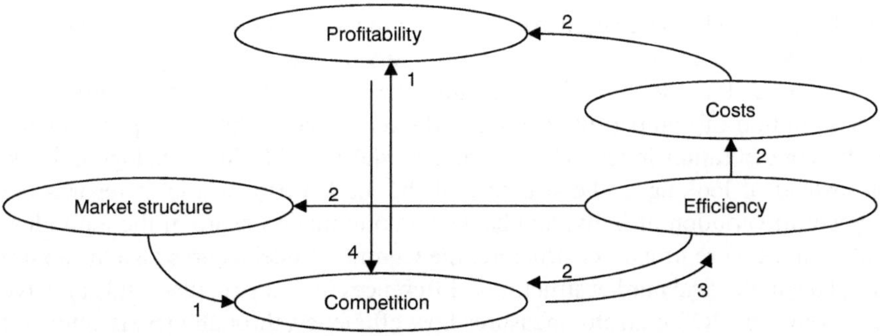

Figure 5.3 Relations between market structure, competition, profitability and efficiency
Explanation: Relations according to the SCP paradigm are indicated by the figure 1, those according to the efficiency hypothesis by the figure 2. Relations according to the 'quiet life' hypothesis (and its reversal) are marked by the figure 3, while the relation following from a general principle is indicated by 4.

and efficiency. At the same time, however, the figure underlines the fact that the measures concerned reflect quite different characteristics of banks and their markets.

5.2.2. Correlation with competition

Before the indicators can be used, it must be established whether the correlation (across all countries) with competition is positive or negative.[6] Figure 5.3 shows that efficiency is positively correlated to competition (for stronger competition leads one to expect higher efficiency) and, for the same reason, that costs are negatively correlated with competition (in other words, stronger competition leads to cost cuts; see Table 5.1). Also, competition is likely to reduce profits. This argument is not entirely convincing, however, because competition may also affect profit in a positive sense through cost reduction. Hence the question mark in Table 5.1.

Where the notion of market structure is represented by the number of banks, a positive correlation with competition is usually assumed; the presence of more banks implies more opportunity for competition. Concentration, indicating mainly the dominant position of a small number of banks, may indicate low competition, because banks may use this to collaborate. A more dynamic interpretation is that such concentration may, on the contrary, be an indication of competition because consolidation may have been enforced by circumstances. Therefore concentration is an ambivalent indicator.

5.2.3. Models and indicators used

Initially, five models were used to estimate competition (see Table 5.2). The Lerner index uses profit margin as an indicator of market power (De Lange van Bergen, 2006). The SCP model measures the influence of market structure on profits via an assumption of competitive conduct. Market structure, here, is approximated by the concentration index. The Cournot model is built along analogous lines, but instead of looking at the structure of the market as a whole, it regards the conjectural variation of individual banks.[7] Taking market share of the individual bank as a measure of market structure, the Cournot model aspires also to capture part of asymmetrical market structures, differences in cost structures and collusive behaviour. The PCS indicator measures how efficiency, through increased market shares and profit margins, is rewarded by higher profits (Chapters 3, 4, 7–9). The Panzar–Rosse model measures to what extent input and output prices move in step (as they would under perfect competition) or out of step (indicating monopoly or a perfect cartel).[8] Other models in the literature (e.g. Bresnahan, Iwata) require datasets that for most countries are simply lacking, while estimations also present high practical barriers (Bikker, 2003). Table 5.2 shows how the different models simulate different aspects of competition.

For the efficiency indicators, cost and profit X-efficiency as well as scale and scope economies were estimated through a model (see Table 5.1). Costs are represented by the cost-to-income ratio and the cost margin, while profit is proxied by return on capital or return on assets (RoA) and by net interest margin (NIM). In the case of market structure, the number of banks, the per capita number of banks and a number of concentration indices are also incorporated.[9]

In all cases this analysis was based on the banking market as a whole, without regard to product differences. It has been argued against this that the situation as regards competition, for instance, may vary depending on the

Table 5.2 Competition models

Model	*Underlying concept*
Lerner index	Profit margin indicates market power
SCP model[a]	Effect of market structure (concentration) on profit through competitive behaviour
Cournot model[b]	Effect of market structure (market share) on profit through competitive behaviour
PCS indicator	Degree into which efficiency is rewarded in the form of higher profits through increased market shares[c]
Panzar–Rosse model	Correlation of input prices and income (revenue)

a Based on the market shares of the largest three banks (C_3) and the Herfindahl–Hirschman concentration index (HHI), respectively, as measures of market structure.

b Based on the market share of the individual bank as a measure of market structure, as an indicator of asymmetrical market structures, differences in cost structures and collusive behaviour.

c Based on the efficiency hypothesis.

market segment. Competition in the mortgage lending market is likely to be much stronger than in the investment counselling market. This is justified criticism; competition may vary from product to product or even from one location to another. However, for most products there are insufficient data available to perform analyses at the product or location level, with a few exceptions.[10] Where approximations for competition and efficiency are used in the economic literature, this is almost invariably done for banks as a whole, so on the highest level of aggregation.

Since all models were estimated on the basis of a single dataset, different outcomes may not be attributed to data differences. The dataset covers a ten-year period (1996–2005) and was obtained from Fitch IBCA's BankScope and from the OECD.[11]

5.3. Critical appraisal of the indicators

This section appraises the indicators presented above against three different criteria: first, two statistical norms – mutual correlations and the principal component analysis[12] and an economic interpretation. Finally, the variation across countries is explained from economic theory.

5.3.1. Correlations

How do the different indicators found correlate to each other? Table 5.3 shows the correlation coefficients between 14 currently used indicators for 46 countries.[13] A correlation between two variables indicates parallel movement, without regard to

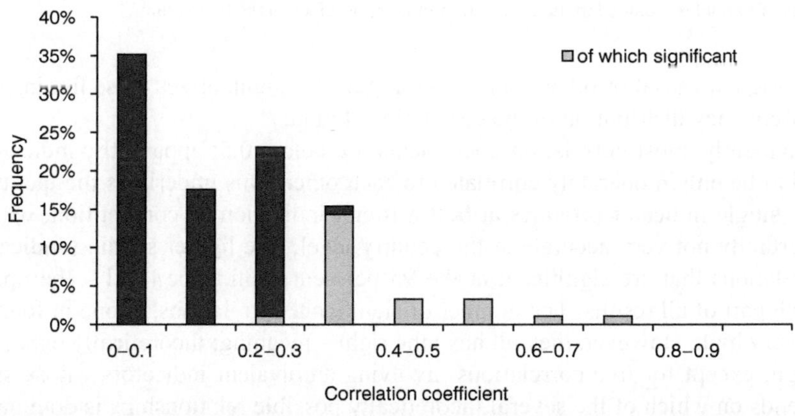

Figure 5.4 Frequency distribution of correlation coefficients between indicators
Explanation: The graph presents the 91 correlations between the 14 indicators used: the Boone, Panzar–Rosse, SCP and Cournot models, cost and profit X-efficiency, return on assets or on equity, cost-to-income ratio, total cost to total income ratio, net interest margin, cost margin, the number of banks and the top 5 banks by market share, C_5 (see Table 5.3). Lighter shading refers to the 22 correlations that are significant at the 5 per cent significance level.

Table 5.3 Correlation coefficients between indicators and the index (46 countries, 1996–2005)

	PCS index	*Panzar–Rosse*	*SCP*	*Cournot*	*Profit eff.*	*Cost-eff.*	*RoC*[c]	*RoA*
	neg[a]	*pos*	*neg*	*neg*	*amb (p)*[b]	*pos*	*neg*	*neg*
PCS	1.00	–0.34**	–0.20	–0.13	0.36	0.11	0.18	0.0
P-R		1.00	–0.04	–0.03	–0.03	0.09	–0.17	–0.2
SCP			1.00	0.29**	–0.07	–0.05	0.12	0.0
Cournot				1.00	–0.12	–0.26*	0.25*	0.1
P. eff.					1.00	0.48***	0.33**	0.1
C. eff.						1.00	–0.02	–0.0
RoC[c]							1.00	0.73
RoA								1.0
C/I								
TC/TI								
NIM								
CM								
# Banks								
C_5								

a Correlation between the PCS indicator and competition is negative, etc.

b Correlation between profit X-efficiency and competition is theoretically ambivalent, but in practice turns out positive (p), or negative (n).

c Return on capital.

Explanation: Asterisks indicate significance levels: 1, 2 or 3 asterisks indicate the 90 per cent, 95 per cent or 99 per cent confidence levels, respectively. Shading of the correlation coefficients indicates where negative correlation is expected. (For the ambivalent Profit efficiency variable, this was done 'in retrospect'.) The names of variables included in the Index are printed in boldface in the first column.

any original causal or other connection. Figure 5.4 summarizes these findings as the frequency distribution of the correlations found.

Evidently, most correlation coefficients are below 0.5; apparently, indicators tend to be only moderately correlated to each other. This underlines the fact that each single indicator provides at best a rough indication of competition, which is certainly not very accurate at the country level. The lighter shading indicates correlations that are significant at the 95 per cent confidence level – the upper fourth part of all results. The number of significant correlations, at one in four, is not very high. However, they all have the right – meaning: theoretically expected – sign, except for five correlations involving ambivalent indicators whose sign depends on which of the several theoretically possible relationships is dominant. The fact that all the other 17 significant correlations bear the right signs without exception is an indication that the indicators behave roughly in accordance with the theoretical framework and hence are not too much distorted by e.g. definition or measurement issues.

/I	*TC/TI*	*NIM*	*Cost margin*	*No. of banks*	C_5	*Index*
mb (n)	*amb (n)*	*neg*	*pos*	*neg*	*neg*	
0.07	–0.23	–0.21	0.00	0.06	0.11	–0.14
0.02	0.17	–0.02	–0.22	0.09	0.03	0.33**
–0.27*	–0.08	0.07	–0.09	–0.02	–0.15	–0.05
–0.21	–0.06	0.20	0.21	–0.31**	0.35**	–0.42***
–0.46***	–0.38**	–0.23	–0.16	0.24	0.06	0.37**
–0.36**	–0.36**	–0.25*	–0.25*	0.32**	0.05	0.53***
–0.39***	–0.34**	0.20	0.18	–0.28*	0.30**	–0.30**
–0.03	–0.34**	0.57***	0.59***	–0.26*	0.21	–0.50***
1.00	0.37**	0.19	0.42***	0.05	–0.08	–0.42***
	1.00	0.11	0.06	–0.05	–0.14	–0.20
		1.00	0.62***	–0.21	0.03	–0.63***
			1.00	–0.18	0.00	–0.58***
				1.00	–0.55***	0.51***
					1.00	–0.37**

5.3.2. Principal components analysis

Another statistical technique is principal components analysis (PCA).[14] To the extent possible, this method attempts to represent the variation across the countries within a set of correlated variables using a few variables called principal components. PCA makes it possible to investigate to what extent the indicators reviewed might all be explained by just a few factors or, in other words, to what extent they overlap. The more successful the analysis, the more similar to each other the indicators would be. Even more important is the possibility to interpret the principal components (PCs) and to see whether they might represent recognizable elements of our performance measures. It would be nice, for instance, if one of the PCs represented competition, another one efficiency and the third one profitability. This way, each PC could, so to speak, filter information from the indicators and represent it in compact form.

Table 5.4 shows the outcome of an analysis with 12 indicators,[15] selected so as to minimize overlap between the indicators considered. Also, the indicators are spread as equally as possible across the categories competition, efficiency, profitability, etc.[16] The shading indicates for each column (i.e. for each principal component) the highest factor or component loading(s). Thus we may infer that the first principal component represents mainly cost and profit margins and profit inefficiency.[17] The second one has the highest factor loading at cost efficiency, while the third one has its highest factor loading

Table 5.4 Factor loadings for the first five principal components (PCs)

	Factor loadings[a]					*Explanation*[b]
	PC1	*PC2*	*PC3*	*PC4*	*PC5*	
Panzar–Rosse model	–0.20	0.18	0.80			0.72
PCS indicator	0.20	0.30	–0.79			0.76
SCP model	–0.80	0.18				0.67
Cournot model	0.18	–0.23	–0.63	–0.42		0.66
Cost efficiency	–0.13	0.81	0.13	0.11		0.70
Profit efficiency	0.84	–0.24				0.76
Return on assets	0.79	0.16	–0.27	–0.24		0.79
Cost-to-income ratio	0.26	–0.60	0.60	0.14		0.81
Net interest margin	0.84	–0.18	0.18			0.77
Number of banks	–0.20	0.13	0.12	0.85	–0.12	0.81
Cost margin	0.85	–0.23	0.12	–0.13		0.81
HHI	0.19	0.13	–0.85	–0.14		0.79
	Explanation of variance per PC					*Total*
	0.19	0.17	0.13	0.15	0.12	0.76

a A factor loading may be regarded as the coordinate of an indicator on a principal component in a coordinate system. In the case of orthogonal components (i.e. forming a right angle), the factor loading of a variable vis-à-vis a component equals the correlation between that variable and that component.

b Explanation of the variance of the indicators based on the first five PCs (equals the sum of squared factor loadings for each variable across the five PCs).

Explanation: The shading indicates the highest factor loading for each column (that is, PC).

at three out of four model-based competition measures, and again at the HHI concentration index. Apparently, this third factor comprises information on competition, being highest correlated with the P-R model, the PCS indicator, the SCP model and the HHI. Moreover, the signs of each factor loadings are correct – that is to say, in accordance with theoretical expectations[18] – so that this PC ought to present a reliable summary of the information content of these competition indicators.

The last line of Table 5.4 shows that the first PC explains almost 20 per cent of the variance in the indicators, falling gradually to 12 per cent for the fifth PC, so that the first five PCs together explain 76 per cent of the variance. Thus less than half of the PCs explain three-quarters of the variance in the indicators. Apparently, the indicators do contain common elements (especially ‘competition’), but also many specific ones (profit, efficiency, concentration and further refinements such as RoA and NRM).

5.3.3. Economic interpretation

What, now, is the economic significance of the indicators, or what are their country-specific values? The answers to these questions are found, for the present estimates of country-level competition and efficiency, in comparing the results to other available sources of a more intuitive or anecdotal nature, or that relate to specific sub-segments or to competition in other sectors. However, there is not much contrastive material around. In practice, there appears to be a degree of consensus to the effect that Anglo-Saxon countries such as the US, the UK and Ireland are highly competitive. Another expert view is that competition in Southern Europe, by contrast, is very modest as a result of lagging development, exemplified by insufficient consolidation and low cost-sensitiveness in bank clients. Along with Italy, France and Germany are also assumed to be less competitive owing to strong public interference and inadequate consolidation. Very recently, we have seen strong government interference with banks in many countries, in response to the financial crisis – good for solvency but bad for competitive conditions and therefore, one hopes, temporary. For Germany, stricter adherence to supervisory rules, financial conservatism and an extensive branch network are mentioned. Another universally accepted truth is that competence is stronger in developed countries than in emerging economies, with the least developed countries bringing up the rear. Table 5.5 presents the country ranking according to the 'expert view'.

Various indicators produce diverging results for the same countries, because they reflect different aspects of competition and also because estimation errors or faulty data distort the result. But there is something else; the outcome suggests that the above generally accepted country ranking is, in fact – or at least according to our estimates – simply wrong. Germany, which is deemed by many to be low on competition, gets good marks for all our criteria: low cost, low profit, high competition, high efficiency – and as measured by nearly all indicators. And a very similar story applies to France. Some Southern European countries live up to their underdeveloped image, yet according to many indicators, Italy – and to some extent Spain – do not. Conversely, the performance measures for the US, the UK and Ireland are less than convincing. Although competition estimates for these countries are favourable, their cost levels (and cost inefficiencies), interest margins and profits are exceptionally high, which is hard to reconcile with a competitive climate. Table 5.5 shows that according to the indicators as measured across 1996–2005, Germany and France take the lead over the Anglo-Saxon countries.

Table 5.5 Competitiveness ranking of EU countries: expert view vs. empiricism

Expert view	*Empiricism (indicators)*
1. UK/US/Ireland	1. Germany/France
2. Western Europe	2. UK/USA/Ireland
3. Germany/France	3. Other EU-15 countries
4. Southern Europe	4. Central and Eastern Europe
5. Central and Eastern Europe	

Whereas the original purpose of the above comparison was to use the 'generally accepted truth' as a benchmark for the indicators, the outcome suggests the reverse, i.e. the urgent need to adjust the expert view.

Causes of country-level deviation among indicators

What causes various measures to reflect somewhat different phenomena for each country? There are three main explanations. First, we are dealing with different concepts. Although mutually correlated, the indicators do in fact measure different things; competition is not the same thing as efficiency, which in turn differs from profitability, etc. Second, there are definition issues; each definition reflects a different aspect of the underlying concept. And finally, imperfections in the data also play a role.

Definition issues also figure in the models that measure competition. Using a standard model of a profit maximizing bank under a regime of oligopolistic competition, one may derive that the theoretical model of competition is as follows (Bikker and Bos, 2005, 2008).

$$\textit{Profit margin} = (-1/\mu)\, \textit{HHI}\, (1 + \lambda) \tag{5.1}$$

Profit margin is assumed to reflect competitiveness: the more market power, or the less competition, the higher profits will be. The μ parameter indicates the price elasticity of demand: the more sensitive consumers are to changes in the prices of bank products, the stronger competition will be. *HHI*, the Herfindahl–Hirschman index of concentration, describes market structure: more banks make for more competition, while a market with few large banks weakens competition. The conjectural (or assumed) variation, λ, indicates how banks will respond to production volumes and prices of other banks. This parameter becomes higher as competition gets stronger. Equation (5.1) may also be derived at the firm level where, applied to bank *i*, it reads:

$$\textit{Profit margin}_i = (-1/\mu)\, \textit{MS}_i\, (1 + \lambda_i) \tag{5.2}$$

where *MS* represents market share. Bikker and Bos (2005, 2008) have demonstrated that existing competition models may be derived from these two, except that they invariably incorporate only one or two of the three components, thereby neglecting one or two others. The SCP model, for instance, assumes that μ and λ in Equation (5.1) are constant (or that (1 + λ) may be approximated by HHI). The same goes for Cournot, albeit at the bank instead of the country level, see Equation (5.2). The PCS indicator is estimated as the μ in Equation (5.2) and assumes λ_i constant. These differences in *a priori* assumptions contribute to the variation in competition estimates. The Lerner index and the Panzar–Rosse model base themselves on the (full) profit margin at the firm level. In the case of the Lerner index, there is the problem that marginal costs have to be estimated, while with Panzar–Rosse the translation from theoretical to empirical model may have a disturbing effect.

5.4. What indicators can do

In the preceding paragraphs on competition it has been shown that competition indicators should not be applied indiscriminately. Time is needed to investigate what information value the indicators do have and whether there is, in fact, a reliable way to gauge competition. In order to find this out, we will concentrate on three aspects: economic interpretation (again), predictive validity and bundling all information into a single index.

5.4.1. Economic interpretation

To see whether any clear structure lies buried inside the data, Table 5.6 presents the estimates of the average cost and profit X-efficiency, costs (averaged across the three cost indicators) and profitability (averaged across the three profit indicators). The table juxtaposes three types of countries (viz . (i) Western Europe and other highly industrialized countries, (ii) emerging economies and other OECD countries, and (iii) Eastern and Central Europe) with efficiency, broken down into five classes in descending order from high to low efficiency countries. Every cell in the table contains the number of countries in that bracket. The table shows a diagonal pattern (see shading). It is evident that the efficiency of banks in the highly developed industrial countries is clearly better than that of banks in emerging countries, while banks in the post-transitional economies of Eastern and Central Europe come out as least efficient. It follows that there is a correlation between efficiency and degree of economic development.

A similar pattern from high to low is to be found, for the same reason, when countries are classified by cost levels or profitability, but then the other way around (from low to high) as high efficiency corresponds to low costs and low profits (see the shaded diagonal in Table 5.6.B and 5.6.C, respectively). In the developed countries, where costs are lower, profits are also lower, whereas costs and profits are higher in the transition countries. It is tempting to attribute this phenomenon to stronger competitive pressure. However, a similar classification does not show an unequivocal pattern for competition. Other investigations have shown that competition in industrial countries is, by contrast, slightly weaker, probably owing to a higher proportion of products such as investment counselling and services and options, where competition is far less energetic than on deposit taking and lending (Bikker et al., 2007). In the course of time, the share of advisory and other services will continue to increase, further weakening competition (Bikker and Spierdijk, 2010a).

5.4.2. Average ranking

In situations where measuring is problematic, a good solution may well be to take the average of several estimations. This is a well-known and frequently used strategy in forecasting; the combination of several forecasts does better than each forecast separately. This strategy was also applied to the set of estimates and

Table 5.6 Distribution of X-efficiency, costs and profitability across countries

		Western Europe and other industrialized	*Emerging economies and other OECD*	*Eastern and Central Europe*
A. X-efficiency				
High	9	8	1	
	9	7		2
Medium	9	3	3	3
	9	5	3	1
Low	9	2	2	5
	45[a]	**25**	**9**	**11**[a]
B. Costs				
Low	9	9		
	8	6	1	1
Medium	10	6	2	2
	9	4	3	2
High	10	.	3	7
	46	**25**	**9**	**12**
C. Profitability				
Low	9	7	1	1
	9	6	2	1
Medium	9	6	2	1
	10	6	1	3
High	9	.	3	6
	46	**25**	**9**	**12**

a The X-efficiency of Romania could not be estimated due to insufficient data.

indicators discussed above. A per-country average of several competition level indicators was used. Because the units of expression of these indicators cannot be compared, their average ranking orders were used instead of their values.[19] For this exercise, 11 measures were selected in such a way that there was as little overlap between them as possible. Wherever the overlap between two measures was substantial, one variable was left out.[20] The 11 eventually selected measures are: PCS indicator, Panzar–Rosse model, SCP model, Cournot model, cost X-efficiency, return on assets, cost-to-income ratio (C/I), total cost to total income ratio, net interest margin (NIM), cost margin (CM) and market share of the top 5 banks (C_5).

Table 5.7 (i.e. the last column 'Index' of Table 5.3) presents the correlations between the 'average ranking', referred to from here on as 'Index', and the underlying variables. Remarkably, 11 of the 14 measures are significantly correlated with the Index, of which seven at the highest confidence level of

Table 5.7 Correlations between the indicators and the index

Indicators	*Correlations*	*Significance*	*Status*	*Index component*
PCS indicator	–0.14			Yes
Panzar–Rosse model	0.33	**		Yes
SCP model	–0.05			Yes
Cournot model	–0.42	***		Yes
Profit efficiency	0.37	**	Amb.	
Cost efficiency	0.53	***		Yes
Return on capital	–0.30	**		
Return on assets (RoA)	–0.50	***		Yes
Cost-to-income ratio (C/I)	–0.42	***	Amb.	Yes
Total cost to total income ratio	–0.20		Amb.	Yes
Net interest margin (NIM)	–0.63	***		Yes
Cost margin (CM)	–0.58	***		Yes
Number of banks	0.51	***		
Concentration index C5	–0.37	**		Yes

Two (three) asterisks indicate a confidence level of 95 per cent (99 per cent). Shading indicates expected positive correlation. (Only where there is ambivalence is there no a priori expectation.) Amb. stands for ambiguous.

99 per cent.[21] This indicates that the ranking picks up an element (interpreted as competition) occurring in many of their underlying indicators. Figure 5.5 shows, moreover, that correlations with the Index are far stronger than those between pairs of indicators.

Reassuringly, all 14 correlations have the correct (theoretically expected) signs,[22] which is, of course, especially significant in the case of the nine significant and non-ambivalent variables: Panzar–Rosse model, Cournot model, cost X-efficiency, return on assets/capital, NIM, CM, number of banks and C_5. Apparently there is, after all, an overall concept of 'competition', which is present in nearly every indicator and is reflected reliably and unequivocally in the resulting Index.[23]

Now that an adequate measure of competition has been found in the Index, it is possible to tell which of the simple indicators, all things considered, does best. Table 5.3 shows that the net interest margin and its relation, return on assets, are the most successful overall performance measures.[24] When the focus is entirely on competition, Panzar–Rosse or Cournot is more satisfactory.

Finally, it should be noted that this ranking-based Index is strongly and significantly (and in declining degrees) correlated with the first three principal components of Table 5.4, which are weighted averages of the original indicators. Both the Index and the principal components aim to present as much of the indicators' information content as possible in summary form.

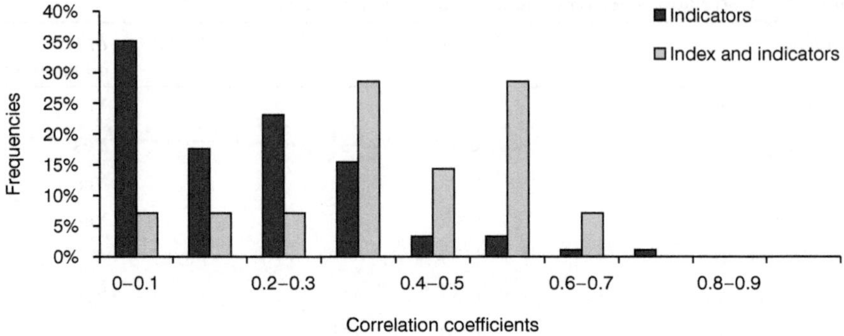

Figure 5.5 Frequency distribution of correlations between indicators and index
Note: Dark shading: frequency distribution of 91 correlations between indicators; light shading: frequency distribution of 14 correlations between indicator and Index.

5.4.3. Predictive validity test

There is another way to test the measures considered, which derives from the psychometric, sociological and marketing literature: the so-termed predictive validity test.[25] The predictive validity test is based on the idea that a constructed variable – such as a survey question – must be correlated to the subsequently observed variable if it is to be a useful predictor. With some adjustment, the indicators in the present analysis could be subjected to the following 'informative validity test'. The test is based on a model in which competition depends on economic variables or, conversely, where an economic variable depends on, among other things, competition. In such a model, each of our indicators might be used as a proxy for competition to see whether it is both significant and (according to theory) correctly signed. If it is, one may conclude that the indicator's relevant information content prevails without its pattern being corrupted by the inherent noise.

Such tests occur frequently in the literature, albeit implicitly, because indicators are usually employed without much ado as competition measures. Examples of this are the SCP and the efficiency hypothesis literatures where concentration and market share, respectively, have been blithely cast in the role of competition. But there are many other fields of study where competition comes into play.[26] As an *ex-post* test, the literature is not a reliable source, since less welcome test results are more likely to be disregarded by authors or else to be rejected by journals.

Three examples of such informative validity tests are now presented. A model-based measure of competition is the H-value from the Panzar–Rosse model which has been estimated for 80 countries. Next, it is explained by means of a large number of carefully selected possible determinants of competition (Bikker et al., 2007). The four (out of nine) determinants that are significant (even at the 99 per cent confidence level), all turn out to carry the right sign (see Table 5.8). Apparently, the H-statistic contains a great deal of – competition-related – information, so that it passes the present test successfully.

Table 5.8 Explanation of bank competition in 76 countries (2004)

Variables	*Coefficients*	*t-value*	*Significance*
Concentration index C_5	–0.001	–0.8	
Activity restrictions	–0.000	–0.7	
Log (Market cap./GDP)	–0.016	–0.4	
Log (per capita GDP)	0.011	0.3	
Real GDP growth	–0.023	–2.8	Sign.
Foreign investment index	–0.132	–3.2	Sign.
Regulation index	0.128	2.5	Sign.
EU-15	–0.129	–1.4	
Former planned economies	–0.435	–5.6	Sign.
R^2, adjusted	0.82		

Source: Bikker et al. (2007).

Our second example concerns monetary transmission, taken from Chapter 8. It is assumed that as competition increases, bank interest rates will be lower and more closely aligned with market rates and the policy rates of the European Central Bank (ECB), so that competition reinforces monetary policy. Models for four types of lending in eight EMU countries[27] explain the spread between the observed four bank rates and the corresponding policy and market rates using competition in the lending market.[28] Competition was in this case measured by means of the PCS indicator, as it permits estimating competition in a partial market (i.e. the lending market). The competition measure carries the correct sign significantly for three out of the four lending rates (see Table 5.9). In the fourth case, the coefficient concerned is not significant. Also, a so-termed 'error correction model' shows that the response of all four lending rates to the market and policy rates is stronger, and hence more closely parallel, as competition increases. Again, the PCS indicator, with seven hits out of eight, appears to have passed the test.[29]

A third example is that of a model which determines the influence of competition on a bank's capital buffer (Bikker and Spierdijk, 2010b). On the one hand it seems self-evident that less competition should lead to higher bank profits, so that banks may add more money to their buffer capital. Here, there is a clear trade-off between the short-term interest of bank customers, characterized by high competition and low prices, and the long-term interest of financial stability, in other words, the certainty that you will get your money back. However, an alternative theory assumes that when fierce competition erodes profit margins, banks will be inclined to take more risks and hold smaller buffers. Also, amid strong competition, banks will be less inclined to invest in inquiries regarding their clients in order to reduce information asymmetry (Marcus, 1984). This, too, increases the risk for banks. To determine which effect is stronger, a model was estimated – by analogy with works by Schaeck et al. (2006) and Schaeck and Cihak (2007) – where the capital buffer depends on variables including

Table 5.9 Effect of competition on spreads between bank and market lending rates

	Effect of competition on spread (t-values)	*Effect of competition times market rate on bank rates (t-values)*
Mortgage loans	**–2.12	***4.29
Consumer credit	***–3.03	***3.21
Short-term corporate loans	***–6.72	***3.47
Long-term corporate loans	0.15	***4.48

Note: Two (three) asterisks indicate a confidence level of 95 per cent (99 per cent).

Source: Chapter 8, Table 8.10, this volume.

competition. Competition was again measured using the Panzar–Rosse model, so that data are available for over 100 countries.

Estimations demonstrate that competition erodes banks' capital buffers, which suggests that the theory claiming that 'weak competition leads to high profits and hence to large buffers' wins out in actual practice. The same is true if, instead of the Panzar–Rosse competition measure, the third principal component derived above (which according to the factor loadings indicated competition) is applied.[30] Again it appears that measuring competition in practice yields plausible results.

5.5. What do the validated measures actually measure?

So far, this chapter has been investigating how bank performance indicators do themselves perform as measures. Next, the question arises as to the banking industry's competition and inefficiency. Earlier studies have tried to capture those variables. For the sake of comparison, two other financial sectors are also considered: insurers and pension funds. Little research has been done in the present area for these types of financial institution, while banking competition measurement has been under-exposed in the literature.

This chapter considers only estimates by methods whose results cover the same 0–100 per cent range, which permits the outcomes to be compared. Disregarding for now the many virtually insurmountable problems besetting the business of measurements and comparisons,[31] Table 5.10 presents several outcomes for scale economies, cost X-inefficiency and competition.

Unused scale economies cannot be present under strong or perfect competition. Estimated unused scale economies increase from banks (5 per cent) via non-life and life insurers (7–14 per cent and 20 per cent, respectively) to 32 per cent for pension fund administrators.[32] Especially insurers and small pension funds could realize hefty cost savings through further consolidation. These outcomes reflect the degree of (overdue) consolidation per sector, and therefore in a sense a lack of competition. For under fierce competition, large-scale cost-saving opportunities would not be left unused.[33] As has been observed many times, the inefficiency of banks and insurers is greater than their scale inefficiency. Bank competition, at 22 per cent worldwide, hovers much closer to monopoly (0 per cent) than to

Table 5.10 Competition among banks, insurers and pension funds (per cent)

	Banks	*Insurers*		*Pension funds*
		Non-life	*Life*	
Scale economies (Int.)	5[a]	–	–	–
Scale economies (Nld.)	–	7/14[b]	20[c]	32[d]
Ditto		21[e]		
Inefficiency (Int.)	18[f]	–	–	–
Inefficiency (Nld.)	18[f]	–	28[c]	–
Competition, P-R (Int.)	22[g]	49[h]	–	–
Competition, PCS (Int.)	–2.5[i]	–	–	–
Competition, PCS (Nld)	–2.5[i]	–0.4[j]	–0.9[k]	
Ditto		–0.5/0.9[l]		

a Scale economies are defined as the average percentage savings on the operating costs of any additional production realized as a result of upscaling. The greater the unused scale economies, the weaker competition will be. Source: own calculations by Jacob Bikker, Marco Hoeberichts and Jurriaan Kalf
b Average and median scale economies, respectively, see Bikker and Gorter (2011), while Bikker and Popescu (2014) find a similar value of 8 per cent for 2006 and before
c Source: Chapter 9, this volume
d Administrative activities in 2010, see Bikker (2013, Table 6.2, Simplified ULM)
e Health care during 2007–2012, see Bikker and Popescu (2014)
f Cost X-inefficiency. Source: Bikker and Bos (2008)
g Sources: H-values from the Panzar–Rosse model by Bikker et al. (2012, Tables 4–6, first columns)
h Sources: H-values from the Panzar–Rosse model by Bikker and Maas (2014)
i See Chapter 7, Table 7.3, this volume
j Fixed effect estimates for health care during 2007–2012, see Bikker and Popescu (2014, Table 9)
k Fixed effect estimates, see Bikker (2012, Table 7.1)
l Fixed effect estimates for fire, transport and other non-life, see Bikker and Popescu (2014, Table 10)

perfect competition (100 per cent), see Bikker et al. (2012).[34] Among non-life insurers, competition is considerably stronger, at 49 per cent (Bikker and Maas, 2014), than among banks. A different pattern is presented by the PCS measure of competition with stronger competition for banks (–2.5, both internationally and for the Netherlands; see Chapter 7) than for non-life insurers (ranging from –0.3 to –0.5) and life insurers (–0.9). Stronger competition for banks than for insurers is in line with the lower inefficiencies for banks compared with insurers. The conclusion is that there is ample room for improvement in competition and efficiency at banks and, especially, insurance companies.

5.6. Summary

While many indicators of competition between banks commonly used in economic literature and in practice do in fact measure something, they do not contribute much to a clear, unambiguous view on bank performance. At the same time it has been established that with the help of appropriate indicators – or, even better, a *combination* of appropriate indicators – we could make a good deal of headway towards a better understanding of competition. The PCS indicator performs quite well in comparison with well-established measures, such as the Panzar–Rosse model, the SCP model and the HHI. The appropriate indicators contain sufficient information on competition to be able to function reliably as explanatory variables in a model where competition plays a dominant role. Finally, the analysis also revealed that some existing expert opinions on the relative competitiveness of notably European countries need to be thoroughly reviewed. Application of several indicators to banks, life and non-life insurers and pension funds has consistently shown that there is a good deal of room for improvement on competition and efficiency at banks and, especially, insurers.

Notes

1 Based on J.A. Bikker, (2009), Sizing up performance measures of the financial services sector, in: M. Balling, E. Gnan, F. Lierman and J.-P. Schoder (eds), *Productivity in the Financial Services Sector*, SUERF Study 2009/4, SUERF – The European Money and Finance Forum, Vienna, 45–69, and J.A. Bikker, (2010), Measuring performance of banks: an assessment, *Journal of Applied Business and Economics* 11 (4), 141–159.
2 Or for a particular bank. This chapter considers country estimates.
3 For the list of these countries, see Bikker and Bos (2008), Table 9.1. Where competition is concerned, one country, Romania, was left out due to data issues.
4 See Bos (2004) for an overview and a critical analysis.
5 Depending on the ambition of efficient firms to expand their market share.
6 Abstracting from causality. In some cases there are more theoretical connections, whereas different empirical results have been obtained. A final choice is made in all cases.
7 Conjectural variation is the degree to which a bank in setting its prices and total production quantity in a business area is aware of its dependency on other banks' behaviour in that area.
8 See Panzar and Rosse (1987).
9 For the exact definitions, see Table 16.1 in Bikker and Bos (2008). Concentration indicators are discussed in Bikker and Haaf (2002a).
10 Bikker and Haaf (2002b) and Bikker et al. (2006b) use the Panzar–Rosse model to disaggregate by bank size, thus going some way towards a breakdown by market type (international vs. local), client type (large corporation vs. medium and small-sized businesses) and product type (wholesale vs. retail). Chapter 7 estimates competition in the lending market and Chapter 9 in the market for life insurance products.
11 The data on individual banks' balance sheets and profit and loss accounts that were used by the five competition measuring models and the models to measure X-efficiency were obtained from BankScope. The dataset contains data on 13,000 private and public banks publishing more or less standardized annual accounts which permit comparison between the different accounting systems. The data underlying the profit and cost indicators for the OECD countries were obtained from the OECD (2000, 2002, 2004). Those data coincide with those used by Bikker and Bos (2008) and are discussed more fully there. The data on concentration indices for all countries and those underlying the profit and cost indicators for the 16 non-OECD countries were calculated on the basis of the banks from those countries that figure in BankScope. Selection rules were applied to the latter set in order to eliminate banks in unusual circumstances (e.g. holdings and banks undergoing a start-up or winding down process). See Bikker *et al.* (2006a).

12 A third statistical method might have been regression analysis. However, the use of this is doubtful given the strongly endogenous nature of nearly all variables used. A counterexample is Koetter et al. (2012).

13 All analyses for 46 countries were made without the Lerner index. Lerner index analyses were performed for 23 countries, but are not discussed here since the index turns out to be significantly correlated only with the PCS indicator. Table 5.3 is part of a larger correlation matrix, because the total number of variables investigated was larger than 14.

14 PCA is a multivariate statistical technique that defines, for a large number of observed variables, a smaller number of underlying series. As a statistical method, PCA is nearly identical to factor analysis. Apart from data reduction, PCA aims to provide an understanding of the dataset's structure.

15 After application of the so-termed varimax rotation for ease of interpretation. The varimax rotation is a change of coordinates used in principal component analysis and factor analysis that maximizes the sum of the variances of the squared loadings (squared correlations between variables and factors).

16 If the selected indicators are varied slightly, the outcome of the PCA will change as well. Typically, the first PCs may usually be interpreted as profit, efficiency and competition – though not always in that order. In some cases, costs appear in combination with profits, while in others they are coupled with efficiency.

17 Note that competition depresses both costs and profits.

18 As competition grows, the *H*-values of the Panzar–Rosse model will also rise (see also note 34), whereas the PCS indicator and the coefficients in the SCP model and the Cournot model decline.

19 The third principle component 'competition' as presented in Table 5.4 is an alternative index, which may be viewed as a weighted (by factor loadings) average of the original normalized series.

20 Cost-based or profit-based scale economies were also disregarded because they show little variation across the countries and because of their ambivalent relation to competition.

21 For the indicators included in the Index, a modicum of correlation with the Index is to be expected, of course. While for some indicators (PCS indicator and SCP model) this does not lead to significance, other indicators show significant correlation without being included in the Index (e.g. profit efficiency and number of banks).

22 The correct sign is negative (owing to the selection made in constructing the Index, because most indicators correlate negatively with competition, see Table 5.3), except in certain cases (shading).

23 A corollary result is that the ambivalent variables are now signed, so as to make clear which relation prevails in practice. In the case of profit efficiency the influence of cost efficiency dominates that of the use of market power. The cost-to-income ratio and the total cost to total income ratio turn out to do well as indicators of efficiency, with the enumerator (costs) dominating the denominator (income) in determining the ratio.

24 In earlier analyses across a smaller number of countries, using a differently composed set of indicators (Bikker and Bos, 2008) or covering other periods (Bikker and Bos, 2005), the net interest margin and the return on assets also came out on top.

25 Predictive validity is the term used if a test is observed before it can be compared to the realization; 'concurrent validity' is applied in cases where observation is simultaneous. The latter term would be applicable if one indicator were to be validated against the other. This option is less useful in the present analysis owing to the endogenous nature of the indicators considered here.

26 Some examples of this are given further below.

27 Austria, Belgium, France, Germany, Italy, the Netherlands, Portugal and Spain (1992–2004).

28 An alternative model, the error correction model, was unable to confirm decreasing spreads amid stronger competition. Apparently, this more complicated model is less capable of measuring the targeted alignment effect.

29 In addition, the spread between two deposit rates and the corresponding market and policy rates is explained by competition on the lending market. It turns out that deposit rates tend to be lower the more competition there is on the lending market. Apparently, competition on lending is not a good indicator for competition in the deposits market. On the contrary, banks compensate for their loss of income as a result of competition on lending by offering lower deposit rates.

30 In fact, the Index turns out not to be significant if replacing the Panzar–Rosse measure.

31 The measurement of scale economies, for instance, is based on the variable 'output', which presents its own measurement issues for each sector.

32 In the Netherlands, health care is included in non-life insurance,

33 It should be noted that these scale effects also concern production structures. In all sectors, fixed costs are high and rising over time, while they are particularly high for pension funds, compared to variable costs.

34 Bikker *et al.* (2012) explain that the *H* value of competition may be interpreted as a continuous measure between monopoly (0) and perfect competition (1) only under stringent assumptions.

References

Bikker, J.A. (2003) Testing for imperfect competition on the EU deposit and loan markets with Bresnahan's market power model, *Kredit und Kapital* 36, 167–212.

Bikker, J.A. (2013) Is there an optimal pension fund size? A scale-economy analysis of administrative and investment costs, DNB Working Paper No. 376, De Nederlandsche Bank, Amsterdam.

Bikker, J.A. and Bos, J.W.B. (2005) Trends in competition and profitability in the banking industry: a basic framework, Suerf Series 2005/2, Vienna: The European Money and Finance Forum.

Bikker, J.A. and Bos, J.W.B. (2008) *Bank Performance: A theoretical and empirical framework for the analysis of profitability, competition and efficiency*, Routledge International Studies in Money and Banking, Routledge, London and New York.

Bikker, J.A. and Gorter, J. (2011) Performance of the Dutch non-life insurance industry: competition, efficiency and focus, *Journal of Risk and Insurance* 78, 163–194.

Bikker, J.A. and Haaf, K. (2002a) Measures of competition and concentration in the banking industry: a review of the literature, *Economic & Financial Modelling* 9, 53–98.

Bikker, J.A. and Haaf, K. (2002b) Competition, concentration and their relationship: an empirical analysis of the banking industry, *Journal of Banking & Finance* 26, 2191–2214.

Bikker, J.A. and Maas, T. (2014) Assessing competition in the non-life insurance industry; an empirical analysis with the Panzar–Rosse model, DNB Working Paper, De Nederlandsche Bank, Amsterdam (forthcoming).

Bikker, J.A. and Popescu, A. (2014) Efficiency and competition in the Dutch non-life insurance industry: effects of the 2006 health care reform, DNB Working Paper, De Nederlandsche Bank, Amsterdam (forthcoming).

Bikker, J.A. and Spierdijk, L. (2010a) Measuring and explaining competition in the financial sector, *Journal of Applied Business and Economics* 11 (1), 11–42.

Bikker, J.A. and Spierdijk, L. (2010b) The impact of competition and concentration on bank solvency (mimeo).

Bikker, J.A., L. Spierdijk, and P. Finnie (2006a) Misspecification in the Panzar-Rosse model: Assessing competition in the banking industry, DNB Working Paper 114, De Nederlandsche Bank, Amsterdam.

Bikker, J.A., L. Spierdijk and P. Finnie (2006b) The impact of bank size on market power, DNB Working Paper 120, De Nederlandsche Bank, Amsterdam.

Bikker, J.A., L. Spierdijk and P. Finnie (2007) The impact of market structure contestability and institutional environment on banking competition, DNB Working Paper 156, De Nederlandsche Bank, Amsterdam.

Bikker, J.A., Shaffer, S. and Spierdijk, L. (2012) Assessing competition with the Panzar–Rosse model: the role of scale, costs, and equilibrium, *Review of Economics and Statistics* 94, 1025–1044.

Bos, J.W.B. (2004) Does market power affect performance in the Dutch banking market? A comparison of reduced form market structure models, *De Economist* 152, 491–512.

De Lange van Bergen, M. (2006) The determinants of banking competition: a world-wide Lerner index approach, Master's thesis, Groningen University.

Demsetz, H. (1973) Industry structure, market rivalry and public policy, *Journal of Law and Economics* 16, 1–9.

Hicks, J. (1935) Annual survey of economic theory: monopoly, *Econometrica*, 3, 1–20.

Koetter, M., Kolari, J. and Spierdijk, L. (2012). Enjoying the quiet life under deregulation? Evidence from adjusted Lerner indices for US banks. *Review of Economics and Statistics* 94, 462–480.

Lamoen, R. van (2011) The relationship between competition and innovation: Measuring innovation and causality, TKI Dissertation Series no. 3, Utrecht University.

Marcus, A.J. (1984) Deregulation and bank financial policy, *Journal of Banking & Finance* 8, 557–565.

OECD (2000, 2002, 2004) *Bank Profitability; Financial Statements of Banks*, OECD, Paris.

Panzar, J. and Rosse, J. (1987) Testing for 'monopoly' equilibrium, *Journal of Industrial Economics*, 35, 443–456.

Schaeck, K. and Cihak, M. (2007) Banking competition and capital ratio, IMF Working Paper WP/07/216, Washington, DC: International Monetary Fund.

Schaeck, K., Cihak, M. and Wolfe, S. (2006) Competition, concentration and bank soundness: New evidence from the micro-level. IMF Working Paper WP/06/185, Washington, DC: International Monetary Fund.

6 Identifying different regimes of competition[1]

Clemens Kool and Michiel van Leuvensteijn

This chapter presents an empirical underpinning of the PCS-indicator. We examine in particular whether this indicator is able to distinguish different regimes of competition over time with respect to the American Sugar Refining Company 1890–1914. We use data from Genesove and Mullin (1998), which includes unique direct observations of marginal costs. Testimonies of the congressional hearings provide information on the level of competition. Genesove and Mullin (1998) validated the elasticity-adjusted Lerner index empirically. The analysis shows that the PCS indicator indeed indicates different regimes of competition and performs equally well as the elasticity-adjusted Lerner index for this application.

6.1. Introduction

This chapter investigates a competition measure which was introduced by both Hay and Liu, and Boone (see Chapters 3 and 4), called the performance-conduct-structure (PCS) indicator. This measure of competition is based on the notion that more efficient companies are likely to gain larger market shares in a competitive than in a non-competitive market. The price-cost margin (PCM) or Lerner index is a widely used measure of competition. However, the PCS approach has advantages over the PCM, because its theoretical foundation is solid, while the theoretical underpinning of the PCM as a competition measure is not robust. Amir (2000), Bulow and Klemperer (1999), Rosenthal (1980) and Stiglitz (1989), for example, present models in which more intense competition leads to higher instead of lower PCM values. Furthermore, Corts (1999) shows that PCM estimates are typically underestimated, which would yield a biased measure of market conduct. The PCS indicator is theoretically robust and does not pose more stringent data requirements than the PCM.

This chapter deals with the empirical qualities of the PCS indicator, as a measure of competition among firms, by using data from Genesove and Mullin (1998, shortened to G&M). These data stem from the US refined sugar industry for the period 1890–1914. This is a well-documented period in terms of competition, due to testimonies of market participants before the US Industrial Commission in 1900 and the US Tariff Commission in 1920. These testimonies make it possible to identify periods with different degrees of competition.

Data with respect to production and prices of refined sugar are available for the market as a whole and for one firm in particular, the American Sugar Refining Company (ASRC), which was the leading company in the sugar industry during 1890–1914. We expect the development of competition in the refined sugar market to be in line with the development of competition that ASRC as the dominant firm encountered. Its market share slowly decreased from 91 per cent in 1892 to 43 per cent in 1914. We have insufficient information to estimate marginal costs of the different producers of refined sugar. It is therefore impossible to estimate the cross-sectional relationship between marginal costs and profits for different sugar refinery firms, in contrast to previous studies that apply the PCS indicator, such as Chapter 7, where a cross-sectional relationship has been estimated between marginal costs and market shares of various countries. Instead, we measure the competitiveness of one firm over time.

The underlying hypothesis is that each sub-period is internally homogenous with respect to the prevailing competition regime, but that regimes differ across sub-periods. The PCS estimates aim to test the existence of different levels of competitiveness of ASRC over time, as derived from the testimonies. G&M used these data to test whether the elasticity-adjusted Lerner index[2] for the entire market is a viable measure of competition. We estimate this index exclusively for ASRC, for the different periods mentioned above and compare the results with those of the PCS indicator. Our analysis shows that the PCS indicator indeed indicates different regimes of competition. For this dataset this indicator performs equally well as the elasticity-adjusted Lerner index.

The structure of this chapter is as follows. Section 6.2 introduces the PCS indicator and explains its advantages. Section 6.3 describes the US sugar industry during 1890–1914 and its different regimes of competition according to the public testimonies available. Special attention will be given to the production technology, which is relevant for calculating the marginal costs. Section 6.4 looks at the data from G&M, while Section 6.5 describes the empirical model. Section 6.6 contains estimates of both the elasticity-adjusted Lerner index and the PCS indicator for the periods with different competition regimes. Finally, we draw conclusions.

6.2. The underpinning of the PCS indicator

The PCS model is based on the notions, first, that more efficient firms (that is, firms with lower marginal costs) gain higher market shares and higher profits and, second, that the heavier the competition in their market, the stronger this effect. Following Boone et al. (2004), we use a standard industrial organization model with a linear demand curve to explain the PCS indicator. We examine its properties in comparison to frequently used measures such as the Herfindahl–Hirschman Index (HHI) and the PCM. We consider an industry in which each firm i produces one product with output q_i. The firm faces a linear demand curve p of the form:

$$p(q_i, q_{j\neq i}) = a - b\,q_i - d\textstyle\sum_{j\neq i} q_j \qquad (6.1)$$

The firm has constant marginal costs, mc_i, and maximizes profits $\pi_i = (p_i - mc_i)\,q_i$ by choosing the optimal output level q_i. We assume that $a > mc_i$ and $0 < d \leq b$. The first-order condition for a Cournot–Nash equilibrium can then be written as:

$$a - 2\,b\,q_i - d\textstyle\sum_{i\neq j} q_j - mc_i = 0 \qquad (6.2)$$

When N firms produce positive output levels, we can solve the N first-order conditions (6.2), yielding:

$$q_i\,(mc_i) = [(2\,b/d - 1)\,a - (2\,b/d + N - 1)\,mc_i + \textstyle\sum_j mc_j]/$$

$$[(2\,b + d\,(N-1))(2\,b/d - 1)] \qquad (6.3)$$

We define profits π_i as variable profits excluding entry costs ε. Hence, a firm enters the industry if, and only if, $\pi_i \geq \varepsilon$ in equilibrium. Note that Equation (6.3) provides a relationship between output and marginal costs. It follows from $\pi_i = (p_i - mc_i)\,q_i$ that profits depend on marginal costs in a quadratic way:

$$\pi_i\,(mc_i) = [(2\,b/d - 1)\,a - (2\,b/d + N - 1)\,mc_i + \textstyle\sum_j mc_j]/$$

$$[(2\,b + d\,(N-1))(2\,b/d - 1)]\,(p_i - mc_i) \qquad (6.4)$$

Therefore, in this market, competition can increase along three channels. First, competition increases when the products of the various firms become closer substitutes (that is, d increases, keeping d below b). In the sugar industry, for example, refined cane and beet sugar became closer substitutes due to the entry of sugar beet producers. Domestic beet sugar supplied less than 1 per cent of US consumption until 1894, but beet supply rose to 5 per cent by 1901 and 15 per cent by 1914, primarily due to a high tax tariff on raw cane sugar and to a lesser extent because of the high profit margin on refined sugar due to ASRC's monopoly (Zerbe, 1969, p. 362, and G&M, p. 358). Second, competition increases when entry costs ε decline and entry occurs, as was the case, for example, with the entry of new companies like Spreckels and Arbuckle in the sugar industry. Boone et al. (2004) proved that profits of more efficient firms (that is, with lower marginal costs mc) increase both under regimes of stronger substitution and amid lower entry costs. Third, changes in b are related to adjustments in preferences of consumers, and thus their willingness to pay for refined sugar. A decrease in b reflects a higher price sensitivity of the demand for sugar and decreases the market power of firm i and all other firms.

The theoretical model above can also be used to explain why widely applied measures such as the HHI and the PCM may fail as reliable competition indicators. The standard intuition of the HHI is based on a Cournot model with symmetric firms, where a fall in entry barriers reduces the HHI. However, with firms that differ in efficiency, an increase in competition through a rise in d reallocates output to the more efficient firms that already had higher output levels. Hence, the increase in competition may raise the HHI.

Other often-used measures of competition, the PCM, and the Lerner index, have similar disadvantages. Graddy (1995), G&M and Wolfram (1999) estimate the elasticity-adjusted Lerner index. They show that the elasticity-adjusted Lerner index is the 'conjectural variation' parameter, which indicates the expectation a firm has of how its competitors would react if it were to vary its output or price. This parameter can be interpreted as a measure of competition. Corts (1999) criticizes the elasticity-adjusted Lerner index and shows that, in general, efficient collusion cannot be distinguished from Cournot competition using the elasticity-adjusted Lerner index. Generally, heavier competition is expected to reduce the PCM of all firms. But since more efficient firms may have a higher PCM (skimming off part of the profits stemming from their efficiency lead), the increase of their market share may raise the industry's average PCM, contrary to common expectations. As such, the PCM typically underestimates the level of competition.

Boone (2000, 2001, 2004), Boone et al. (2004) and CPB (2000) consider firms in a market with homogenous goods at time *t* and estimate the cross-sectional PCS indicator. This indicator measures competition between firms in the market by measuring the strength of the relationship between profits and marginal costs at one moment in time. This chapter applies the indicator to compare the relative competitiveness of one firm in different sub-periods to its average competitiveness in the long term. Thus the PCS indicator does not measure the competitiveness of a market, but indicates whether a specific firm in one period is more or less competitive compared with another period. Of course, comparing competitiveness of one firm over time implies that we assume that the competitive conditions may change in the course of time.

Following Equation (6.4), we can write the relationship between profits and marginal costs as:

$$\pi_{1,t}(mc_{1,t}) = [(2\, b_p/d_p - 1)\, a_p - (2\, b_p/d_p + N_p - 1)\, mc_{1,t} + \textstyle\sum_j mc_{j,t}]$$
$$/[(2\, b_p + d_p\,(N_p - 1))(2\, b_p/d_p - 1)]\,(p_t - mc_{1,t}) \qquad (6.5)$$

where the subscript *1* refers to ASRC, *j* to the competitors of ASRC, *p* refers to the subperiods in which distinct competition regimes are operational and *t* to calender time in quarters.

The PCS indicator is the profit elasticity of marginal costs derived from Equation (6.5):

$$PCS_t = d\,\pi_{1,t}/d\,mc_{1,t}\,(mc_{1,t}/\pi_{1,t}) < 0$$

The expectation is that PCS is negative, where $mc_{1,t}$ is the value of marginal cost in quarter *t* and $\pi_{1,t}$ is profit in quarter *t*.

Competition can increase over time when (i) the products of the various firms become closer substitutes (that is, d_p increases, keeping d_p below b_p), (ii) entry costs fall (ε_p) or (iii) the number of firms N_p increases. Finally, a decrease in b_p reflects a higher price sensitivity of the demand for sugar in period *p* and leads to increased competition as well. ASRC's competitive behaviour will be compared across four different episodes: a period of oligopoly, the combination of two short price war periods, a period in which the cartel is split up and a period between the last price war and the break-up of the cartel.

6.3. The sugar industry

6.3.1. History: 1887–1914

To verify whether the PCS indicator properly tracks different regimes of competition, we use the case of the US sugar industry between 1887 and 1914. Genesove and Mullin (1995, 1997, 1998, 2006) provide a detailed description of the sugar industry in this period. Based on the testimonies before the US Industrial Commission 1899/1900 described in their work, we identify four different regimes of competition in the period 1887–1914.

From 1887 until 1889, the sugar industry can be characterized as oligopolistic. The Sugar Trust, formed in December 1887 as a consolidation of 18 firms, controlled 80 per cent of the sugar industry's capacity. The 20 plants owned by the original 18 trust members were quickly reduced to ten plants. Refined sugar prices increased by 16 per cent.

The high prices attracted a new entrant to the market: Claus Spreckels began production in early 1890: Q1.[3] This led to the first price war. In 1891, the Sugar Trust was reorganized as a corporation, the American Sugar Refining Company (ASRC). ASRC acquired Spreckel's plant. By April 1892, the acquisition had ended the price war. Due to the acquisition, ASRC's share of the refined sugar industry capacity rose to 95 per cent.

In the subsequent period, from 1892 to 1897, the sugar industry was characterized by high levels of concentration; with a maximum of concentration of 95 per cent of the market, the ASRC was an oligopoly. A total of five firms entered the market, each with a single plant, with an average capacity of 1,340 barrels of refined sugar per day. The ASRC and associated firms had a capacity of 49,500 barrels. Contemporary publications indicate that by 1896 American Sugar, leader of the cartel, had agreements with the new entrants.

In 1898, the next phase of competition started with the construction of a plant by the Arbuckle Brothers, which came into production in August 1898. The Doscher refinery, another entrant, began production in November 1898. These new plants had a capacity of 3,000 barrels per day. This led to a severe price war, marked by pricing at or below cost. As a result, the smaller independent refiners were shut down and one of the new entrants left the market. The second price war started in August 1898 and ended in May 1900.

After this price war, competition entered another phase in which its regime and level were unclear. Competition increased, for instance, in the period 1900:Q3–end 1909, compared with the oligopolistic period with the gradual decline of ASRC's market share, during 1892:Q2–1898:Q2. Competitive pressure from cheap raw beet sugar imports from abroad was strongly reduced, however, because the American refined sugar industry was able to produce refined sugar at low cost thanks to a relatively low duty tariff structure on Cuban raw sugar reducing the price of raw sugar. The tariff structure contained two main components: the duty on raw sugar (input) and the duty on refined sugar (the final edible product). The latter tariff protected the US refining industry from foreign, chiefly European, competition. In 1903, an important preference was granted to raw Cuban sugar. Under the Cuban reciprocity treaty, Cuban raw cane sugar was imported to the US at a tariff rate of 80 per cent of full duty. This lowered the price of raw cane sugar in New York, the main trading place for sugar, relative to the price of German raw beet sugar and protected the American sugar refining industry that produced refined cane sugar against their American counterparts that produced refined beet sugar using German raw beet sugar.

After 1909, antitrust regulation increased competition. Seeking the dissolution of ASRC in 1910, the federal government filed suit with regard to the antitrust regulation, charging monopolization and restraint of trade. Although this case was not formally resolved until a consent decree was signed in 1922, the government victories in the American Tobacco and Standard Oil cases in 1911 led ASRC to initiate partial, voluntary, dissolution. In the weekly journal *Chronicle* of January 1910, the Board of ASRC recognized that the Circuit Court of Appeals gave the competition law a much wider interpretation in the American Tobacco case than it had previously. The break-up of the cartel took place between 1910 and 1914.

Given that we have data only from 1890 onwards, only five of these six episodes in the history of the US sugar industry will be used in our analysis. The two price wars will be taken together, because of their small number of observations. Table 6.1 summarizes these episodes. We define two periods of price war, i.e. 1890:Q1–1892:Q2, with the entry of Claus Spreckels in early 1890 and the subsequent takeover of his plant by ASRC in 1892:Q3, and 1900:Q3–1909, with the entry of the Arbuckle Brothers. The period of oligopoly is defined as 1892:Q2–1898:Q2, the period between two price wars – a time by which ASRC had acquired 95 per cent of production. From 1900:Q3 to 1909, the cartel saw competition increase due to the rise in raw imports from Cuba and due to the preferential treatment in tariffs in 1903. The slow break-up of the cartel was in the period 1910:Q1–1914:Q2, beginning with the first successes in anti-trust

Table 6.1 The US competition regimes during 1887–1914

Periods	*Competition regimes*	*Used in analyses*
1887–1889	Sugar Trust possesses 80 per cent of the market: oligopoly	No
1890–1892:Q1	Spreckels' entry, price war	Yes
1892:Q2–1898:Q2	Cartel operation, small-scale entry, acquisition of Spreckels: oligopoly	Yes
1898:Q3–1900:Q2	Entry by Arbuckle Brothers and Doscher, price war	Yes
1900:Q3–1909	Mixed competition regime	Yes
1910–1914	Government antitrust suit, break-up of cartel: end of oligopoly	Yes

regulation against American Tobacco and Standard Oil and the voluntary split-up of the cartel (see also Genesove and Mullin, 1995, 1998, 2006).

6.3.2. Technology of sugar production

The technology to produce sugar is a very straightforward process. In the period under review, raw sugar consisted of 96 per cent pure sugar and 4 per cent water and impurities. To transform raw sugar into refined sugar, all sugar refiners used the same process and the same technology. Therefore, marginal costs are a linear function of the price of raw sugar, p_{raw}, with a fixed coefficient k. In the calculation of the marginal costs of producing refined sugar, variable costs such as labour and other costs must also be included. This leads to the following formula for marginal costs:

$$m_{ct} = mc_0 + k \times p_{raw,t} \tag{6.6}$$

where mc_t, the marginal costs, depend on all variable costs other than the cost of raw sugar, e.g. wages, mc_0, and the price of raw sugar, $p_{raw,t}$, and t is measured in quarters.

The fixed coefficient, k, is equal to 1.075 according to Genesove and Mullin (1995, 1998), because the production of one pound of refined sugar requires 1.075 pounds of raw sugar. The value of mc_0 is less straightforward. G&M put 26 cents as – a constant – best guess for mc_0. This estimate is based on the testimony of a partner in Arbuckle Brothers (an entrant in the second price war). In this testimony, it is said that if raw sugar costs 4.5 cents a pound, it will cost somewhere over 5 up to 5.1 cents to produce one pound of refined sugar. Other than the cost of raw sugar, mc_0 is equal to the true net-of-raw-sugar-costs margin, $p_t - p_{raw,t} \times 1.075$, where p_t is the price of refined sugar. Subtracting 4.5 × 1.075 from a total cost of 5 or 5.1 cents, we obtain a value of mc_0 ranging between 16 and 26 cents (per hundred pounds). The upper limit of these other marginal costs of non-raw sugar is still small compared with the mean raw price of 3.31 US dollars, amounting to 7.5 per cent of the price of raw sugar. A commission merchant of the independent firms testified, 'it is possible that the [larger houses] can refine at smaller margin than the others. … [but] it can[not] amount to a great deal: We suppose 3 to 5 cents a hundred would represent the difference' (Genesove and Mullin 1995, p. 13). So there could be slight differences in marginal costs between producers depending on the scale of their production capacity. In line with G&M, we use the estimate of 26 cents for the costs component in marginal costs, mc_0, for each quarter t, to calculate ASRC's marginal costs.

In theory, the variation in marginal cost could have been enough to estimate the PCS indicator cross-sectionally, as different marginal costs lead to different marginal profit margins, profits and market shares. The differences in marginal cost of 3 to 5 cents per hundred pounds may seem small, but compared with an average profit margin of 22 cents (see Table 6.2 for the average difference between price and marginal cost, mc), 3 to 5 cents represents 13.6 to 22.7 per cent of the profit margin. Unfortunately, data for of ASRC's competitors are unavailable, so the analysis is limited to a time-series perspective.

Table 6.2 Descriptive statistics

Variable	*Obser-vations*	*Mean*	*Std. Dev.*	*Min*	*Max*
Total production in long tons	97	4.43	1.11	2.35	7.80
Cuban imports of raw sugar in long tons	97	2.18	1.73	8.62	7.07
Price of refined sugar (p) in dollars	97	4.03	0.62	2.75	5.51
Price of raw sugar (p_{raw}) in dollars	97	3.30	0.59	2.25	4.87
Market share in %	97	63.00	12.00	43.00	91.00
Marginal cost (mc) in dollars	97	3.81	0.64	2.68	5.50
Calculating the PCS indicator					
Profit price war in dollars	17	2.52	12.00	–11.95	36.56
Profit oligopoly in dollars	24	28.12	12.67	3.93	49.51
Profit break-up cartel in dollars	18	6.58	5.00	0.87	17.20
Profit mixed regime war in dollars	38	13.35	7.68	–1.65	27.36
mc price war in dollars	17	4.47	0.80	3.25	5.50
mc oligopoly in dollars	24	3.97	0.47	3.27	4.82
mc break-up cartel in dollars	18	3.34	0.47	2.68	4.37
mc mixed regime in dollars	38	3.63	0.42	3.06	4.74

Explanation: All prices are reported in dollars per hundred pounds. All quantities are reported in 100,000 of long tons (one long ton is equal to 2,240 pounds), while profits are in 100,000 dollars. Price war: 1890–1892:Q1 and 1898:Q3–1900:Q2, mixed regime: 1900:Q3–1909.

6.4. The US sugar market data

Profits and marginal costs are the key variables to calculate the PCS indicator. Profits cannot be directly observed from the data from G&M. First, data from ASRC's profit and loss accounts can be retrieved only for the period after 1906, because in the period 1890–1906 the profit and loss accounts were not reported.[4] Second, ASRC admitted that the figures presented in their profit and loss accounts did not accurately describe the company's actual profits. This policy of secrecy was intended to avoid attracting the attention of potential competitors (*NY Times*, 30 March 1908). Even shareholders were misled. Havemeijer, director of ASRC, declared that this was done only to serve their best interests.

In this chapter, a proxy for ASRC's profits is constructed by using information on market shares quoted on a *yearly* basis, the total demand in the market, quoted on a *quarterly* basis, and the difference between the price of refined sugar, p_t, and marginal costs, mc_t, both also on a *quarterly* basis. As described above, the marginal costs are calculated following a G&M formula: $mc_t = 0.26 + 1.075 \times p_{raw,t}$. The proxy for profits is calculated as the profit margin multiplied by the quantities of refined sugar sold. The profit margin is equal to the difference between price p and marginal costs, mc. The quantity sold by ASRC, Q_{1t}, is equal to the total demand in the market multiplied by ASRC's market share, where subscript *1* represents ASRC. In formula terms, the proxy for profits is $(p_t - mc_t)\, Q_{it}$. These data are also available on a quarterly basis for the period 1890:Q1–1914:Q2.

Table 6.2 presents a number of stylized data characteristics. In line with G&M, the observation of 1897:Q4 is omitted from the estimation because reported Cuban raw sugar imports were zero in this quarter. As a result the dataset contains 97 observations which are divided into four periods: price war with 17 observations, oligopoly with 24 observations, break-up of the cartel with 18 observations and a period with a mixed competition regime with 38 observations. The total production of refined sugar, on average, amounted to 443,000 long tons of sugar per quarter.[5] Cuban import of raw sugar averaged 218,000 long tons per quarter. Total production reached its highest level after the break-up of the cartel with the entry of more producers. Production was kept low during the period of oligopoly. The sugar price was at its highest level during the second price war, 4.51 dollars, due to high raw sugar prices during the Spanish–American War of 1898, and at its lowest level after the break-up of the cartel, 3.45 dollars. This may have been related to the high level of production of refined sugar at the time. The prices of both refined and raw sugar are expressed in dollars per hundred pounds. ASRC's average market share was 63 per cent and gradually moved from 91 per cent during the time of oligopoly to 43 per cent after the break-up of the cartel.

Quarterly profits varied strongly across the different periods. They were at their lowest level during the price wars with considerably negative values in some quarters. During the period of oligopoly, the profits reached their highest level, nearly ten times as high as during the price war. After the break-up of the cartel, profits decreased strongly compared with the intermediate period between oligopoly and the break-up of the cartel. Marginal costs were relatively high during the period of oligopoly and price war, due to the high raw sugar prices. The tariff preferences granted to imports of Cuban raw sugar reduced marginal costs substantially in the period after the price war and in the period after the break-up of the cartel.

Our calculation of the PCS indicator has two potential weaknesses. First, due to data limitations, we use a proxy for profits that is partially based on information contained in marginal costs. The analysis is therefore vulnerable to the critique that this proxy may not accurately describe actual earnings from operations. Figure 6.1 shows that the proxy for profits follows the same pattern as the earnings from operations. Here, we are able to compare the calculated profit proxy with the actual earnings on operations as reported in the *Chronicles* and in ASRC's the annual reports for 1909–1913. During 1890–1906, ASRC published only balance sheet data and did not provide profit and loss accounts. In 1907 and 1908, only total earnings were published, which were not broken down into earnings from operations and other earnings.

Our proxy for profits reasonably describes profits actually earned. Smoothing the earnings figures by calculating a two-year moving average actually provides a very accurate picture of the earned profits. As some of the reported profits were actually earned in the previous year, but accounted for in the current year, it is

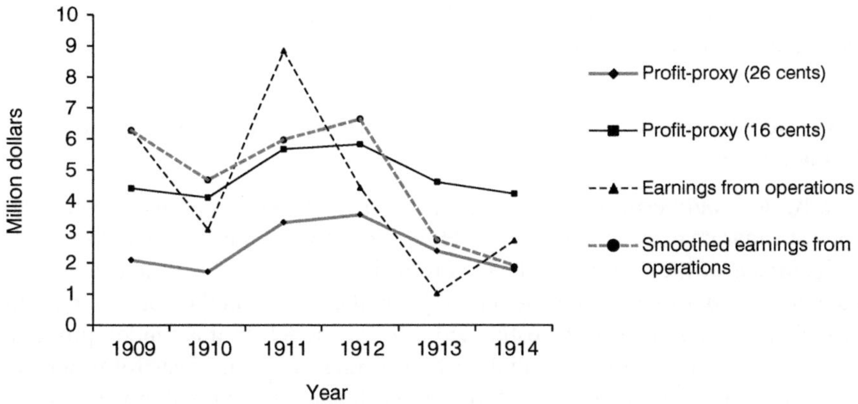

Figure 6.1. Profit-proxy compared with earnings from operations
Note: Since we only had the figures for the first six months of each year, we obtained the calculated profit proxy by doubling these first half-year figures.

reasonable to smooth the data. Figure 6.1 shows that our profits proxy is lower than the actual reported profits (with 1913 as an exception). As mentioned earlier, profit and loss accounts were available only after 1906 and retractable for the years 1909–1913. For these years, the Pearson correlation between the proxy and the reported earnings on operations is 0.43 before and 0.47 after smoothing. Taking into account the figures for 1914, of which only the first six months are available in the G&M dataset, would raise the correlation to 0.50 (reported earnings) and 0.61 (smoothed earnings). The proxy for profits and the actual smoothed figures for earnings from operations clearly move at the same pace. Therefore, using the proxy for profits as a representation of earnings of operations is warranted, in our view.

All in all, the comparison between our calculation of profits from the G&M dataset with those of the profit and loss accounts shows an overestimation of the marginal costs. G&M suggest that the (assumed) fixed component of marginal costs, namely stemming from personnel expenses, ranges between 16 and 26 cents. As shown in Figure 6.1, a profit-proxy in which the additional marginal costs are set at 16 cents indicates a better fit to the earnings data. As a robustness check, we therefore provide an additional estimate of the PCS indicator using 16 cents as additional marginal costs, mc_0.

The second critique is that the proxy for profits is calculated using information on marginal costs and, hence, is not independent from marginal costs. As a robustness check, we estimate the relationship between profits and instrumented marginal costs. The estimated value of marginal costs is derived from a regression of marginal costs as dependent variables and lagged values of marginal costs as independent variables. Recall that the proxy for profit uses information on marginal costs rather than information on the instrumented marginal costs. If the profit proxy were determined significantly by the instrumented marginal costs, then this would indicate that the relationship between the proxy for profit and marginal costs is not significantly influenced by the fact that profits are partly calculated on the basis of information on marginal costs.

6.5. The empirical model of PCS indicator and elasticity-adjusted Lerner index

Ideally, we would estimate Equation (6.5), which shows a nonlinear relationship between marginal costs and profits. However, most parameters would then be insignificant at the 5 per cent level. From this, we draw the conclusion that a nonlinear model may be too demanding for the small number of observations available. For that reason we estimated a linear model. In this model, profits of firm *1*, $\pi_{1,t}$, are related to marginal costs of firm *1*, $mc_{1,t}$, in linear form, where t refers to quarters. Equation (6.5) can be rewritten as an empirical model:

$$\pi_{1t} = \psi s + \sum d_p \delta_p mc_{1t} \tag{6.7}$$

where d_p is a dummy equal to 1 if t is an element in the sub-period p and zero otherwise. We have defined four sub-periods so that $p = 1, ..., 4$. The profit of firm *1*, π_{1t}, in period t depends on the marginal cost in different sub-periods of period t. The PCS indicator for sub-period p is equal to $\delta_p \, mc_{1p} / \pi_{1p}$, the elasticity of profits, π, to mc. The period 1890–1914 is divided into the previously defined sub-periods, i.e. of price war, oligopoly, break-up of the cartel and mixed competition regime. ψ_s is a constant with quarterly dummies, $s = 1, ..., 4$.

G&M explicitly test whether the elasticity-adjusted Lerner index, that is the PCM multiplied by the absolute value of the price elasticity of sugar demand, is able to distinguish between periods of price war and periods in which there was no price war in the sugar industry. To investigate whether the PCS indicator is able to identify the different sub-periods, we use the Wald test to ascertain whether its values in the different sub-periods are significantly different from each other. Given the fact that there are four periods, we have in principle six hypotheses. Of these six, we leave out the hypotheses that test whether competition in the mixed regime period was more or less intense than it was during the period of oligopoly or the period of the break-up of the cartel, because it is impossible to have priors on these hypotheses. It is difficult to classify the mixed competition regime of the period 1900–1909, the period after the Arbuckle war. The price war was not an outright win over the Arbuckle group. After the price war, the Arbuckle group was incorporated into the cartel. Based on the aforementioned testimonies, it is unclear whether competition had been improved or the degree of competition had returned to pre-price-war days. Therefore, it is hard to set prior beliefs on whether competition during the period 1900–1909 should be higher or lower than during the period of break-up of the cartel or oligopoly.

The four remaining hypotheses are all one-sided tests. The prior for Hypothesis I is that the value of the PCS indicator, *PCS*, in a period of oligopoly is larger than its value during the break-up of the cartel. Recall that the value of the PCS indicator is always negative or zero. In other words, we expect competition to have been fiercer during the period after the break-up of the cartel compared with the period when the cartel was still intact, because sugar firms no longer colluded after the cartel had broken up. Therefore, Hypothesis I is as follows:

$$H_0\text{: } PCS_{oligopoly} \leq PCS_{break\text{-}up}$$

$$H_1\text{: } PCS_{oligopoly} > PCS_{break\text{-}up}$$

Furthermore, following G&M, competition must have been fiercer during a price war than in other periods, such as the period during which the cartel was split up. Competition during the price war was very strong, as is shown by the drastic reductions in price at the time. Prices were even temporarily lower than marginal costs, resulting in losses for ASRC. After the break-up of the cartel, ASRC was still making profits (Genesove and Mullin 2006). Therefore, our prior belief for Hypothesis II is that competition during the price war was heavier than after the break-up of the cartel, which implicates a rejection of H_0 of Hypothesis II:

$$H_0\text{: } PCS_{break\text{-}up} \leq PCS_{price\ war}$$

$$H_1\text{: } PCS_{break\text{-}up} > PCS_{price\ war}$$

Of course, the entry of firms like Spreckels and Arbuckle, and the ensuing price war to fend off these entrants, must have increased the level of competition compared with the period of oligopoly in which ASRC's market share reached 95 per cent. Thus, Hypothesis III is expected to be rejected:

$$H_0\text{: } PCS_{oligopoly} \leq PCS_{price\ war}$$

$$H_1\text{: } PCS_{oligopoly} > PCS_{price\ war}$$

Based on the testimonies, the PCS indicator should indicate more competition during the periods of price wars than during the period with a mixed competition regime. Given these considerations, we test the following Hypothesis IV:

$$H_0\text{: } PCS_{mixed\ regime} \leq PCS_{\text{price war}}$$

$$H_1\text{: } PCS_{mixed\ regime} > PCS_{\text{price war}}$$

6.6. Empirical results

This section compares the elasticity-adjusted Lerner index with the new indicator. First, both measures of competition are calculated from the data for the sugar industry. Then, Hypotheses I–IV defined above are tested for both these measures of competition. There are several reasons why we would like to make this comparison. The first is that Boone already explained in Chapter 4 that the PCS indicator is theoretically a better indicator for competition than the PCM. The elasticity-adjusted Lerner index is an improved version of the PCM, and so the question remains, whether the PCS indicator is also empirically a better indicator than the Lerner index. The other reasons are more of a practical nature. G&M calculated the elasticity-adjusted Lerner index for the overall sugar industry, rather than for one firm, which complicates the comparison of our results for the new indicator of competition with those of G&M. The other reason is that G&M only consider price wars versus absence of price wars. Our analysis of different regimes of competition is more demanding. Therefore, Section 6.6.1 presents the results for the elasticity-adjusted Lerner index and Section 6.6.2 presents those for the PCS indicator. Finally, Section 6.6.3 compares the results.

6.6.1. The elasticity-adjusted Lerner index revisited

The elasticity-adjusted Lerner index, L_η, is defined as

$$L_{\eta,t} = \eta(p_t)\,(p_t - mc_t)/\,p_t \tag{6.8}$$

where $(p_t - mc_t)/p_t$ is the PCM, and $\eta(p_t)$ is the absolute value of the price elasticity of demand for sugar. For a monopolist or a functioning cartel, we would expect $L_{\eta,t} = 1$, and in a perfectly competitive or Bertrand market, $L_{\eta,t} = 0$. We estimate the price elasticity of demand in the following model:

$$D_t = \gamma_0 + \gamma_1 Q_3 + \sum d_p\, \eta\, p_t \tag{6.9}$$

where D, total demand in the market, depends on the price set in the market, p, and a dummy for the high season, Q_3. Equation (6.9) is estimated with an instrumental variable (IV) to allow for endogeneity between the sugar price and demand.[6] The instrumental variable used is the Cuban import of raw sugar, which most probably reduced the price of raw sugar and thus the price of refined sugar, but not the demand for sugar or the firm's profits. With respect to the potential endogeneity of Cuban imports, G&M point out that this would depend upon the sources of variation in Cuban production: the seasonality of the yearly production, yearly climate variation, the Cuban Revolution (1895–1898), the subsequent Spanish–American War and a spectacular increase in planting of sugar cane. Only the latter factor could theoretically be related to demand shocks if a shock in US demand for sugar induced speculative raw sugar storage in Cuba. The only storage of raw sugar happened at the shipping docks. Storage meant a delay in the cane harvest, which in turn led to sucrose loss. Postponing the harvest in hopes of receiving higher prices involved the significant risk of the rainy season beginning before all cane could be harvested (G&M, pp. 363–364). Decreased Cuban imports could increase the price of raw sugar. Overall, this makes the endogeneity of Cuban sugar imports unlikely. We use Newey and West's kernel-based heteroskedasticity and autocorrelation-consistent (HAC) variance estimators, where the bandwidth was set at four periods, as before in the estimation of the PCS indicator. This model provides the results shown in Table 6.3. Here, it follows that the price parameters do not vary significantly among the different regimes of competition. Furthermore, as expected, the demand for sugar during the high season is higher than during the low season.

Table 6.3 Instrumental variable-estimation results for the demand for refined sugar

Demand (production)	*Parameter*	*z-value*
p oligopoly	–39.68	**–3.32
p price war	–39.57	**–3.60
p break-up cartel	–35.73	*–2.35
p mixed regime	–39.17	**–2.93
Q_3 effect	26.64	**5.67
Constant	248.98	**4.99
R^2-adjusted	0.139	
Anderson correlation test (*p*-value)	12.83 (0.00)	
Hansen *J*-statistic	Exactly identified	
Number of observations	97	

Note: * and ** means significance at the 5 per cent and 1 per cent level, respectively.

Elasticity-adjusted Lerner index

The elasticity-adjusted Lerner index is calculated by means of the following formula:

$$L_{\eta,p} = \eta_p(p_p\text{-}mc_{1,p})/p_p \qquad (6.10)$$

where p_p is the price, $D_{1,p}$ is ASRC's production, $(p_p\text{-}mc_{1,p})/p_p$ is ASRC's price-cost margin (see Table 6.A in Appendix 6.I) and η_p is the estimated price elasticity of demand in period *p*, see Table 6.3. L_η has an average value of 0.123, a minimum of 0.037 and a maximum of 0.261. G&M use D_t, the average total production in the market, to calculate the elasticity-adjusted Lerner index for the total market. We only look at ASRC's competitiveness. Therefore, we use the production of this company to evaluate the elasticity-adjusted Lerner index, assuming that all sugar firms face the same demand curve in period *p*. This assumption is reasonable, given the small quality differences between the firms' products, as sugar is a bulk good.[7]

Figure 6.2 shows the different values of the elasticity-adjusted Lerner index, and reveals that competition was at its highest level during the price wars of 1890–1891 and 1899–1900. The PCM was at its lowest level in these periods, as was the elasticity-adjusted Lerner index. Competition was at its lowest level during the period of oligopoly, i.e. 1892–1898. The level of competition increased after the second price war and after the cartel broke up in 1910. The hypotheses tested in Table 6.4 confirm that the differences in the elasticity-adjusted Lerner index are significant between the regime of price war and the other regimes of competition at the 1 per cent significance level, with one exception; the elasticity-adjusted Lerner index can only identify differences in competition between price war and the break-up of the cartel at the 10 per cent level.

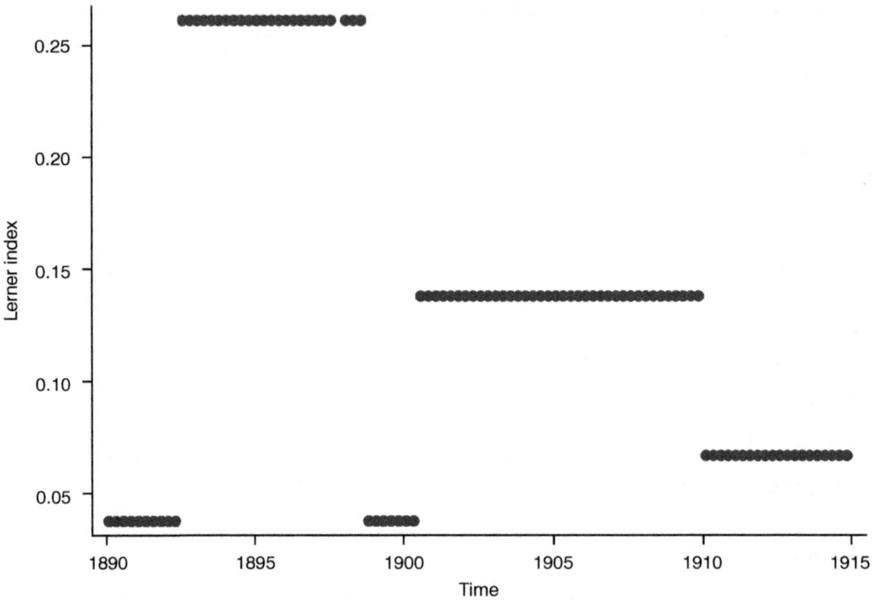

Figure 6.2. ASRC's elasticity-adjusted Lerner index

Table 6.4 Wald tests of the elasticity-adjusted Lerner index

	IV	
Hypotheses	$\chi^2(1)$	*p-values*
Test H_0: Lerner oligopoly ≤ Lerner break-up	14.79	0.00
Test H_0: Lerner break-up ≤ Lerner price war	2.50	0.06
Test H_0: Lerner oligopoly ≤ Lerner price war	10.65	0.00
Test H_0: Lerner mixed regime ≤ Lerner price war	7.35	0.00

6.6.2. Results for the PCS indicator

We now estimate the linear model from Equation (6.7) to determine the PCS indicator. We take mc_0 to be equal to 26 cents. As was explained previously, we use instrumental variables to correct for endogenous shifts in the demand curve. We use Cuban imports of raw sugar as our preferred instrumental variable. The second and third columns of Table 6.5 show the results of the IV estimation. The standard errors are computed using Newey and West's kernel-based heteroskedasticity and autocorrelation-consistent (HAC) variance estimators, where the bandwidth was set at four periods, as was done by G&M. The estimations are adjusted for seasonal effects by introducing three quarterly dummies, Q_1–Q_3.

The results of the benchmark IV estimation in the second and third column of Table 6.5 indicate that the parameter for the marginal cost variable differs significantly from zero at the 1 per cent level during all periods, with the exception

Table 6.5 Empirical results of the PCS indicator based on profits

mc_o estimation approach	*26 cents/IV*		*26 cents/GMM*		*16 cents/IV*	
	Parameter	*z-value*	*Parameter*	*z-value*	*Parameter*	*z-value*
mc oligopoly	–6.56	–1.83	–8.40	**–3.18	–6.82	–1.83
mc price war	–11.43	**–3.49	–14.06	**–5.60	–11.99	**–3.59
mc break-up cartel	–14.89	**–3.42	–15.97	**–4.84	–15.65	**–3.45
mc mixed regime	–11.76	**–3.00	–13.59	**–4.69	–12.39	**–3.05
Q_1 effect	0.04	0.02	0.17	0.09	–0.07	–0.04
Q_2 effect	7.25	**3.38	7.41	**3.48	8.52	**3.86
Q_3 effect	9.22	**4.43	8.74	**4.28	10.93	**5.00
Constant	51.09	**3.67	57.65	**5.55	57.38	**4.07
R^2, adjusted	0.546		0.516		0.562	
Anderson correlation test (*p*-value)	32.88 (0.00)		51.71 (0.00)		32.79 (0.00)	
Hansen *J*-statistic (*p*-value)	Exactly identified		6.712 (0.15)		Exactly identified	
Number of observations	97		92		97	

* and ** mean significance at the 5 per cent and 1 per cent level, respectively.

of the period of oligopoly. Marginal costs do not appear to bear any relationship with profits in the period of oligopoly. The marginal cost parameter is at its lowest level during the price war regime and at its highest during the oligopoly regime. The difference between the marginal cost parameters is significant only between the period of oligopoly and all the other periods. In all other cases, these differences are not significant.[8] In addition, the estimations show that the high seasons of spring and summer (Q_2 and Q_3, respectively) were more profitable than the low season of winter, Q_1, and the benchmark season of autumn.

We perform two robustness checks. In Section 6.4, we pointed out that the proxy for profits is calculated using information on marginal costs and is therefore not fully independent of marginal costs. As a robustness check we estimate the same equation with the General Method of Moments (GMM) using additional instrumental variables – the marginal costs lagged four quarters – to analyse whether the instrumented marginal costs are related to profits in the same way as marginal costs. If this is the case, it suggests that our profit-proxy based on marginal costs does not distort the results significantly. To test for over-identification of the instrument, we apply the Hansen J-test for GMM (Hayashi, 2000). The joint null hypothesis is that the instruments are valid, i.e. uncorrelated with the error term. Under the null hypothesis, the test statistic is chi-squared with the number of degrees of freedom equal to the number of over-identifying restrictions. A rejection would cast doubt on the validity of the instruments. Only instruments with four periods lagged rejected the Hansen J-statistic with more than 5 per cent significance. The final results, presented in columns 4 and 5 of Table 6.5, show the same picture as the first column. The parameters are of the same order of magnitude as those in the first column and are even more significant. Therefore, we conclude that the use of a profit proxy based on marginal costs is appropriate and does not bias the results.

As a second robustness check, we estimate the same relationship in IV but this time with an estimate for mc_0 of 16 cents instead of 26 cents, resulting in lower marginal cost and profits. We use 16 cents, as this best mimics the figures for earnings from operations acquired from the *Chronicles* and ASRC's annual reports. Columns 6 and 7 of Table 6.5 show that the estimates based on a 16-cent marginal cost assumption do not differ substantially from the original ones based on a 26-cent marginal cost assumption. Overall, we conclude that the results are insensitive to the chosen level of additional marginal costs, mc_0.

6.6.2. The PCS indicator

The PCS indicator is the elasticity of profits to marginal costs, i.e. $\delta\ mc_p/\pi_p$. The PCS indicator for the different sub-periods is calculated by multiplying the IV estimates of parameter δ of *mc* in sub-period *p* from the benchmark regressions (column 2) in Table 6.5 by the ratio of average marginal costs, $mc_{p,}$ and average profits, $\pi_{p'}$ in the same sub-period *p* (as presented in Table 6.2).

Figure 6.3 presents the values of the PCS indicator for the different regimes of competition and shows that competition during the price wars of 1890–1891 and 1899–1900 was very strong compared with other periods, as indicated by its significantly negative values. Competition was at its lowest point (and the PCS at its highest value) during the period of oligopoly, i.e. 1892–1898. After the break-up of the cartel in 1910, its values again became more negative, indicating that ASRC became more competitive compared with the previous period of oligopoly. The period 1900–1909 shows that competition in the sugar market was moderate during the mixed regime, higher than during the previous period of oligopoly, but lower than during the period after the break-up of the cartel.[9] Next we examine the significance of these differences by testing the hypotheses of Section 6.5.

Hypotheses

To test the different hypotheses, we used a Chi-squared distributed Wald test with one degree of freedom to determine whether the PCS indicator was significantly different between two periods. Table 6.6, second column, presents the results and shows that the PCS indicator during the break-up of the cartel was significantly more negative than the PCS indicator in times of an oligopoly (H_0: 'PCS oligopoly > PCS break-up cartel'). The null hypothesis I is thus rejected at the 1 per cent level. Furthermore, for all the other hypotheses, all the null hypotheses are also rejected, which indicates that the PCS is fully able to distinguish between the

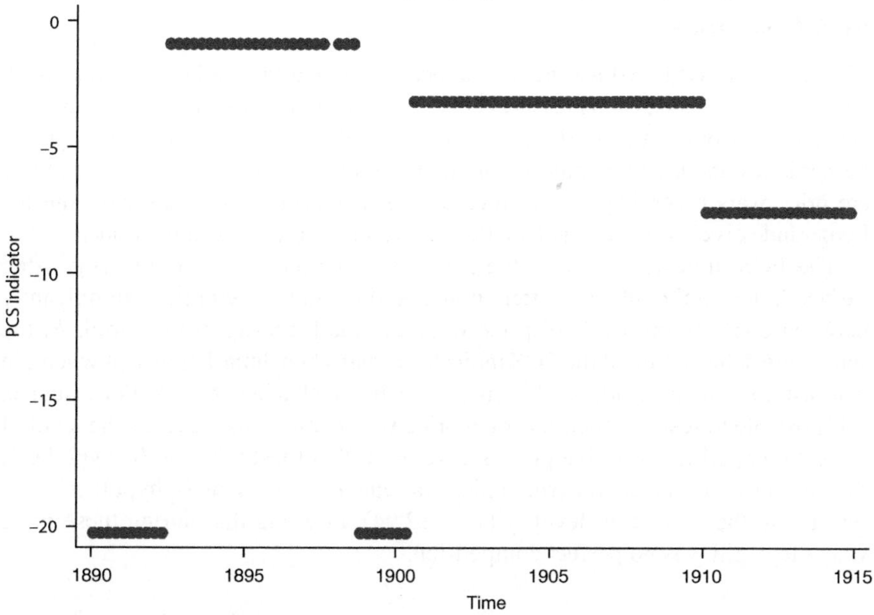

Figure 6.3 ASRC's PCS indicator over time. In line with G&M, the observation of 1897:Q4 is omitted from the estimation because the instrumental variable, i.e. Cuban imports of raw sugar, was zero.

Table 6.6 Testing hypotheses on the PCS indicator

Hypotheses	*26 cents/IV*		*26 cents/GMM*		*16 cents/IV*	
Wald test	$\chi^2(1)$	*p-values*	$\chi^2(1)$	*p-values*	$\chi^2(1)$	*p-values*
Test H_0: PCS oligopoly ≤ PCS break-up	14.87	0.00	27.56	0.00	17.77	0.00
Test H_0: PCS break-up ≤ PCS price war	11.67	0.00	34.07	0.00	10.21	0.00
Test H_0: PCS oligopoly ≤ PCS price war	13.30	0.00	33.71	0.00	16.95	0.00
Test H_0: PCS mixed regime ≤ PCS price war	12.83	0.00	33.00	0.00	15.09	0.00

The PCS_mixed_regime indicator was significantly different from the other periods at the 1 per cent level. The Wald tests are available upon request.

different regimes of competition. Therefore, our measure of competition could very well be used to measure the different regimes of competition. The second and third columns of Table 6.6 also show that with instrumented marginal cost or with additional marginal costs of 16 cents, the PCS is capable of identifying the different regimes of competition. Again, the conclusion is that the degree to which the PCS indicator is able to identify different regimes of competition is not affected by the fact that the proxy for profits is based on marginal costs.

6.6.3. Comparison

Above we discussed two measures of competition: the elasticity-adjusted Lerner index and the PCS indicator. Both measures provide a similar picture with regard to levels of competition. Competition is low in times of oligopoly, and both the elasticity-adjusted Lerner index and the PCS indicator are high. Competition is most fierce when there are price wars according to both measures of competition; the elasticity-adjusted Lerner index is close to zero and the PCS indicator has a very negative value.

The PCS indicator provides the same information as the elasticity-adjusted Lerner index, although the latter indicator does not differentiate significantly between competition levels of price wars and the break-up of the cartel. At the same time, a limitation of the PCS indicator is that a benchmark is absent where, in contrast, the elasticity-adjusted Lerner index has such a benchmark. For instance, it is possible to test whether, during a price war, competition reaches the level of perfect competition. For that purpose, we use a Wald-test with the H_0 hypothesis that the elasticity-adjusted Lerner index was equal to zero. This H_0 hypothesis was rejected at the 1 per cent level ($\chi^2(1) = 12.94$), meaning that during these price wars there still was no perfect competition.

6.7. Conclusion

This chapter tested whether the PCS indicator is able to identify empirically significant differences in competitive pressure between periods of oligopoly, price war and split-up of cartels. A limitation of the PCS indicator, compared with the elasticity-adjusted Lerner index, is that it cannot measure the absolute level of a firm's competitiveness, as it can only tell whether, on average, the firm is more or less competitive in a certain period than in another period. For this purpose, a linear model is estimated between a proxy for profits and marginal costs by using data of the dominant firm in the sugar industry, ASRC, during 1890–1914, as used by Genesove and Mullin (1998). The profit proxy is based on information on marginal costs. From these estimates, it follows that the PCS indicator indeed is able to identify the different regimes of competition empirically. The results show that competition is significantly more intense during a price war than it is in a period of an oligopoly. Our indicator also demonstrates that competition during the break-up of the cartel is significantly higher than during an oligopoly, which is in line with expectation. Finally, the PCS indicator's value during a price war is lower than in the period after the break-up of the cartel, indicating that competition is fiercer in the former than in the latter period. Robustness checks with regard to the appropriate measurement of profits by means of the proxy of profits show that the results are insensitive to variation in the specification of the profit proxy. Estimations with instrumented marginal costs reveal that the results of the PCS indicator are not substantially influenced by the fact that the proxy is based on marginal costs. From a comparison of these results with those of the elasticity-adjusted Lerner index, it follows that the new indicator performs just as well as the adjusted Lerner index.

Appendix 6.I: Descriptive statistics for calculating the elasticity-adjusted Lerner index

From Table 6.A, it follows that the price-cost margin as a percentage of price was at its lowest level during the price wars, 1 per cent of the price, and at its highest level during the period of oligopoly, 10 per cent of the price. Furthermore, production increased over time, from around 0.83 million long tons to 0.124 million long tons after the break-up of the cartel, as the entry of firms increased. Market shares declined gradually from 78 per cent on average during the oligopoly period to 47 per cent after the break-up of the cartel. Prices were indeed high during the times of oligopoly, but this was partly due to high raw sugar prices. Prices reached their lowest levels after the break-up of the cartel.

Notes

1 Based on Chapter 5 of the PhD thesis 'Measuring competition in financial markets' by Michiel van Leuvensteijn (2009).

2 The elasticity-adjusted Lerner index is the Lerner index multiplied by the price elasticity of demand.

Table 6.A Descriptive statistics for calculating the elasticity-adjusted Lerner index

	Observations	*Mean*	*Std. dev.*	*Min*	*Max*
PCM price war (in terms of price)	17	0.01	0.05	–0.04	0.14
PCM oligopoly (in terms of price)	24	0.10	0.04	0.02	0.15
PCM break-up cartel (in terms of price)	18	0.03	0.02	0.01	0.07
PCM mixed regime (in terms of price)	38	0.06	0.03	–0.01	0.10
Production price war in long tons	17	82.37	15.47	55.54	118.94
Production oligopoly in long tons	24	83.39	16.64	52.66	122.08
Production break-up cartel in long tons	18	124.90	28.65	81.09	165.54
Production mixed regime in long tons	38	104.46	17.67	74.26	145.18
Market share price war (in %)	17	71	8	65	91
Market share oligopoly (in %)	24	78	6	70	91
Market share break-up cartel (in %)	18	47	3	43	50
Market share mixed regime (in %)	38	59	5	50	70
Price war (in dollars)	17	4.51	0.68	3.55	5.50
Price oligopoly (in dollars)	24	4.40	0.412	3.72	5.07
Price break-up cartel (in dollars)	18	3.45	0.47	2.75	4.44
Price mixed regime (in dollars)	38	3.85	0.44	3.38	5.02

Note: All prices are reported in dollars per hundred pounds. All quantities are reported in 100,000 of long tons (one long ton is 2240 pounds). Profits are in 100,000 dollars.

3 See Genesove and Mullin (1997, p. 21) and Genesove and Mullin (2006).
4 Only ASRC's balance sheet was reported (as required under the laws of the State of Massachusetts) in the period 1890–1906.
5 One long ton is equal to 2,240 pounds (1,016 kg).
6 G&M differentiate between low and high season by estimating different price elasticities for demand. Introducing three quarterly dummies yields positive price elasticities for demand during the price war, due to the small database.
7 Had we used total production of the market, the Wald test of Hypothesis II would have been equal to 0.471 with a p-value of 0.77 and would have been rejected at the 10 per cent level.
8 The Wald tests are available on request. The estimations presented use yearly data for market shares. As a robustness check, we have also used a moving average over four quarters from 1891 onwards for market shares. Using this smoothed version of market share did not change the results significantly.
9 The figures of the PCS indicator with the estimates of the fourth and sixth columns of Table 6.5 are not shown because they are almost identical to Figure 6.2. They are available upon request.

References

Amir, R. (2000) Market structure, scale economies and industry performance, CIE discussion papers, University of Copenhagen. Department of Economics. Centre for Industrial Economics.

Boone, J. (2000) Competition, CEPR discussion paper series no. 2636, December.

Boone, J. (2001) Intensity of competition and the incentive to innovate, *International Journal of Industrial Organization*, vol. 19(5): 705–726.

Boone, J. (2004) A new way to measure competition, CEPR discussion paper series no. 4330, March.

Boone, J., R. Griffith and R. Harrison (2004) Measuring competition, presented at the Encore Meeting 2004: Measuring competition.

Bulow, J. and P. Klemperer, (1999). Prices and the winner's curse, *RAND Journal of Economics*, vol. 33(1): 1–21.

Corts, K. (1999) Conduct parameters and the measurement of market power, *Journal of Econometrics*, vol. 88(2): 227–250.

CPB (2000) Measuring competition: How are cost differentials mapped into profit differentials? Working paper no. 131, CPB Netherlands Bureau for Economic Policy Analysis, The Hague.

Genesove, D. and W.P. Mullin (1995) Validating the conjectural variation method: The sugar industry, 1890–1914, NBER paper 5314.

Genesove, D. and W.P. Mullin (1997) Predation and its rate of return: The sugar industry, 1890–1914, NBER paper 6032.

Genesove, D. and W.P. Mullin (1998) Testing static oligopoly models: Conduct and cost in the sugar industry, 1890–1914, *Rand Journal of Economics*, vol. 29: 355–377.

Genesove, D. and W.P. Mullin (2006) Predation and its rate of return: The sugar industry, 1887–1914, *Rand Journal of Economics*, vol. 37(1): 47–69.

Graddy, K. (1995) Testing for imperfect competition of the Fulton fish market, *RAND Journal of Economics*, vol. 26(1): 75–92.

Hayashi, F. (2000) *Econometrics*, Princeton University Press.

Leuvensteijn, M. Van (2009) Measuring competition in financial markets, PhD thesis, Utrecht University.

New York Times (1908) Sugar Trust makes first open report, 25 March 1908.

Rosenthal, R. (1980) A model in which an increase in the number of sellers leads to a higher price, *Econometrica*, vol. 48(6): 1575–1579.

Stiglitz, J. (1989) Imperfect information in the product market, in: R. Schmalensee and R. Willig, eds., *Handbook of Industrial Organization*, vol. I, Elsevier Science Publishers.

Wolfram, C. (1999) Measuring duopoly power in the British electricity spot market, *American Economic Review*, vol. 89(4): 805–826.

Zerbe, R.O. (1969) The American Sugar Refining Company 1887–1914: The Story of a Monopoly, *Journal of Law and Economics,* 12, 339–375.

7 A new approach to measuring competition in the loan markets of the euro area[1]

Jacob A. Bikker, Michiel van Leuvensteijn, Adrian van Rixtel and Christoffer Kok

This chapter is the first that applies a new measure of competition, the PCS indicator, to the banking industry. This approach is able to measure competition within segments of the banking market, such as the loan market, whereas many well-known measures of competition can consider the entire banking market only. Like most other model-based measures, this approach ignores differences in bank product quality and design, as well as the attractiveness of innovations. We measure loan market competition in the five largest EU countries as well as, for comparison, the UK, the US and Japan. Our findings indicate that over the 1994–2004 period the US had the most competitive loan market, whereas overall loan markets in Germany and Spain were among the most competitive in the EU. The Netherlands occupied an intermediate position, whereas in Italy competition declined significantly over time. The French, Japanese and UK loan markets were generally less competitive.

7.1. Introduction

This chapter investigates the measurement of competition in the EU banking sector. Competition is a key driver of social welfare, as it may push down prices (i.e. interest rates) and improves services for consumers and enterprises (Cetorelli, 2001).[2] Also, competition is pivotal to monetary policy; in a competitive market, changes in the policy rates of the European Central Bank (ECB) are passed on more quickly into the interest rates that banks offer their customers.

This chapter presents estimates of competition in loan markets of the major EU countries using the PCS indicator. This indicator measures the impact of efficiency on performance in terms of profits or market shares. The idea behind this indicator is that competition enhances the performance of efficient firms and impairs the performance of inefficient firms, which is reflected in their respective profits or market shares. This approach is related to the well-known efficiency hypothesis, which also explains banks' performances from differences in efficiency (Goldberg and Rai, 1996; Smirlock, 1985).

A well-known problem in the banking industry is that competition cannot be measured directly, as cost data and often also price data of single banking products are usually unavailable. Hence, indirect measures are needed. This chapter adds to the competition literature in applying a new competition indicator to the banking sector which is an improvement on widely accepted concentration measures, such as the Herfindahl–Hirschmann Index (HHI). The HHI has the disadvantage that it ignores the difference between large and small countries. Furthermore, concentration may also be due to consolidation forced by severe competition. Hence, the concentration index is an ambiguous measure.[3]

Our approach to competition is also innovative in the sense that we can measure competition not only for the entire banking market, but also for various product markets, such as the loan market, and for several types of banks, such as commercial, savings banks and cooperative banks. An often applied measure such as the Panzar–Rosse model only investigates the overall competitive nature of all banking activities. Another advantage of the PCS indicator is that it requires relatively little data, unlike, e.g. the Bresnahan model which is very data intensive. This allows the estimation of competition on an annual basis to assess developments over time. Like many other model-based measures, our approach ignores differences in bank product quality and design, as well as the attractiveness of innovations.

The structure of this chapter is as follows. Section 7.2 presents an overview of different approaches to the measurement of banking competition in the literature. Section 7.3 provides a theoretical basis for the indicator as a new measure for competition and discusses its properties. The data are described in the following section. The applied econometric method and the estimation results of the PCS indicator are presented in Section 7.5. Finally, Section 7.6 concludes.

7.2. Literature on measuring competition

Competition in the banking sector has been analysed by measuring market power and efficiency. A well-known approach to measuring market power is suggested by Bresnahan (1982) and Lau (1982), and was recently used by Bikker (2003) and Uchida and Tsutsui (2005). They analyse bank behaviour on an aggregate level and estimate the banks' average conjectural variation. High conjectural variation implies that a bank is highly aware of its interdependence with other firms in terms of output and prices (via the demand equation). Under perfect competition where output price equals marginal costs, banks' conjectural variation should be zero, whereas a value of one would indicate monopoly.

Panzar and Rosse (1987) propose an approach based on the so-called *H*-statistic which is the sum of the elasticities of the reduced-form revenues with respect to the input prices. This *H*-statistic ranges from $-\infty$ to 1. An *H*-value equal to or smaller than zero indicates monopoly or perfect collusion, whereas a value between zero and one provides evidence of a range of oligopolistic or monopolistic types of competition. A value of one points to perfect competition. This approach has been applied to all EU countries by Bikker and Haaf (2002) and to the Turkish banking industry by Günalp and Celik (2006).

A third indicator for market power is the Hirschman–Herfindahl index, which measures the degree of market concentration. This indicator is often used in the context of the 'Structure Conduct Performance' (SCP) model (see e.g. Berger et al., 2004, and Bos, 2002), which assumes that market structure affects banks' behaviour, which in turn determines their performance.[4] The idea is that banks with larger market shares may have more market power and use it. Moreover, a smaller number of banks make collusion more likely. To test the SCP hypothesis, performance (profit) is explained by market structure (as measured by the HHI).

Market power may also be related to profit, in the sense that extremely high profits may point to a lack of competition. A traditional measure of profitability is the price-cost margin (PCM), which is equal to the output price minus marginal costs, divided by the output price. The PCM is frequently used in the empirical industrial organization literature as an empirical approximation of the theoretical Lerner index.[5] In the literature, banks' efficiency is often seen as a proxy of competition. The existence of scale and scope economies has in the past been investigated thoroughly. It is often assumed that unused scale economies would be exploited, and thus reduced under strong competition.[6] Hence, the existence of non-exhausted scale economies is an indication that the potential to reduce costs has not been exhausted and, therefore, can be seen as an indirect indicator of (a lack of) competition (see Chapter 9). The existence of scale efficiency is also important as regards the potential entry of new firms, which is a major determinant of competition. Strong scale effects would put new firms into an unfavourable position.

A whole strand of literature explores X-efficiency, which reflects managerial ability to drive down production costs, controlled for output volumes and input price levels. The X-efficiency of firm i is defined as the difference in costs between that firm and the best practice firms of similar size and with similar input prices (Leibenstein, 1966). Heavy competition is expected to force banks to drive down their X-inefficiency, so that the latter is often used as an indirect measure of competition. An overview of the empirical literature is presented in Bikker (2004) and Bikker and Bos (2008).

A final area in the literature is given over to the Structure Conduct Performance (SCP) model where conduct reflects competitive behaviour. This hypothesis assumes that market structure affects competitive behaviour and, hence, performance. Many articles test this model jointly with an alternative explanation of performance, namely the efficiency hypothesis, which attributes differences in performance (or profit) to differences in efficiency (e.g. Goldberg and Rai, 1996, and Smirlock, 1985). As mentioned above, the PCS indicator can be seen as an elaboration on this efficiency hypothesis. This test is based on estimating an equation which explains profits by market structure variables and measures of efficiency. The efficiency hypothesis assumes that market structure variables no longer contribute to profits once efficiency is considered as the cause of profit. As Bikker and Bos (2005) show, this test suffers from a multicollinearity problem if the efficiency hypothesis holds.

Summarizing, there are indicators of competition, like the *H*-statistic, the approach of Bresnahan and Lau and the different efficiency indicators that focus on the entire banking sector. Other indicators, like the price-cost margin, are related to product markets, but require very detailed information. As will be shown below, our new indicator, which is related to the efficiency hypothesis, focuses on one product market, in our case the loan market, and is not very information intensive.

7.3. The PCS indicator model

The PCS indicator is based on the notions, first, that more efficient firms (that is, firms with lower marginal costs) gain higher market shares or profits and, second, that this effect is stronger the heavier the competition in that market. The theoretical relationship between market shares and marginal costs, as has been developed in Chapters 3 and 4, and Section 6.2, is nonlinear. Chapter 3 proposes a Box–Cox test to choose between linear and log-linear. We also take a practical view and take empirical results into account. Following most other studies we choose a log-linear relationship:

$$\ln s_i = \alpha + \beta \ln mc_i \qquad (7.1)$$

The market shares of banks with lower marginal costs are expected to increase, so that β is negative. The stronger competition is, the stronger this effect will be, and the larger, in absolute terms, this (negative) value of β. We refer to the β parameter as the *PCS indicator.* The specification of Equation (7.1) implies that β is an elasticity, which facilitates interpretation, particularly across equations.[7] In Section 7.5, we will find that the results of the linear model are very similar to those of the log-linear model.

The theoretical model above can also be used to explain why widely applied measures such as the HHI and the PCM fail as reliable competition indicators. The standard intuition of the HHI is based on a Cournot model with symmetric banks, where a fall in entry barriers reduces the HHI. However, where banks differ in efficiency, an increase in competition through a rise in d reallocates output to the more efficient banks that already had higher output levels. Hence, the increase in competition raises the HHI. The effect of increased competition on the industry's PCM may also be perverse. Generally, heavier competition reduces the PCM of all banks. But since more efficient banks may have a higher PCM (skimming off part of the profits stemming from their efficiency lead), the increase of their market share may raise the industry's average PCM, contrary to common expectations.

We note that the PCS indicator model, like every other model, is a simplification of reality. First, efficient banks may choose to translate lower costs either into higher profits or into lower output prices in order to gain market share. Our approach assumes that the behaviour of banks is between these two extreme cases, so that banks generally pass on at least part of their efficiency gains to their clients. More precisely, we assume that the banks' passing-on behaviour, which drives Equation (7.1), does not diverge too strongly across the banks. Second, our approach ignores differences in bank product quality and design, as well as the attractiveness of innovations. We assume that over time banks are forced to provide quality levels that are more or less similar. By the same token, we presume that banks have to follow the innovations of their peers. Hence, like many other model-based measures, the PCS indicator approach focuses on one important relationship, and disregard other aspects (see also Bikker and Bos, 2005). Also, compared with direct measures of competition, the PCS indicator may have the disadvantage of being an estimate and thus surrounded by a degree of uncertainty. Of course, other model-based measures, such as Panzar and Rosse's *H*-statistic, suffer from the same disadvantage. One advantage of the PCS indicator in comparison to the *H*-statistic, as suggested by Panzar and Rosse (1987), is that the PCS indicator may focus on one sub-market only, here the loan market, and not on the entire banking market.

As the PCS indicator may be time dependent, reflecting changes in competition over time, we estimate β separately for every year (hence, β_t). We do not have an absolute benchmark for the level of β. We only know that the more negative β is, the stronger competition must be. Comparing the indicator across regions or countries, or even across industries, may help to interpret estimation results. For that reason, Boone and Weigand in Centraal Planbureau (2000) and Boone et al. (2004) applied the model to different manufacturing industries. Since measurement errors – including unobserved country or industry specific factors – are less likely to vary over time than across industries, the time series interpretation of β is probably more robust than the cross-sector one (that is, comparison of β for various countries or industries at a specific moment in time). Therefore, Boone focuses mainly on the *change* in β_t over time within a given industry, rather than comparing β between industries.

Because marginal costs cannot be observed directly, Centraal Planbureau (2000) and Boone et al. (2004) approximate a firm's marginal costs by the ratio of average costs to revenues. As dependent variable in Equation (7.1), Centraal Planbureau (2000) uses the *relative* values of profits and as explanatory variable the ratio of variable costs to revenues, whereas Boone et al. (2004) consider *absolute* instead of relative values.

We improve on Boone's approach in two ways. First, we calculate marginal costs rather than approximating them by average variable costs. We are able to do so by using a translog cost function, which is more precise and more closely in line with theory. An important advantage is that these marginal costs allow us to focus on segments of the market, such as the loan market, where no direct observations of individual cost items are available. Second, we use market share as dependent variable instead of profits. The latter is, by definition, the product of market shares and profit margin. We expect that efficiency gains lead to lower output prices, which increase market shares and, further, that in more competitive markets efficiency will increase market share more than in non-competitive markets. This is supported by the theoretical framework above. We have no a priori knowledge about the effect of efficiency on the profit margin. Hence, a market share model will be more precise. Another great advantage of using market shares is that they are always positive, whereas the range of profits (or losses) includes negative values. A log-linear specification would exclude negative profits (losses) by definition, so that the estimation results would be distorted by sample bias, because inefficient, loss-making banks would have to be ignored.

7.3.1. The translog function and marginal costs

In order to be able to calculate marginal costs, we first estimate, for each country, a translog cost function (TCF) using individual bank observations. Such a function assumes that the technology of an individual bank can be described by one multiproduct production function. Under proper conditions, a dual cost function can be derived from such a production function, using output levels and factor prices as arguments. A TCF is a second-order Taylor expansion around the mean of a generic dual cost function with all variables appearing as logarithms. It is a flexible functional form that has proved to be an effective tool in explaining multiproduct bank services. The TCF has the following form:

$$\ln c_{it}^{h} = \alpha_0 + \sum_{h=1,\dots,(H-1)} \alpha_h d_i^h + \sum_{t=1,\dots,(T-1)} \delta_t d_t + \sum_{h=1,\dots,H} \sum_{j=1,\dots,K} \beta_{jh} \ln x_{ijt} d_i^h + \sum_{h=1,\dots,H} \sum_{j=1,\dots,K} \sum_{k=1,\dots,K} \gamma_{jkh} \ln x_{ijt} \ln x_{ikt} d_i^h + v_{it} \quad (7.2)$$

where the dependent variable c_{it}^{h} reflects the production costs of bank i ($i = 1, \dots, N$) in year t ($t = 1, \dots, T$). The sub-index h ($h = 1, \dots, H$) refers to the type category of the bank, that is, commercial bank, savings bank or cooperative bank. The variable d_i^h is a dummy variable, which is 1 if bank i is of type h and zero otherwise. The variable d_t is another dummy variable, which is 1 in year t and otherwise zero. The explanatory variables x_{ikt} represent three groups of variables ($k = 1, \dots, K$.). The first group consists of (K_1) bank output components, such as loans, securities and other services (proxied by other income). The second group consists of (K_2) input prices, such as wage rates, deposit rates (as price of funding) and the price of other expenses (proxied as the ratio of other expenses to fixed assets). The third group consists of ($K - K_1 \quad K_2$) control variables (also called 'netputs'), e.g. the equity ratio. In line with Berger and Mester (1997), the equity ratio corrects for differences in loan portfolio risk across banks. The coefficients α_h, β_{jh} and γ_{jkh}, all vary with h, the bank type. The parameters δ_t are the coefficients of the time dummies and v_{it} is the error term. This specification is also in line with Shen (2005) and Kasman and Yildirim (2006).

Two standard properties of cost functions are linear homogeneity in the input prices and cost-exhaustion (see e.g. Beattie and Taylor, 1985, and Jorgenson, 1986). They imply the following restrictions on the parameters, assuming – without loss of generality – that the indices j and k of the two sum terms in Equation (7.2) are equal to 1, 2 or 3, respectively, for wages, funding rates and prices of other expenses (disregarding the sub-index h):

$$\beta_1 + \beta_2 + \beta_3 = 1, \gamma_{1,k} + \gamma_{2,k} + \gamma_{3,k} = 0 \text{ for } k = 1, 2, 3, \text{ and}$$

$$\gamma_{k,1} + \gamma_{k,2} + \gamma_{k,3} = 0 \text{ for } k = 4, \dots, K \quad (7.3)$$

The first restriction stems from cost exhaustion, reflecting the fact that the sum of cost shares is equal to unity. In other words, the value of the three inputs is equal to total costs. Linear homogeneity in the input prices requires that the three linear input price elasticities (β_i) add up to 1, whereas the squared and cross terms of all explanatory variables ($\gamma_{i,j}$) add up to zero. Again without loss of generality, we also apply the symmetry restrictions $\gamma_{j,k} = \gamma_{k,j}$ for j, $k = 1, \ldots, K$.[8] As Equation (7.2) expresses that we assume different cost functions for each type of bank, the restrictions (7.3) apply to each type of bank.

The marginal costs of output category $j = l$ (of loans) for bank i of category h in year t, $mc_{ilt}^{\ h}$ are defined as:

$$mc_{ilt}^{\ h} = \partial c_{it}^{\ h} / \partial x_{ilt} = (c_{it}^{\ h} / x_{ilt}) \partial \ln c_{it}^{\ h} / \partial \ln x_{ilt} \qquad (7.4)$$

The term $\partial \ln c_{it}^{\ h} / \partial \ln x_{ilt}$ is the first derivative of Equation (7.2) of costs to loans. We use the marginal costs of the output component 'loans' only (and not for the other K_l components) as we investigate the loan markets. We estimate a separate translog cost function for each individual sector in each individual country, allowing for differences in the production structure across bank types within a country. This leads to the following equation of the marginal costs for output category loans (l) for bank i in category h during year t:

$$mc_{ilt}^{\ h} = c_{it}^{\ h} / x_{ilt} \left(\beta_{lh} + 2\, \gamma_{llh} \ln x_{ilt} + \textstyle\sum_{k=1,\ldots,K;\, k \neq l} \gamma_{lkh} \ln x_{ikt}\right) d_i^h \qquad (7.5)$$

7.4. Banks' balance sheet data

This chapter uses an extended BankScope database of banks' balance sheet data running from 1992 to 2004. We investigate banking markets of the major euro area economies, i.e. France, Germany, Italy, the Netherlands and Spain, as well as, for comparison, the UK, the US and Japan. The focus is on commercial banks, savings banks, cooperative banks and mortgage banks and, for most countries, ignores specialized banks, such as investment banks, securities firms and specialized governmental credit institutions. For Germany, some specialized governmental credit institutions, that is, the major *Landesbanks*, are included in the sample in order to have a more adequate coverage of the German banking system. In addition to certain public finance duties, these *Landesbanks* also offer banking activities in competition with the private sector banks (Hackethal, 2004). For Japan, in contrast with Uchida and Tsutsui (2005), we also include three long-term credit banks, because they have traditionally offered long-term loans to the corporate sector and have increasingly become competitors of the commercial banks, due to the ongoing process of financial liberalization in Japan which has eroded the traditional segmentation of the Japanese banking sector (Van Rixtel, 2002).

In order to exclude irrelevant and unreliable observations, banks are incorporated in our sample only if they fulfil the following conditions: total assets, loans, deposits, equity and other non-interest income should be positive; the deposits-to-assets ratio and loans-to-assets ratio should be less than, respectively, 0.98 and 1; the income-to-assets ratio should be below 20 per cent; personnel expenses-to-assets and other expenses-to-assets ratios should be between 0.05 and 5 per cent; and finally, the equity-to-assets ratio should be between 1 and 50 per cent. These restrictions reduced the sample by 3,980 observations mainly due to the equity-to-assets ratio restriction. As the Japanese banking sector experienced a deep crisis during most of our sample period, we have relaxed the equity ratio restriction for Japanese banks.

As a result, the dataset for 2002 totals 8,605 commercial banks (including *Landesbanks*), 2,121 cooperative banks, 1,545 savings banks and 109 mortgage banks, plus 31 other banks, making 12,411 banks in all (see Table 7.1). Over all years of the sample, the number of observations is 88,647. German and, particularly, US banks dominate the sample with, respectively, 1,570 and 8,837 banks (in 2002). Before 1999, the number of US banks is only around one quarter of this number.

Table 7.2 provides a summary description of the variables used in the estimations, such as costs, loans, securities and other services, each expressed as a share of total assets, income or funding. Costs are defined as the sum of interest expenses, personnel expenses and other non-interest expenses. Costs, loans and securities are, respectively, 6 per cent, 61 per cent and 25 per cent of total assets. Average market shares differ strongly across countries, due mainly to country-size effects. The output factor 'other services' is proxied by non-interest income, which is around 12 per cent of total income. Wage rates are proxied by personnel expenses as a share of total assets, as for most banks the staff numbers are not available. Wages average 1.5 per cent of total assets. The other-expenses-to-fixed-assets ratio provides an input price for this input factor. Finally, interest rate costs, proxied by the ratio of interest expenses and total funding, run to around 3.1 per cent.

7.5. Estimation results of the PCS indicator

After calculating marginal costs – see Section 7.3.1 and Appendix 7.I – we are able to estimate the PCS indicator. For each country we use the relationship between the marginal costs of individual banks and their market shares as in Equation (7.1):

$$\ln s_{ilt} = \alpha + \sum_{t=1,\dots,T} \beta_t d_t \ln mc_{ilt} + \sum_{t=1,\dots,(T-1)} \gamma_t d_t + u_{ilt} \qquad (7.6)$$

where s stands for market share, mc for marginal costs, i refers to bank i, l to output type 'loans', and t to year t; d_t are time dummies – as in Equation (7.2) – and u_{ilt} is the error term. This provides us with the coefficient β_t, the PCS indicator. Note that the indicator β_t is time dependent. We will observe some notable differences across countries in the PCS indicator's development during the sample period. In most countries, the β_t do not differ significantly from zero in any year.

Higher market shares may diminish marginal costs due to scale economies. Therefore, we expect larger market shares to go hand in hand with lower marginal costs so that marginal costs may be endogenous. To correct for this possible endogeneity, we use the Generalized Method of Moments (GMM) approach with as instrument variables the one-, two- or three-year lagged values of the explanatory variable, marginal costs.[9] To test for over-identification of the instruments, we apply the Hansen J-test for GMM (Hayashi, 2000). The joint null hypothesis is that the instruments are valid instruments, i.e. uncorrelated with the error term. Under the null hypothesis, the test statistic is chi-squared with the number of degrees of freedom equal to the number of over-identification restrictions. Rejection would cast doubt on the validity of the instruments. Further, the Anderson canonical

Table 7.1 Number of banks by country and by type in 2002

Country	*Commercial banks*	*Cooperative banks*	*Long-term credit banks*	*Real estate banks/ Mortgage banks*	*Savings banks*	*Special governmental credit institutions*	*Total*
Germany	130	867	0	44	501	28	1,570
Spain	61	17	0	0	43	0	121
France	115	83	0	2	30	0	230
United Kingdom	80	0	0	57	3	0	140
Italy	105	476	0	1	52	0	634
Japan	169	676	3	0	1	0	849
Netherlands	24	1	0	4	1	0	30
United States	7,921	1	0	1	914	0	8,837
Total	8,605	2,121	3	109	1,545	28	12,411

Table 7.2 Mean values of key variables by countries for the 1992–2004 period (%)

Country	*Total costs as a share of total assets*	*Average market share of lending*	*Loans as a share of total assets*	*Securities as a share of total assets*	*Other services as a share of total income*	*Other expenses as a share of fixed assets*	*Wages as a share of total assets*	*Interest expenses as a share of total funding*
Germany	6.44	0.06	60	22	12	227	1.5	3.7
Spain	6.63	0.98	58	14	16	167	1.5	4.1
France	7.42	0.41	54	4	20	537	1.5	4.8
United Kingdom	6.29	0.78	59	11	14	885	0.9	5.1
Italy	6.67	0.22	53	26	16	261	1.7	3.5
Japan	2.89	0.25	58	20	14	128	0.1	0.4
Netherlands	6.59	3.02	54	15	13	340	0.9	5.4
United States	5.63	0.01	63	28	11	148	1.6	2.8
Total	5.82	0.12	61	25	12	203	1.5	3.1

Table 7.3 Summary statistics of the PCS indicator for eight countries (1994–2004)

	DE	*ES*	*FR*	*IT*	*NL*	*UK*	*US*	*JP*
Average	–4.0	–4.8	–0.6	–4.0	–2.5	–1.00	–5.60	2.44
Standard deviation	1.5	1.8	0.5	1.8	1.5	0.66	0.95	5.74
Maximum	–2.5	–2.7	0.3	–1.6	1.0	0.36	–4.54	13.88
Minimum	–7.1	–9.6	–1.3	–7.3	–4.4	–1.87	–6.89	–3.63

correlation likelihood ratio is used to test for the relevance of excluded instrument variables (Hayashi, 2000). The null hypothesis of this test is that the matrix of reduced form coefficients has rank $K - 1$, where K is the number of regressors, meaning that the equation is under-identified. Under the null hypothesis of under-identification, the statistic is chi-squared distributed with $L - K + 1$ degrees of freedom, where L is the number of instruments (whether or not included in the equation). This statistic provides a measure of instrument relevance, and rejection of the null hypothesis indicates that the model is identified. We use kernel-based heteroskedastic and autocorrelation consistent (HAC) variance estimations. The bandwidth in the estimation is set at two periods and the Newey–West kernel is applied. Where the instruments are over-identified, 2SLS is used instead of GMM. For this 2SLS estimator, Sargan's statistic is used instead of the Hansen J-test.

Table 7.3 presents averages of the PCS indicator over 1994–2004 by country (first row). We observe that the US had the most competitive loan market, whereas overall loan markets in Germany and Spain were among the most competitive within the EU. The Netherlands occupied an intermediate position, whereas in Italy competition declined significantly over time. The French, Japanese and UK loan markets were generally less competitive. To explain these different levels of competition we turn to the yearly estimations of the PCS indicator as presented in Table 7.4.

Table 7.4 shows that only for the US, the betas differ significantly from zero for all years. For Spain and the Netherlands, we observe substantial jumps in the series over time (see also Figure 7.1). However, generally speaking, the estimated successive annual betas for each country do not differ significantly from each other.[10] Japan (for six years), France (for two years) and the Netherlands as well as the UK (for one year) sometimes show positive β_t values instead of the expected negative values, in line with the rationale of Equation (7.6).[11]

Contrary to recent criticism regarding the functioning of the German banking sector (e.g. IMF, 2004), our estimates suggest that this sector is among the most competitive of the euro area countries considered. Most likely, this result for Germany hinges in part on the special structure of its banking system, being built on three pillars, namely commercial banks, publicly-owned savings banks and cooperative banks (see Hackethal, 2004). The PCS indicator for Germany likely reflects the competitive environment of the commercial banking sector, which operates countrywide, rather than the competitiveness of the savings and cooperative banks that are, generally, active in regional markets only.[12]

Table 7.4 Development of the PCS indicator over time for eight countries[b]

	Germany[a]		*France*		*Italy*[a]	
PCS indicator	β_t	*z-value*	β_t	*z-value*	β_t	*z-value*
1993					–5.90	–1.18
1994					**–7.25	–3.24
1995	–4.47	–1.40	**–1.28	–3.36	**–4.51	–3.53
1996	**–7.09	–2.92	**–1.28	–3.56	**–5.58	–3.98
1997	**–4.64	–3.41	**–1.11	–3.55	**–5.89	–4.08
1998	**–5.10	–3.97	*–0.79	–1.99	**–4.60	–6.08
1999	**–2.60	–4.04	*–0.78	–2.30	**–4.05	–4.39
2000	**–2.50	–4.60	–0.46	–1.34	**–3.32	–4.39
2001	**–3.31	–7.02	–0.68	–1.67	**–2.66	–3.62
2002	**–4.53	–4.71	–0.40	–0.78	–1.59.	–1.82
2003	**–2.73	–5.62	0.27	0.39	**–2.42	–3.69
2004	**–2.66	–4.15	0.10.	0.12	**–1.81	–2.79
F-test	10.70		5.10		13.23	
Anderson canon corr. LR-test	185.2		1,023.7		300.3	
Hansen *J*-test (*p*-value)	0.00		19.69 (0.48)		0.00	
Number of observations	14,534		918		4,918	

	Spain[a]		*Netherlands*		*US*[a]	
PCS indicator	β_t	*z-value*	β_t	*z-value*	β_t	*z-value*
1993	*–4.21	–2.49				
1994	*–4.80	–2.28	–1.92	–1.42		
1995	–5.20	–1.92	*–4.42	–2.42		
1996	–9.61	–0.67	**–2.09	–2.58		
1997	–4.36	–1.78	–3.57	–1.70		
1998	–5.40	–0.86	1.04	0.38		
1999	*–5.46	–2.21	–1.44	–0.85		
2000	–3.44	–1.93	**–3.26	–3.00	**–6.89	–20.34
2001	**–4.38	–2.55	**–3.91	–4.71	**–6.16	–20.94
2002	*–3.88	–2.09	*–2.45	–2.44	**–5.54	–22.61
2003	–3.42	–1.20	–2.22	–1.80	**–4.87	–22.15
2004	**–2.69	–5.62	**–3.09	–2.85	**–4.54	–25.53
F-test	3.33		3.90			198.30
Anderson canon corr. LR-test	38.8		31.7		7,084.3	
Hansen *J*-test (*p*-value)	0.00		20.5 (0.04)		0.00	
Number of observations	1,015		241		40,177	

continued…

Table 7.4 continued

	United Kingdom		*Japan*	
PCS indicator	β_t	*z-value*	β_t	*z-value*
1994	0.36	0.55		
1995	–0.95	–1.57	**7.30	4.93
1996	–0.48	–0.64	**13.88	6.63
1997	–1.33	–1.52	**5.98	3.97
1998	*–1.87	–2.17	**3.97	4.04
1999	*–1.52	–1.96	**4.85	2.58
2000	*–1.56	–2.05	0.11	0.03
2001	*–1.46	–1.97	**–2.52	–4.04
2002	–1.22	–1.65	**–2.63	–3.73
2003	–0.43	–0.66	**–2.90	–6.56
2004	–0.49	–0.93	**–3.63	–5.95
F-test	1.25		23.48	
Anderson canon corr. LR-test	1,468.2		214.8	
Hansen *J*-test (*p*-value)	20.88 (0.03)		34.43 (0.02)	
Number of observations	912		1476	

Notes: Asterisks indicate 95 per cent (*) and 99 per cent (**) levels of confidence. Coefficients of time dummies are not shown.

a 2SLS is used and the equation is exactly identified, so that the Hansen J-test is 0.00.

b Equation (7.6) is estimated with the GMM. The numbers of observations for Italy, Japan, the Netherlands, Spain and the UK are higher than in Table 7.3, due to the use of instrumental variables with lags of higher order in Table 7.3.

The results for Spain and Italy seem to be driven mainly by the boost to competition following the deregulation and liberalization of the banking sectors in both countries during the early 1990s[13] (see also Figure 7.2).[14] In the Netherlands, the banking sector went through a process of profound reorganization and consolidation during the 1980s and 1990s.[15] This development increased concentration in the Dutch banking sector, but may also have led to efficiency improvements. All in all, the PCS indicator suggests that, from an international perspective, competitive conditions in the Dutch banking sector take up an intermediate position.[16] Finally, the French banking sector is found to be the least competitive of the euro area countries considered. This finding may stem in part from the fact that although most French banks have now been privatized and the government continues its withdrawal from the banking industry, the role of the State in the French banking sector remains non-negligible, in that some important entities remain State-controlled (see for example: Fitch Ratings, 2001; Moody's Investors Service, 2004; Standard & Poor's, 2005).

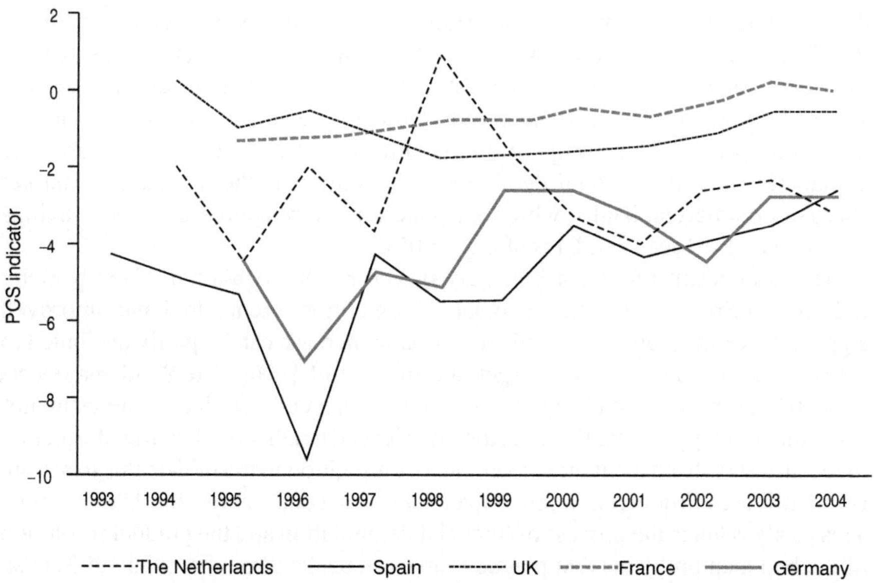

Figure 7.1 Indicators of the countries with no significant change in competition over time

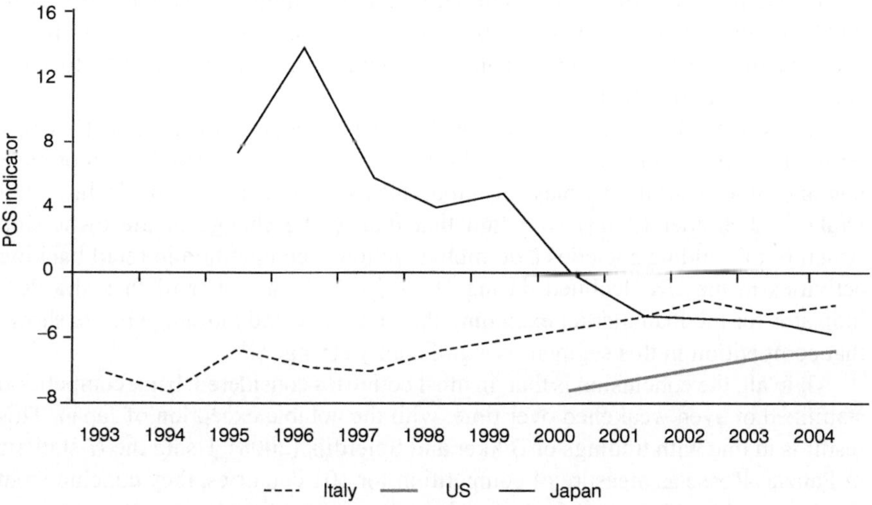

Figure 7.2 Indicators of the countries with significant change in competition over time

Turning to the non-euro area countries, the PCS indicator suggests that the US banking sector is the most competitive among the countries in our sample, reflecting the significant changes in the US banking system over the past two decades. While it remains largely bifurcated along metropolitan and rural lines and continues to hinge on the principles of specialization and regionalism (basically stemming from legislation enacted following the Great Depression), the US banking system has undergone a transformation, owing mainly to the lifting of restrictions on the range of banking activities and of the ban on interstate banking.[17] Although our estimates of the PCS indicator for the US show a significantly increasing trend (indicating a decline in competition),[18] the (average) level of competition remains comparatively high. A possible explanation for this gradual decline of competition is the decrease in market share of commercial banks, which are generally more competitive than savings banks (see also Jones and Critchfield, 2005).

The poor result for Japan is largely driven by the regulation of the banking industry during the 1990s. In Japan, competition seems to have improved significantly (see Figure 7.2). This remarkable increase can be partly attributed to a history of very low, if any, competition in the mid-1990s. The Wald test rejects the null hypothesis of no change at 1 per cent for Japan. In particular, our estimates show that the Japanese banking sector experienced a rather marked transformation in recent years, from a climate of very low competition in the mid-1990s to a more competitive environment, where Japan ranked second behind the US, in 2004. This partly reflects the process of financial deregulation and the gradual resolution of the bad loan problems that plagued Japanese banks throughout the 1990s (Van Rixtel, 2002). Eventually, this development involved the *de facto* nationalization of the worst-performing institutions and a major wave of consolidation, resulting in the establishment of a small number of large commercial banking groups in 2000 and 2001 (Van Rixtel et al., 2004). Our estimates suggest that the profound and structural changes in the Japanese banking sector have helped to foster a competitive environment.

Finally, in the UK, competition in the loan market appears to be weak. This may be because in specific segments of the UK loan market, in particular mortgage lending, other institutions play an important role.[19] Our results are in line with Drake and Simper (2003) who find that due to the change in the ownership structure of building societies ('de-mutualization'), competition in retail banking activities in the UK declined during 1999–2001. As a matter of fact, the PCS indicator for the loan market excluding the real estate and mortgage banks shows that competition in this segment is significantly stronger.[20]

All in all, the conclusion is that, in most countries considered, bank competition stabilized or even weakened over time, with the notable exception of Japan. This result is in line with findings of Bikker and Spierdijk (2008). Using the *H*-statistic of Panzar–Rosse as measure of competition for 101 countries, they conclude that the dominant trend is towards weaker banking competition.

7.6. Conclusions

This chapter uses a measure for competition, the PCS indicator, and is the first study that applies this approach to banking markets. The PCS indicator quantifies the impact of marginal costs on bank performance, as measured in terms of market shares. We improve the original PCS indicator by calculating marginal costs instead of approximating marginal costs by average variable costs. In the latter case, the results are distorted by the impact of scale effects, due to the fixed costs. This approach has the advantage of being able to measure bank market segments, such as the loan market, whereas many well-known measures of competition, such as the Panzar–Rosse method, consider only the entire banking market. Moreover, estimation of the PCS indicator requires relatively moderate amounts of data. Like many other model-based measures, our approach ignores quality and design differences between bank products, as well as the attractiveness of innovations. Finally, as for all model-based measures, the PCS indicator should only be regarded as an estimate.

We apply the PCS indicator to the loan markets of the five major countries in the euro area plus, for comparison, the UK, the US and Japan over the 1994–2004 period. Our findings indicate that during this period the US had the most competitive loan market, whereas overall loan markets in Germany and Spain were among the most competitive in the EU. The German results seem to be driven partly by a competitive commercial banking sector reflecting the distinct nature of its 'three-pillar' banking system. In Spain, competition remained strong and relatively stable over the full sample period, indicating the progress the Spanish banking system has made since the major liberalization reforms of the late 1980s and early 1990s. The Netherlands occupied an intermediate position among the countries in our sample, despite having a relatively concentrated banking market dominated by a small number of very large players. Italian competition declined significantly over time, which may be due to the partial reconstitution of market power by the banking groups formed in the early 1990s. French and British loan markets were less competitive overall. In Japan, competition in loan markets was found to increase dramatically over the years, in line with the consolidation and revitalization of the Japanese banking industry in recent years.

All in all, according to the PCS indicator, competitive conditions in the loan markets and their developments over time are found to differ considerably across countries. These differences seem largely to reflect distinct characteristics of the national banking sectors, such as the relative importance of commercial, cooperative and savings banks respectively, and changes to the banks' institutional and regulatory environment during our sample period.

Appendix 7.I: Estimation results for marginal costs

We estimate a separate translog cost function for each country and take the first derivative of loans to obtain the marginal costs of lending, see Section 7.3.1. As an example, Table 7.A.1 presents estimation results of the translog cost function for Germany. Table 7.A.2 shows the marginal costs estimates of loans, both across countries and over time. Marginal costs decline strongly over time, reflecting the significant decreases in funding rates during 1992–2004 and possibly also technological improvements. Germany, France and Spain have relatively high marginal costs compared with the Netherlands and Belgium. Apart from differences in funding rates, this may also be explained by lower efficiency in the former countries.

Table 7.A.1 Estimates of the translog cost function for Germany

Dependent variable: ln(costs) – ln(other expenses)	*Coef-ficient*	*t-value*	*P > |t|*
Outputs			
ln(loans)_comm. banks	0.01	0.43	0.67
(ln(loans))²_comm. banks	0.08	45.14	0.00
ln(securities)_comm. banks	0.11	9.32	0.00
(ln(securities))²_comm. banks	0.04	39.84	0.00
ln(other services)_comm. banks	0.66	34.45	0.00
(ln(other services))²_comm. banks	0.06	24.31	0.00
ln(loans)_savings banks	–0.55	–5.16	0.00
(ln(loans))²_savings banks	0.21	20.25	0.00
ln(securities)_savings banks	0.60	10.79	0.00
(ln(securities))²_savings banks	0.05	24.39	0.00
ln(other services)_savings banks	0.92	7.93	0.00
(ln(other services))²_savings banks	0.07	5.73	0.00
ln(loans)_coop. banks	0.19	6.02	0.00
(ln(loans))²_coop. banks	0.11	26.79	0.00
ln(securities)_coop. banks	0.42	27.56	0.00
(ln(securities))²_coop. banks	0.04	42.97	0.00
ln(other services)_coop. banks	0.42	14.93	0.00
(ln(other services))²_coop. banks	0.05	13.86	0.00
Input prices			
ln(wage) – ln(other expenses)_comm. banks	–0.02	–0.78	0.44
(ln(wage) – ln(other expenses))²_comm. banks	0.12	26.00	0.00
ln(funding rate) – ln(other expenses)_comm. banks	0.85	28.35	0.00
(ln(funding rate) – ln(other expenses))²_comm. banks	0.15	22.66	0.00
ln(wage) – ln(other expenses)_savings banks	0.79	5.55	0.00
(ln(wage) – ln(other expenses))²_savings banks	0.06	2.18	0.03
ln(funding rate) – ln(other expenses)_savings banks	0.14	0.94	0.35
(ln(funding rate) – ln(other expenses))²_savings banks	0.08	2.91	0.00
ln(wage) – ln(other expenses)_coop. banks	0.15	4.16	0.00
(ln(wage) – ln(other expenses))²_coop. banks	0.65	15.58	0.00
ln(funding rate) – ln(other expenses)_coop. banks	0.09	15.26	0.00
(ln(funding rate) – ln(other expenses))²_coop. banks	0.10	12.40	0.00
Cross-products between input prices			
(ln(wage) – ln(other expenses)) * (ln(funding rate) – ln(other expenses))_ comm. banks	–0.27	–26.54	0.00
(ln(wage) – ln(other expenses)) * (ln(funding rate) – ln(other expenses))_savings banks	–0.15	–2.84	0.01
(ln(wage) – ln(other expenses)) * (ln(funding rate) – ln(other expenses))_coop. banks	–0.20	–14.82	0.00
Cross-products between outputs			
ln(loans) * ln(securities)_comm. banks	–0.03	–16.25	0.00
ln(loans) * ln(other services)_comm. banks	–0.10	–27.25	0.00
ln(securities) * ln(other services)_comm. banks	–0.03	–15.70	0.00

Dependent variable: ln(costs) – ln(other expenses)	*Coef-ficient*	*t-value*	*P > |t|*
ln(loans) * ln(securities)_savings banks	–0.21	–20.79	0.00
ln(loans) * ln(other services)_savings banks	–0.21	–10.44	0.00
ln(securities) * ln(other services)_savings banks	0.08	7.58	0.00
ln(loans) * ln(securities)_coop. banks	–0.12	–34.04	0.00
ln(loans) * ln(other services)_ coop. banks	–0.10	–15.55	0.00
ln(securities) * ln(other services)_coop. banks	0.03	9.17	0.00
Cross-products between outputs and input prices			
ln(loans) * (ln(wage) – ln(other expenses))_comm. banks	0.06	13.48	0.00
ln(loans) * (ln(funding rate) – ln(other expenses))_comm. banks	–0.04	–8.27	0.00
ln(loans) * (ln(wage) – ln(other expenses))_savings banks	0.00	–0.11	0.91
ln(loans) * (ln(funding rate) – ln(other expenses))_savings banks	0.02	0.78	0.44
ln(loans) * (ln(wage) – ln(other expenses))_coop. banks	0.10	11.44	0.00
ln(loans) * (ln(funding rate) – ln(other expenses))_coop. banks	–0.08	–8.09	0.00
ln(securities) * (ln(wage) – ln(other expenses))_comm. banks	0.03	11.11	0.00
ln(securities) * (ln(funding rate) – ln(other expenses))_comm. banks	–0.04	–10.00	0.00
ln(securities) * (ln(wage) – ln(other expenses))_savings banks	–0.10	–6.34	0.00
ln(securities) * (ln(funding rate) – ln(other expenses))_savings banks	0.06	3.88	0.00
ln(securities) * (ln(wage) – ln(other expenses))_coop. banks	–0.06	–14.28	0.00
ln(securities) * (ln(funding rate) – ln(other expenses))_coop. banks	0.05	10.49	0.00
ln(other services) * (ln(wage) – ln(other expenses))_comm. banks	–0.05	–9.36	0.00
ln(other services) * (ln(funding rate) – ln(other expenses))_comm. banks	0.04	6.74	0.00
ln(other services) * (ln(wage) – ln(other expenses))_savings banks	0.07	2.22	0.03
ln(other services) * (ln(funding rate) – ln(other expenses))_savings banks	–0.06	–1.89	0.06
ln(other services) * (ln(wage) – ln(other expenses))_coop. banks	–0.04	–4.48	0.00
ln(other services) * (ln(funding rate) – ln(other expenses))_coop. banks	0.03	2.79	0.01
Control variables			
ln(equity/assets)_comm. banks	–0.15	–4.26	0.00
$\ln(\text{equity/assets})^2$_comm. banks	0.01	1.96	0.05
ln(equity/assets)_savings banks	1.11	6.80	0.00
$\ln(\text{equity/assets})^2$_savings banks	0.21	7.86	0.00
ln(equity/assets)_coop. banks	0.51	10.03	0.00
$\ln(\text{equity/assets})^2$_coop. banks	0.10	11.86	0.00
dummy savings banks	2.63	6.12	0.00
dummy coop. banks	–0.15	–13.49	0.00
Intercept	3.07	48.08	0.00
Number of observations	19,551		
F(80, 19,470)	25,462.91		
Adjusted R-square	0.99		

Notes: Coefficients of time dummies not shown.

Table 7.A.2 Marginal cost estimates of loans across countries and over time (%)

	AT	*BE*	*DE*	*ES*	*FR*	*IT*	*NL*	*PT*
1992	10.3	7.1	10.2	15.9	13.8	13.2	9.2	21.3
1993	9.4	6.9	9.4	17.2	13.4	12.0	8.1	18.8
1994	7.1	6.4	9.2	14.3	11.9	12.2	7.4	16.6
1995	7.3	5.8	8.9	15.4	11.7	11.8	7.1	15.4
1996	7.1	5.2	8.5	14.3	10.9	11.3	6.3	13.4
1997	6.1	4.6	7.4	11.7	10.9	9.7	6.4	12.3
1998	6.0	3.6	7.1	11.1	11.2	7.5	7.4	9.4
1999	5.5	3.2	6.4	8.8	10.0	6.7	6.4	6.1
2000	6.1	3.3	7.1	9.9	11.2	6.7	6.5	6.3
2001	6.1	3.1	7.3	9.6	11.7	6.6	6.4	5.9
2002	5.7	3.1	7.1	7.8	10.7	6.1	5.7	5.2
2003	5.5	2.7	6.4	5.9	8.9	5.3	4.9	5.3
2004	5.2	2.5	6.0	4.8	7.9	4.9	4.6	5.5

Notes

1 Based on M. van Leuvensteijn, J.A. Bikker, A.A.R.J.M. van Rixtel, C. Kok Sørensen, (2011), A new approach to measuring competition in the loan markets of the euro area, *Applied Economics* 43, 3155–3167.

2 However, as is stressed by Allen et al. (2001), there is a conflict between this traditional view, stemming from the industrial organization literature, and more recent theoretical models of bank competition, which raise the question whether competition between banks is good or bad. See, for example, Cetorelli and Strahan (2006).

3 A world-wide study by Claessens and Laeven (2004) found that bank concentration was positively instead of negatively related to competition.

4 Bikker and Bos (2005), pages 22 and 23.

5 The Lerner index derives from the monopolist's profit maximization condition as price minus marginal cost, divided by price. The monopolist maximizes profits when the Lerner index is equal to the inverse price elasticity of market demand. Under perfect competition, the Lerner index is zero (market demand is infinitely elastic), in monopoly it approaches one for positive non-zero marginal cost. The Lerner index can be derived for intermediary cases as well. For a discussion see Church and Ware (2000).

6 This interpretation would be different in a market numbering only a few firms. Furthermore, this interpretation would also change when many new entries incur unfavourable scale effects during the initial phase of their growth path.

7 The few existing empirical studies based on the PCS indicator have all used a log linear relationship. See, for example, Chapter 9.

8 The restrictions are imposed on Equation (7.2) so that the equation is reformulated with a lower number of parameters (see Chapter 9).

9 For Germany, the one-, two- or three-year lagged values of the average costs are used.

10 'Significant' refers always to the 95 per cent level of confidence all along.

11 An alternative explanation is that competition on quality may lead to both higher marginal costs and higher market shares.

12 Savings banks have small market shares and comparable marginal costs, so that the overall PCS indicator is determined mainly by the few commercial banks with large market shares and varying marginal cost.

13 See for example S&P (2004) and Moody's Investors Service (2006). Our results are in line with Maudos et al. (2002), who find that profit margins during that decade declined significantly in Spain, especially for commercial banks and, to a lesser extent, for savings banks. For Italy, Coccorese (2005) presents evidence for the largest eight Italian banks during 1988–2000 that despite increased concentration the degree of competition remained considerable. Agostino et al. (2005), find high concentrations of ownership and related profit persistency.

14 In 2005 and 2006, a new wave of consolidation in the Italian banking sector was initiated. However, as our sample ends in 2004, our results do not capture these events.

15 See for example Moody's Investors Service (2005a).

16 Our results are in line with other empirical investigations, such as on competition in the Dutch market for revolving consumer credit, which showed that this market is competitive indeed (see Toolsema, 2002).

17 See for overviews of the various legislative changes for example Cetorelli (2001), Clarke (2004) and Fitch Ratings (2005). Emmons and Schmid (2000) find evidence that even before most of this new legislation was enacted, banks and credit unions competed directly.

18 The Wald test rejects the null hypothesis of no change at the 1 per cent level of significance.

19 The UK has over 100 mortgage lenders. See also Moody's Investors Service (2005b).

20 According to Heffernan (2002), the mortgage market in the UK is relatively competitive, but in other market segments such as personal loans there is substantially less competition. Results for the UK of estimations using a sample, in which the mortgage lenders are excluded, can be obtained from the authors upon request.

References

Agostino, M., L. Leonida and F. Trivieri (2005) Profit persistence and ownership: evidence from the Italian banking sector, *Applied Economics* 37, 1615–1621.

Allen, F., H. Gersbach, J.-P. Krahnen and A.M. Santomero (2001) Competition among banks: Introduction and conference overview, *European Finance Review* 5 (1–2), 1–11.

Beattie, B.R., and C.R. Taylor (1985) *The Economics of Production*, John Wiley & Sons.

Berger, A.N., and L.J. Mester (1997) Inside the black box: What explains differences in the efficiencies of financial institutions? *Journal of Banking & Finance* 21, 895–947.

Berger, A.N, A. Demirgüç-Kunt, R. Levine and J.G. Haubrich (2004) Bank concentration and competition: An evolution in the making, *Journal of Money, Credit, and Banking* 36, 433–451.

Bikker, J.A. (2003) Testing for imperfect competition on the EU deposit and loan markets with Bresnahan's market power model, *Kredit und Kapital* 36, 167–212.

Bikker, J.A. (2004) *Competition and Efficiency in a Unified European Banking Market*, Edward Elgar.

Bikker, J.A. and J.W.B. Bos (2005) Trends in competition and profitability in the banking industry: a basic framework, SUERF Studies No. 2005/2. Vienna: The European Money and Finance Forum.

Bikker, J.A. and J.W.B. Bos (2008) *Bank Performance: A theoretical and empirical framework for the analysis of profitability, competition and efficiency*, Routledge International Studies in Money and Banking, Routledge, London and New York.

Bikker, J.A. and K. Haaf (2002) Competition, concentration and their relationship: an empirical analysis of the banking industry, *Journal of Banking & Finance* 26, 2191–2214.

Bikker, J.A. and L. Spierdijk (2008) How banking competition changed over time, DNB Working Paper 167, De Nederlandsche Bank, Amsterdam.

Boone J., R. Griffith and R. Harrison (2004) Measuring Competition, presented at the Encore Meeting 2004 'Measuring competition'.

Bos, J.W.B. (2002) European Banking: Market Power and Efficiency, PhD thesis, Maastricht University.

Bresnahan, T.F. (1982) The oligopoly solution concept is identified, *Economics Letters* 10, 87–92.

Centraal Planbureau (2000) Measuring competition; how are cost differentials mapped into profit differentials, CPB Working Document nr. 131.

Cetorelli, N. (2001) Competition among banks: Good or bad? *Federal Reserve Bank of Chicago, Economic Perspectives* 2Q/2001, 38–48.

Cetorelli, N. and P.E. Strahan (2006) Finance as a barrier to entry: Bank competition and industry structure in local U.S. markets, *Journal of Finance* 61 (1), 437–461.

Church, J., and R. Ware (2000) *Industrial Organization: A Strategic Approach*, McGraw Hill.

Claessens, S. and L. Laeven (2004) What drives bank competition? Some international evidence, *Journal of Money, Credit and Banking* 36 (3), 563–83.

Clarke, M.Z. (2004) Geographic deregulation of banking and economic growth, *Journal of Money, Credit, and Banking* 36, 929–942.

Coccorese, P. (2005) Competition in markets with dominant firms: A note on the evidence from the Italian banking industry, *Journal of Banking & Finance* 29, 1083–1093.

Drake, L., and R. Simper (2003) Competition and Efficiency in UK Banking: The Impact of Corporate Ownership Structure, mimeograph.

Emmons, W.R, and F.A. Schmid (2000) Bank competition and concentration: Do credit unions matter? *Federal Reserve Bank of St. Louis, Review,* May/June, 29–42.

Fitch Ratings (2001) *The French Banking System*, July.

Fitch Ratings (2005) *U.S. Banking System*, 12 January.

Goldberg, L.G., and A. Rai (1996) The structure-performance relationship for European banking, *Journal of Banking & Finance* 20, 745–771.

Günalp, B. and T. Celik (2006) Competition in the Turkish banking industry, *Applied Economics* 38, 1335–1342.

Hackethal, A. (2004) German banks and banking structure, in: J.P. Krahnen and R.H. Schmidt (eds), *The German Financial System*, Oxford University Press, 71–105.

Hayashi, F. (2000) *Econometrics*, Princeton University Press.

Heffernan, S.A. (2002) How do UK financial institutions really price their banking products? *Journal of Banking & Finance* 26, 1997–2016.

*nternational Monetary Fund (2004) Germany's three-pillar banking system: Cross country perspectives in Europe, IMF Occasional Paper No. 233.

Jones, D.K., and T. Critchfield (2005) Consolidation in the U.S. banking industry: Is the 'long strange trip' about to end? *FDIC Banking Review* 17, 31–61.

Jorgenson, D.W. (1986) Econometric methods for modelling producer behaviour, in: E. Grilliches and M. Intrilligator (eds), *Handbook for Econometrics*, Vol. III, Elsevier Science Publishers.

Kasman, A. and C. Yidirim (2006) Cost and profit efficiencies in transition banking: the case of new EU members, *Applied Economics* 38, 1079–1090.

Lau, L. (1982) On identifying the degree of competitiveness from industry price and output data, *Economics Letters* 10, 93–99.

Leibenstein, H. (1966) Allocative Efficiency vs. 'X-Efficiency', *American Economic Review* 56, 392–415.

Maudos, J., J.M. Pastor and F. Perez (2002) Competition and efficiency in the Spanish banking sector: The importance of specialisation, *Applied Financial Economics* 12, 505–516.

Moody's Investors Service (2004) *Banking System Outlook: France*, October.

Moody's Investors Service (2005a) *Banking System Outlook: The Netherlands*, September.

Moody's Investors Service (2005b) *UK Mortgage Lenders*, August.

Moody's Investors Service (2006) *Banking System Outlook: Spain*, January.

Panzar, J.C., and J.N. Rosse (1987) Testing for 'monopoly' equilibrium, *Journal of Industrial Economics* 35, 443–456.

Rixtel, A. van (2002) *Informality and Monetary Policy in Japan: The Political Economy of Bank Performance*, Cambridge University Press.

Rixtel, A. van, Y. Wiwattanakantang, T. Souma and K. Suzuki (2004) Banking in Japan: will too big to fail prevail? In: B.E. Gup (ed.), *Too Big to Fail: Policies and Practices in Government Bailouts*, Praeger, 253–283.

Shen, C.-H. (2005) Cost efficiency and banking performance in a partial universal banking system: application of the panel smooth threshold model, *Applied Economics*, 37, 993–1009.

Smirlock, M. (1985) Evidence of the (non)relationship between concentration and profitability in banking, *Journal of Money, Credit and Banking* 17, 69–83.

Standard & Poor's (2005) *Bank Industry Risk Analysis: France*, 15 February.

Toolsema, L.A. (2002) Competition in the Dutch consumer credit market, *Journal of Banking & Finance* 26, 2215–2229.

Uchida, H. and Y. Tsutsui (2005) Has competition in the Japanese banking sector improved? *Journal of Banking & Finance* 29, 419–439.

8 Impact of bank competition on the interest rate pass-through in the euro area[1]

Jacob A. Bikker, Michiel van Leuvensteijn, Christoffer Kok and Adrian van Rixtel

This chapter analyses the impact of loan market competition on the interest rates applied by euro-area banks to loans during the 1994–2004 period, using the PCS indicator. We find evidence that stronger competition implies significantly lower spreads between bank and market interest rates for most loan market products, in line with expectations. This result implies that stronger competition causes both lower bank interest rates and a stronger pass-through of market rate changes into bank rates. Evidence of the latter is also presented by our error correction model for bank rates. Further, banks compensate income losses from increased loan market competition by offering lower deposit rates. Our findings with respect to the loan market rates have important monetary policy implications, as they suggest that measures to promote competition in the European banking sector are likely to render the monetary policy transmission mechanism more effective.

8.1. Introduction

This chapter discusses the effects of bank competition on bank loan interest rates, and their responses to changes in market rates, as well as on deposit rates. Given the prominent role of the banking sector in the euro area's financial system, it is of significant importance for the European Central Bank (ECB) to monitor the degree of competitive behaviour in the euro-area bank loan market. A more competitive banking market is expected to drive down bank loan rates, adding to the welfare of households and enterprises in a financially stable environment. This is particularly true for competitive edges resulting from efficiency gains. At the same time, competition may increase instability through two channels: by exacerbating both the problem of depositor (investor) coordination on the liability side and the risk of panics; and by increasing incentives to take risks, and thus raising the probability of failure (Vives, 2010). Further, in a more competitive market, changes in the ECB's main policy rates are assumed to pass through more strongly and more quickly into banking rates, enhancing the monetary policy transmission mechanism.

This chapter extends the existing empirical evidence, which suggests that the degree of bank competition has a significant effect on both the level of bank rates and the pass-through of market rates to bank rates. It assesses the impact of monetary policy actions, via changes in market interest rates, on bank interest rates. Understanding this pass-through mechanism is crucially important to central banks. Most studies that analyse the relationship between competition and banks' pricing behaviour apply a concentration index such as the Herfindahl–Hirschman index (HHI) as a measure of competition. However, we question the suitability of such indices as measures of competition. Where the traditional interpretation is that concentration erodes competition, concentration and competition may instead increase simultaneously where competition forces consolidation. For example, in a market where inefficient banking firms are taken over by efficient peers, strengthened competition may go hand in hand with an increased concentration ratio. In addition, the HHI suffers from a serious weakness in that it does not distinguish between small and large countries. In small countries, the concentration ratio is likely to be higher, precisely because the economy is small.

The main innovation of our chapter is that it applies the PCS indicator. The basic notion underlying this indicator is that in a competitive market, the more efficient companies are likely to have bigger market shares. Hence, the stronger the impact of efficiency on market shares, the stronger competition will be. Further, by analysing how this efficiency–market share relationship changes over time, our approach provides a measure which can be employed to assess how changes in competition affect the cost of borrowing for both households and enterprises, and how they affect the pass-through of policy rates into bank lending rates.

This chapter also contributes to the pass-through literature in the sense that it uses a newly constructed dataset on bank lending rates for eight euro-area countries covering the period from January 1994 to December 2004. These data cover a longer period and are based on more harmonized principles than those used by previous pass-through studies for the euro area.[2] The dataset regards Austria, Belgium, France, Germany, Italy, the Netherlands, Portugal and Spain.[3] We consider four types of loan products: mortgage loans, consumer loans and both short-term and long-term loans to enterprises as well as two types of savings: time deposits and current-account deposits.[4] We apply recently developed dynamic panel estimates of the pass-through model. Our approach is closely related to that of Kok Sørensen and Werner (2006), on which it expands by directly linking the degree of competition to the pass-through estimates.

Against this background, we test the following three hypotheses:

1 Loan interest rates are lower in more competitive loan markets than in less competitive loan markets. Similarly, deposit interest rates are higher in more competitive banking markets than in less competitive markets.
2 Long-run responses of bank interest rates to the corresponding market rates are stronger in more competitive markets than in less competitive markets.
3 Bank interest rates in more competitive markets adjust faster to changes in market interest rates than in less competitive markets.

We find that stronger competition implies significantly lower interest rate spreads for most loan market products, as we expected. This result implies that the more fiercely banks compete with each other, the lower bank interest rates will be and the more strongly market rates will be passed through. We find evidence of stronger pass-through in our error correction model of bank interest rates. Furthermore, in more competitive markets, corporate lending rates respond more rapidly to changes in market interest rates. Finally, we observe for the two deposit categories, that stronger competition in the loan market increases the (negative) spread between bank and market rates significantly. Apparently, banks compensate income losses due to stronger loan market competition by offering lower deposit rates.

The structure of this chapter is as follows. Section 8.2 discusses the literature on competition and bank interest rate pass-through. Section 8.3 describes the PCS indicator of competition and provides country estimates of this indicator. Section 8.4 presents the employed interest rate pass-through model of the error-correction type and explains the use of panel unit root and co-integration tests. Section 8.5 introduces the bank and market interest rate data and investigates their properties. Empirical evidence on competition and the bank interest rate pass-through based on the spread model and the error-correction model equations is shown in Section 8.6. Finally, Section 8.7 summarizes and concludes.

8.2. Literature on competition and monetary transmission

According to the seminal papers by Klein (1971) and Monti (1972) on banks' interest rate setting behaviour, banks wield a degree of market pricing power in determining loan interest rates. The Monti–Klein model demonstrates that interest rates on bank products with lower demand elasticities are priced less competitively. Hence both the levels of bank interest rates and their changes over time are expected to depend on the degree of competition. With respect to the level of bank interest rates, Maudos and Fernández de Guevara (2004) show that an increase in banks' market power (i.e. a reduction in competitive pressure) results in higher net interest margins.[5] In addition, Corvoisier and Gropp (2002) explain the difference between bank retail interest rates and money market rates from banks' product-specific concentration indices. They find that in concentrated markets, retail lending rates are substantially higher.

Regarding the effect of competition on the way banks adjust their lending rates, both Cottarelli and Kourelis (1994) and Borio and Fritz (1995) performed cross-country analyses and found a significant effect of constrained competition on the monetary transmission mechanism. Thus lending rates tend to be stickier when banks operate in a less competitive environment, due to, *inter alia,* the existence of barriers to entry. This finding was confirmed in an Italian setting by Cottarelli et al. (1995). Reflecting the existence of bank market power and collusive behaviour as well as potential switching costs for bank customers (or other factors affecting demand elasticities), the degree of price stickiness is likely to be asymmetric over the (monetary policy) interest rate cycle.[6] Against this background, Mojon (2001) tests for the impact of banking competition on the transmission process related to euro-area bank lending rates, using an index of deregulation constructed by Gual

(1999). He finds that higher competition tends to put pressure on banks to adjust lending rates more quickly when money market rates are decreasing. Furthermore, higher competition tends to reduce the ability of banks to increase lending rates (although not significantly), when money market rates are moving up.[7] Similar findings of asymmetric pass-through effects have been found by Scholnick (1996), Heinemann and Schüler (2002), Sander and Kleimeier (2002, 2004) and Kuan-Min and Thanh-Binh Nguyen (2010).[8] Moreover, De Bondt (2005) argues that stronger competition from other banks and from capital markets has helped to speed up the adjustment of interest rates to changes in market rates by banks in the euro area.

A number of country-specific studies also provide evidence of sluggish pass-through from market rates into bank rates when competition is weak. For example, Heffernan (1997) finds that British banks' interest rate adjustment behaviour is compatible with imperfect competition whereas Weth (2002), by using various proxies for bank market power, provides evidence of sluggish and asymmetric pass-through among German banks. De Graeve et al. (2007) estimate the determinants of the interest rate pass-through behaviour of Belgian banks and find that banks with more market power pursue a less competitive pricing policy. In a microeconomic analysis of Spanish banks, Lago-González and Salas-Fumás (2005) provide evidence that a mixture of price adjustment costs and bank market power causes price rigidity and asymmetric pass-through. The impact on interest rates will have wider implications for the development of output and prices as shown, for example, for Ireland by Bredin and O'Reilly (2004). In a cross-country study, Kok Sørensen and Werner (2006) show that differences in the pass-through process across the euro-area countries may to some extent be explained by national differences in bank competition. Finally, in another euro area based study, Gropp et al. (2007) provide evidence that the level of banking competition has a positive impact on the degree of bank interest rate pass-through using the *H*-statistic.

8.3. The PCS indicator

The PCS indicator assumes that more efficient firms (that is, firms with lower marginal costs) will gain higher market shares or profits, and that this effect will be stronger the fiercer competition in that market is. Using the same data as Genesove and Mullin (1998), Boone and Van Leuvensteijn (2010) show that this indicator is able to identify different regimes of competition empirically. In line with Hay, Liu and Boone (Chapters 3 and 4) we have the following model for market shares:

$$\ln(ms_{it}) = \alpha + \beta_t \ln(mc_{it}) + \sum_{t=1,\ldots,(T-1)} \gamma_t d_t + \varepsilon_{it} \quad (8.1)$$

where α, β_t and γ are parameters, ms_{it} denotes the market share of bank i in year t, mc_{it} stands for the marginal costs of the respective bank, d_t is a time dummy and ε_{it} an error term. The parameter of interest, β_t, is expected to have a negative sign, because relatively efficient banks will gain higher market shares. Equation (8.1) has been specified in log-linear terms in order to deal with heteroskedasticity.

Moreover, this specification implies that β_t is an elasticity, which facilitates its interpretation, particularly across countries.[9] We will refer to β_t as the PCS indicator in year *t*. When differences in performance in terms of market shares are increasingly determined by marginal cost differences, this indicates increased competition. The PCS indicator requires data on fairly homogeneous products.

An advantage of the PCS indicator is that it is linked more directly to competition than frequently used but often misleading measures such as the Herfindahl–Hirschman Index (HHI) and other concentration indices. The standard intuition of the HHI is based on a Cournot model with symmetric banks, where a relaxation of entry barriers reduces the HHI. However, where banks differ in efficiency, an increase in competition reallocates output to the more efficient banks that already had higher output levels. Hence, the increase in competition raises the HHI.[10]In order to estimate the PCS indicator from Equation (8.1), we will use the data described in the next subsection.

8.3.1. Data on euro-area banks

Our first empirical analysis is the estimation of the PCS indicator model, following Equation (8.1). The PCS indicator model uses annual BankScope data on banks from eight euro-area countries during 1992–2004.[11] This model is based on marginal costs which are derived from a translog cost function with output components and input prices (see Section 7.3.1, and Appendix 7.I). In order to exclude irrelevant and unreliable observations, banks are only incorporated in our sample if they fulfil the following conditions: total assets, loans, deposits, equity and 'other non-interest income' must be positive; the deposits-to-assets ratio and loans-to-assets ratio must be less than 0.98 and 1, respectively; the income-to-assets ratio must be below 0.20; the personnel expenses-to-assets and other expenses-to-assets ratios must be between 0.05 and 5 per cent; and, finally, the equity-to-assets ratio must be between 0.01 and 0.50. These conditions are set to capture, for each variable, the range between the 5 per cent and 95 per cent percentiles in order to reduce outliers. As a result, our final dataset totals 520 commercial banks, 1,506 cooperative banks, 699 savings banks, 28 specialized governmental credit institutions (*Landesbanken*) and 62 real estate banks (see Table 8.1).

Table 8.2 provides a short description of the model variables. To grasp the relative magnitude of the key variables, such as costs, loans, security investment and other services, we present them as shares of corresponding balance-sheet items. Total costs are defined as total expenses. They vary, as country averages, between 6.3 and 8.6 per cent of total assets, whereas market shares in the loan market vary between 0.06 and 5.8 per cent. Across countries, loans and securities are in the ranges of, respectively, 35–60 per cent and 4–37 per cent of total assets. One of the output components we distinguish is other services. For lack of direct observations, this variable is proxied by non-interest income. Non-interest income ranges from 12 to 20 per cent of total income. Wage rates are proxied as the ratio of personnel expenses and total assets, since for many banks the number of staff is not available. Wages vary across countries between 0.9 and 1.7 per cent of total

Table 8.1 Total number of banks by country and by type (over the period 1992–2004)

Country	*Commercial banks*	*Cooperative banks*	*Real estate banks*	*Savings banks*	*Specialized governmental credit institutions*	*Total*
AT	52	54	10	65	0	181
BE	24	6	0	5	0	35
DE	130	867	44	501	28	1570
ES	61	17	0	43	0	121
FR	115	83	2	30	0	230
IT	105	476	1	52	0	634
NL	24	1	4	1	0	30
PT	9	2	1	2	0	14
Total	520	1506	62	699	28	2815

Note: Country name abbreviations are for, respectively, Austria, Belgium, Germany, Spain, France, Italy, the Netherlands and Portugal.

Table 8.2 Mean values of key variables for various countries (1992–2004)

	PCS model	*Translog cost function*						
Country	*Average loans market shares in %*	*Total costs as % of total assets*	*Loans as % of total assets*	*Securities as % of total assets*	*Other services as % of total income*	*Other expenses as % of fixed assets*	*Wages as % of total assets*	*Interest expenses as % of total funding*
AT	0.87	6.34	56	22	20	229	1.4	3.2
BE	2.27	6.49	35	37	16	594	1.0	4.5
DE	0.06	6.44	60	22	12	227	1.5	3.7
ES	0.98	6.63	58	14	16	167	1.5	4.1
FR	0.41	7.42	54	4	20	537	1.5	4.8
IT	0.22	6.67	53	26	16	261	1.7	3.5
NL	3.02	6.59	54	15	13	340	0.9	5.4
PT	5.83	8.62	52	8	18	191	1.3	5.9

assets. The input price of capital is proxied by the ratio of other expenses and fixed assets. Finally, interest rates are proxied as interest expenses divided by total funding and range from 3.2 to 5.9 per cent.

8.3.2. Estimation results for the PCS indicator

Table 8.3 shows the country estimates of the time-dependent PCS indicator based on the dataset described above, across countries and over time, in most cases 1994–2004, depending on the country. The results are based on Equation (8.1). The estimations are carried out using the Generalized Moment Method (GMM) with one-, two- or three-year lagged values of the explanatory variable, marginal costs, or average costs as instrument variables.[12] To test for over-identification of the instruments, we apply the Hansen J-test to the GMM (Hayashi, 2000). The joint null hypothesis is that the instruments are valid as such, i.e. uncorrelated with the error term. Under the null hypothesis, the test statistic is chi-squared distributed with the number of degrees of freedom equal to the number of over-identification restrictions. A rejection would cast doubt on the validity of the instruments. Furthermore, the Anderson canonical correlation likelihood ratio is used to test for the relevance of excluded instrument variables (Hayashi, 2000). The null hypothesis of this test is that the matrix of reduced-form coefficients has rank $K - 1$, where K is the number of regressors, meaning that the equation is

Table 8.3 PCS indicator estimates over time and across eight euro-area countries

	Germany		*France*		*Italy*	
	β_t	*z-value*	β_t	*z-value*	β_t	*z-value*
1993					–5.90	–1.18
1994					**–7.25	–3.24
1995	–4.47	–1.40	**–1.28	–3.36	**–4.51	–3.53
1996	**–7.09	–2.92	**–1.28	–3.56	**–5.58	–3.98
1997	**–4.64	–3.41	**–1.11	–3.55	**–5.89	–4.08
1998	**–5.10	–3.97	*–0.79	–1.99	**–4.60	–6.08
1999	**–2.60	–4.04	*–0.7	–2.30	**–4.05	–4.39
2000	**–2.50	–4.60	–0.46	–1.34	**–3.32	–4.39
2001	**–3.31	–7.02	–0.68	–1.67	**–2.66	–3.62
2002	**–4.53	–4.71	–0.40	–0.78	–1.59	–1.82
2003	**–2.73	–5.62	0.27	0.39	**–2.42	–3.69
2004	**–2.66	–4.15	0.10	0.12	**–1.81	–2.79
F-test	10.70		5.01	13.23		
Anderson canon corr. LR-test	185.20		1023.66	300.34		
Hansen *J*-test (*p*-value)	0.00		19.69 (0.48)	0.00		
Number of observations	14,534		918	4,918		

	Spain		*Netherlands*		*Belgium*	
	β_t	*z-value*	β_t	*z-value*	β_t	*z-value*
1993	*–4.21	–2.49				
1994	*–4.80	–2.28	–1.92	–1.42		
1995	–5.20	–1.92	*–4.42	–2.42	–1.48	–1.59
1996	–9.61	–0.67	**–2.09	–2.58	**–1.74	–2.93
1997	–4.36	–1.78	–3.57	–1.70	**–2.02	–3.78
1998	–5.40	–0.86	1.04	0.38	**–1.98	–3.19
1999	*–5.46	–2.21	–1.44	–0.85	**–2.62	–4.65
2000	–3.44	–1.93	**–3.26	–3.00	**–3.41	–6.10
2001	**–4.38	–2.55	**–3.91	–4.71	**–3.00	–4.51
2002	*–3.88	–2.09	*–2.45	–2.44	**–3.42	–4.34
2003	–3.42	–1.20	–2.22	–1.80	**–2.79	–3.18
2004	**–2.69	–5.62	**–3.09	–2.85	**–3.12	–4.02
F-test	3.33		3.90		6.35	
Anderson canon corr. LR-test	38.78		31.71		178.10	
Hansen *J*-test (*p*-value)	0.00		20.5 (0.039)	8.34 (0.60)		
Number of observations	1,015		241		269	

	Austria		*Portugal*	
	β_t	*z-value*	β_t	*z-value*
1994	11.2	1.01	0.05	0.05
1995	–4.03	–0.94	1.57	0.91
1996	*–2.31	–1.93	0.09	0.16
1997	4.25	0.93	–0.04	–0.08
1998	0.91	–0.52	–0.55	–0.76
1999	–2.98	–0.73	–1.51	–1.40
2000	–2.31	–0.50	**–2.43	–4.03
2001	–0.96	–1.30	**–1.92	–3.77
2002	*–1.49	–1.97	**–2.16	–7.33
2003	**–1.26	–3.52	*–1.74	–2.05
2004	**–2.99	–2.23	–1.53	–1.69
F-test	2.21		3.94	
Anderson canon corr. LR-test	28.89		77.92	
Hansen *J*-test, (*p*-value)	9.308 (0.59)	11.71 (0.38)		
Number of observations	988		134	

Notes: This table presents GMM estimates of Equation (8.1). For Italy and Spain, 2SLS has been used where the equation is exactly identified, so that the Hansen J-test equals 0.00. Asterisks indicate 95 per cent (*) and 99 per cent (**) levels of confidence. Coefficients of time dummies are not shown.

under-identified. Under the null hypothesis of under-identification, the statistic is chi-squared distributed with $L - K + 1$ degrees of freedom, where L is the number of instruments (whether included in the equation or excluded from it). This statistic provides a measure of instrument relevance, and rejection of the null hypothesis indicates that the model is identified. We use kernel-based heteroskedastic and autocorrelation consistent (HAC) variance estimations. The bandwidth in the estimation is set at two periods and the Newey–West kernel is applied. Where the instruments are over-identified, 2SLS is used instead of GMM. For this 2SLS estimator, Sargan's statistic is used instead of the Hansen J-test.

Over the sample period, the PCS indicator for Belgium, Germany, and Italy is highly significant, except for one or two years, suggesting stronger loan market competition then elsewhere in the euro area.[13] The Dutch and Spanish loan markets take up an intermediate position with significant PCS indicators for at least a number of years. For France, the degree of competition declined over the years, whereas the reverse development is observed for Austria and Portugal. If, for each country, we had estimated only one beta for the full-sample period instead of annual ones (that is, $\beta_t = \beta$ for all t), we would have obtained significant values for all countries except Portugal, reflecting a certain degree of competition across the entire area (see Chapter 7). For a number of countries, the PCS indicator has positive values, though not significantly different from zero, which indicates low levels of competition. These PCS indicator estimates enable us to analyse the impact of competition on the interest rate pass-through, using a model described in the next section.

8.4. The specification of the interest rate pass-through model

Our analysis of the pass-through of market interest rates to bank rates takes into account that economic variables may be non-stationary.[14] The relationship between non-stationary but co-integrated variables should preferably be analysed using an error-correction model (ECM), by which the long-run co-movement of the variables may be disentangled from the short-run adjustment towards the equilibrium.[15] Accordingly, most of the pass-through studies conducted in recent years apply an ECM, which allows testing for both the long-run equilibrium pass-through of bank rates to changes in market rates and the speed of adjustment towards the equilibrium.[16] Using a panel-econometric approach, we test for the impact of banking competition – measured by the PCS indicator – on the long-run equilibrium of market rate pass-through.

8.4.1. The error-correction model

If bank interest rates and their corresponding market rates are co-integrated, the error-correction framework is the most appropriate model. We propose the following two model equations for each of the six considered product related bank interest rates,[17] which will be used to test the three hypotheses as developed in the introduction:

$$BR_{i,t} = \zeta PCS_{i,t} + \eta_i MR_{i,t} + \theta\ PCS_{i,t} MR_{i,t} + \kappa_i D_i + u_{i,t} \tag{8.2.a}$$

$$\Delta BR_{i,t} = \lambda_i u_{i,t-1} + \mu_i \Delta MR_{i,t} + \xi\ PCS_{i,t} \Delta MR_{i,t} + v_{i,t} \tag{8.2.b}$$

where i refers to countries ($i = 1, \ldots, N$) and t to months ($t = 1, \ldots, T$). Equation (8.2.a) reflects the long-run equilibrium pass-through, while Equation (8.2.b) presents the short-term adjustments of bank interest rates to their long-run equilibrium. We first discuss the long-run effects of Equation (8.2.a) because the short-run effects of Equation (8.2.b) depend on the error term $u_{i,t}$ of Equation (8.2.a). *BR* represents bank interest rates (loan rates or deposit rates) and ΔBR is the monthly change in bank interest rates. $PCS_{i,t}$ is the indicator of country i at time t. To simplify interpretation, the PCS indicator is redefined in absolute terms, where an increase in the PCS indicator reflects stronger competition, so that $PCS = -\beta$.[18] For each of the six considered interest rates, we include the market rates in the various countries separately ($\eta_i\ MR_{i,t}$ and $\mu_i\ \Delta MR_{i,t}$, respectively, in the long and the short run), in order to observe country-specific effects. The market rates, $MR_{i,t}$, are multiplied by the PCS indicator ($\theta\ PCS_{i,t}\ MR_{i,t}$ and $\zeta\ PCS_{i,t}\ \Delta MR_{i,t}$, respectively, for the long and the short run), in order to capture the (overall) impact of competition on the pass-through. Furthermore, we account for country effects in the long-run model by using country dummies (D_i). The short-run model includes the error correction term ($\lambda_i\ u_{i,t-1}$), the effects of competition on short-term adjustments in market rates ($\zeta\ PCS_{i,t}\ \Delta MR_{i,t}$) for all countries simultaneously and the change in the market rate for each country separately ($\mu_i\ \Delta MR_{i,t}$). Alternatively, Equations (8.2.a) and (8.2.b) can be extended by a risk measure to capture the risk premium in bank interest rates.

In Equations (8.2.a) and (8.2.b), we estimate euro-area wide (panel) parameters for the various competition effects (ζ, θ and ξ), because competition is supposed to change only gradually over time and the estimated PCS indicator appears to vary insufficiently over time to capture reliable country-specific competition effects. The other parameters (η_i, μ_i and λ_i) remain country-specific, unless their equality across all countries considered should pass a Wald test.

The three hypotheses to be tested are, expressed in the parameters of Equations (8.2.a) and (8.2.b):

1. Loan interest rates are lower in more competitive loan markets than in less competitive loan markets, that is, H_0: $\zeta + \theta\ MR_{i,t} < 0$ and H_1: $\zeta + \theta\ MR_{i,t} \geq 0$.[19] Similarly, deposit rates are higher in more competitive markets than in less competitive ones (hence, H_0: $\zeta + \theta\ MR_{i,t} > 0$ and H_1: $\zeta + \theta\ MR_{i,t} \leq 0$).
2. In more competitive markets, long-run loan and deposit rates respond more strongly to the corresponding market rates than in less competitive markets, or H_0: $\theta > 0$ and H_1: $\theta \leq 0$.
3. Bank interest rates in more competitive markets adjust more quickly in the short run to changes in market rates than in less competitive markets, so H_0: $\xi > 0$ and H_1: $\xi \leq 0$.

As the PCS indicator measures competition in the loan market, the competition effect on the deposit rate pass-through may be less reliable. Loan market competition may have a positive impact on deposit markets as well, implying $\zeta + \theta\, MR_{i,t} > 0$. Alternatively, banks may try to compensate for strong loan market competition by exploiting their market power in the deposit market, in which case $\zeta + \theta\, MR_{i,t} < 0$. This would assume that banks act as price makers in the deposit market and as price takers in the loan market.

As a simpler, alternative modelling approach, we also consider that in Equation (8.2.a) the pass-through effect may be immediate and complete, that is, we assume that $\eta_i = 1$ and $\theta = 0$, so that the bank's interest rate spread, $(BR_{i,t} - MR_{i,t})$, is explained by competition indicator $PCS_{i,t}$ and fixed effects (that is, country dummies, D_i, and monthly dummies, D_t):

$$(BR_{i,t} - MR_{i,t}) = \zeta\ PCS_{i,t} + \kappa_i D_i + \psi_t D_t + u_{i,t} \tag{8.3}$$

Using this interest rate spread model, the first hypothesis ('Loan interest rates are lower in more competitive loan markets than in less competitive loan markets') is reformulated as H_0: $\zeta < 0$ and H_1: $\zeta \geq 0$.

8.4.2. Unit root and panel co-integration tests

Unit root tests

The pass-through of interest rates can only be specified as an error correction framework if the variables are non-stationary and a long-term relationship between the variables is established. Therefore, as a first preparatory step, we investigate the unit root properties of the variables and verify through a co-integration test in the next section whether a long-term relationship is established between the variables.[20] We apply two types of tests based on two different null hypotheses. The Im, Pesaran and Shin (2003) test (referred to as IPS test) is a panel version of the Augmented Dickey–Fuller (ADF) test on unit roots. It is based on the following regression equation:

$$\Delta Y_{i,t} = \alpha_i + \rho_i Y_{i,t-1} + \sum_{j=1}^{p_j} \tau_{i,j} \Delta Y_{i,t-j} + \varepsilon_{i,t} \tag{8.4}$$

where Y stands for BR, MR, PCS, and $PCS \times MR$, i refers to countries ($i = 1, \ldots, N$) and t points to months ($t = 1, \ldots, T$). The autoregressive parameter ρ_i is estimated for each country separately, which allows for a large degree of heterogeneity. The null hypothesis is H_0: $\rho_i = 0$ for all i, against the alternative hypothesis H_1: $\rho_i < 0$ for some countries. The test statistic Z_{t_bar} of the IPS test is constructed by cross-section averaging the individual t-statistics for ρ_i. Rejection of the null hypothesis indicates stationariness.

As a cross-check, we add results based on Hadri's (2000) test, which is a panel version of the Kwiatkowski, Phillips, Schmidt, and Shin (KPSS) test, testing the null hypothesis of stationarity. The model underlying the Hadri test can be written as:

$$Y_{i,t} = \alpha_i + \sum_{\tau=1}^{t} u_{i,\tau} + \varepsilon_{i,t} \tag{8.5}$$

with Y as above. The time series $Y_{i,t}$ are broken down into two components, a random walk component $\Sigma_\tau u_{i,\tau}$ and a stationary component $\varepsilon_{i,t}$. The test statistic Z_τ is based on the ratio of the variances $\sigma^2_u / \sigma^2_\varepsilon$. The null hypothesis of the test assumes that this ratio is zero, implying that the interest rate contains no random walk component. By contrast, rejection of the null hypothesis indicates the presence of unit root behaviour in the variable under investigation. Both panel series test statistics are asymptotically normal.

Co-integration tests

The second preliminary step tests for co-integration using panel co-integration tests by Pedroni (1999, 2004), which are based on the following regression model for each product-related bank interest rate:

$$\text{BR}_{i,t} = \omega\ \text{PCS}_{i,t} + \psi_{i,1}\text{MR}_{i,t} + \psi_{i,2}\text{PCS}_{i,t}\text{MR}_{i,t} + \upsilon_{i,t} \tag{8.6}$$

The long-run coefficients $\psi_{i,j}$ ($j = 1, 2$) may be different across the euro-area countries. We use the group mean panel version of the Pedroni test. The null hypothesis of this test assumes a unit root in the residuals of the co-integration regression, which implies absence of co-integration. The alternative hypothesis assumes a root less than one, but allows for different roots across the euro-area countries.[21] We use three different types of test statistics: an ADF type that is similar to the ADF statistic used in univariate unit root tests, a non-parametric Phillips–Perron (PP) version, and a version which is based directly on the autoregressive coefficient (ρ-test). These tests will be applied to the bank and market interest data described in the next section.

8.5. Bank and market interest rate data and their properties

Our retail bank interest rates are from the ECB's monthly MFI Interest Rate (MIR) statistics, which have been compiled on a harmonized basis across all euro-area countries since January 2003. For the period prior to January 2003, the series have been extended backwards to January 1994 using the non-harmonized national retail interest rate (NRIR) statistics compiled by the national central banks of the (later) Eurosystem.[22] The MIR statistics consist of more detailed breakdowns than the NRIR statistics, particularly in terms of loan size and rate fixation periods. In order to link the two sets of statistics, the MIR series have been aggregated (using new business volumes as weights) to the broader product categories of the NRIR statistics, which include rates on (i) mortgage loans, (ii) consumer loans, (iii) short-term loans to non-financial corporations (≤ 1 year), (iv) long-term loans to non-financial corporations (> 1 year), (v) current-account deposits, and (vi) time deposits.[23] The sample period covers 147 monthly observations ranging from January 1994 to March 2006 (used up to the end of 2004).

We select market rates which correspond most closely to these bank interest rates in terms of rate-fixation period. Hence, a three-month money market rate is selected to correspond with bank rates that are either floating or fixed for short

Table 8.4 Availability of six bank interest rates and corresponding market rates with equivalent fixation periods

	Mortgage loans	*Consumer loans*	*Short-term enterprise loans*	*Long-term enterprise loans*	*Current account deposits*	*Time deposits*
AT	April 1995 3M MR	April 1995 3M MR	April 1995 3M MR		April 1995 3M MR	April 1995 3M MR
BE	Jan. 1994 3M MR	Jan. 1994 5Y MR	Jan. 1994 3M MR	Jan. 1994 5Y MR		Jan. 1994 3M MR
DE	Jan. 1994 10Y MR	Jan. 1994 5Y MR	Jan. 1994 3M MR	Nov. 1996 5Y MR		Jan. 1994 3M MR
ES	Jan. 1994 3M MR	Jan. 1994 3M MR	Jan. 1994 3M MR	Jan. 1994 3M MR	Jan. 1994 3M MR	Jan. 1994 3M MR
FR	Jan. 1994 10Y MR	Jan. 1994 5Y MR	Jan. 1994 3M MR	Jan. 1994 5Y MR		Jan. 1994 3M MR
IT	Jan. 1995 3M MR		Jan. 1994 3M MR	Jan. 1995 3M MR	Jan. 1994 3M MR	Feb. 1995 3M MR
NL	Jan. 1994 10Y MR		Jan. 1994 3M MR		Jan. 1994 3M MR	Jan. 1994 3M MR
PT	Jan. 1994 3M MR	Jan. 1994 3M MR	Jan. 1994 3M MR			Jan. 1994 3M MR

Sources: ECB and Bloomberg.

Note: Date indicates: 'available since'; '3M MR' is the 3-month money market rate (MR). '5Y MR' and '10Y MR' are the 5-year and 10-year government bond yields, all applying in the respective countries.

periods (below one year), while longer-term government bond yields are paired with long-term fixed bank rates.[24] Table 8.4 presents the data availability of bank interest rates in each country together with the corresponding market rates for each product category. Note that there is strong variation in rate fixation periods across both products and countries. For instance, in many euro-area countries the predominant fixation period for mortgages is rather short, proxied by three months (see ECB, 2006). In Germany and France, however, the typical fixation period on consumer loans is quite long, approximated here by five years.

Table 8.5 shows summary statistics of the bank interest rate data. Bank interest rates differ substantially across countries, across products and, of course, over time. On average, over the 1994–2004 period, mortgage rates and consumer lending rates were highest in Portugal and lowest in Austria. Average rates on short-term loans to enterprises were highest in Portugal and lowest in Germany, whereas the rates on long-term loans to enterprises were highest in Italy and lowest in Belgium. On the deposit side, current-account deposit rates were lowest in Austria and highest in Italy, while time deposit rates were lowest in Italy and highest in Germany.

Table 8.6 details the market interest rates for the considered countries. We find that Italy has, on average, the highest three-month money market rate and the

Table 8.5 Summary statistics of six bank interest rates (%) (1994–2004)

	AT	*BE*	*DE*	*ES*	*FR*	*IT*	*NL*	*PT*
Mortgage rates								
Average	5.6	5.9	6.4	6.6	6.1	7.0	5.7	7.6
Standard deviation	1.0	1.2	1.1	2.7	1.5	3.2	1.0	3.5
Maximum	7.9	8.8	9.1	11.5	8.9	13.0	8.0	14.5
Minimum	3.8	3.8	4.5	3.1	3.9	3.7	3.8	3.4
Consumer lending rates								
Average	6.6	8.1	7.5	10.4	8.8			13.1
Standard deviation	1.1	0.5	1.0	2.8	1.7			3.6
Maximum	9.5	9.1	10.2	16.2	12.1			19.6
Minimum	5.0	7.3	6.3	7.1	6.2			8.6
Rates on short-term loans to enterprises								
Average	4.8	4.6	4.0	5.9	4.5	6.7	4.2	8.8
Standard deviation	1.0	1.1	0.7	2.2	1.5	2.8	1.0	3.8
Maximum	7.2	7.6	5.8	10.5	7.8	11.7	6.5	16.8
Minimum	2.9	2.9	3.1	3.2	2.6	3.3	2.8	4.4
Rates on long-term loans to enterprises								
Average		5.1	5.2	5.7	5.9	6.3		
Standard deviation		1.1	0.5	2.4	1.4	2.7		
Maximum		8.2	6.1	10.4	8.8	11.8		
Minimum		3.4	4.2	3.0	4.0	3.1		
Current account deposit rates								
Average	1.3			1.8		2.6	1.7	
Standard deviation	0.2			1.2		1.8	0.3	
Maximum	1.7			4.6		5.7	2.0	
Minimum	1.0			0.5		0.7	1.1	
Time deposit rates								
Average	3.5	3.4	4.4	3.8	4.0	3.3	4.1	3.4
Standard deviation	1.0	0.9	2.1	1.3	2.3	0.9	2.2	0.8
Maximum	6.3	5.4	8.9	8.0	9.1	5.4	8.7	5.1
Minimum	1.9	2.0	1.9	2.0	1.6	2.0	1.8	2.0

Netherlands has the lowest. The same picture emerges for the 5-year government bond yield. The minima for the three-month money market rates and the yields on government bonds with, respectively, 5-year and a 10-year fixation periods are very similar across all countries; these minima were reached after the introduction of the euro in 1999.

Table 8.6 Summary statistics of three market rates (%) (1994–2004)

	AT	*BE*	*DE*	*ES*	*FR*	*IT*	*NL*	*PT*
3-month money market rate								
Average	3.6	3.6	3.6	4.9	3.9	5.4	3.5	5.3
Standard deviation	0.9	1.1	1.0	2.3	1.4	2.8	1.0	2.9
Maximum	5.5	7.0	5.9	9.7	8.1	11.0	5.4	12.7
Minimum	2.0	2.0	2.0	2.0	2.0	2.0	2.0	2.0
5-year government bond yield								
Average	4.7	4.8	4.5	5.7	4.8	6.1	4.6	5.9
Standard deviation	1.1	1.2	1.0	2.6	1.3	2.9	1.1	2.7
Maximum	7.3	8.0	7.1	12.2	7.9	13.4	7.3	12.2
Minimum	2.8	2.9	2.8	2.7	2.7	2.9	2.8	2.7
10-year government bond yield								
Average			5.2		5.4		5.3	
Standard deviation			1.0		1.2		1.0	
Maximum			7.6		8.2		7.7	
Minimum			3.6		3.6		3.6	

Table 8.7 presents the spreads between the various bank and market rates. Spreads on deposits are negative as, on these products, the market rates exceed the bank lending rates. On average, the spreads are quite narrow, ranging from 0.5 to 2.0 per cent, with the notable exception of consumer loans, where bank interest rates often include very high risk premiums.

8.5.1 Unit roots and co-integration

Table 8.8 reports the panel unit root tests for the bank and market interest rate series for the considered eight euro-area countries simultaneously. The IPS test on the null hypothesis of a unit root cannot be rejected at the 5 per cent significance level for either the bank rates or the market rates, indicating non-stationary interest rates. This result for the interest rates is confirmed by the Hadri test.

For the PCS indicator and the interaction variables of the PCS indicator and market interest rates, the evidence is mixed. The IPS tests indicate stationarity for the PCS indicator and interaction terms with three out of six interest rates, while the Hadri test clearly rejects stationarity for all terms. Where the evidence is mixed, we accept non-stationarity for the PCS indicator and the cross terms, since the majority of test results indicate this. We also apply the panel unit root tests to the first differences of the interest rates, the PCS indicator and the interaction terms to test on second-order non-stationarity. In all cases, the test results reject I(2) and, hence, support the conclusion that the interest rate series are integrated of order 1, so that I(1) holds. Given these findings, we proceed to test for co-integration between bank interest rates and the corresponding market rates.

Table 8.7 Summary statistics of six bank rate spreads (%) (1994–2004)

	AT	*BE*	*DE*	*ES*	*FR*	*IT*	*NL*	*PT*
Mortgage rates								
Average	2.1	2.2	1.8	1.6	1.3	1.9	1.1	2.2
Standard deviation	0.6	0.6	0.3	0.5	0.7	0.7	0.2	1.0
Maximum	3.6	3.5	2.4	2.9	3.8	3.7	1.7	4.5
Minimum	0.8	0.3	1.0	0.8	0.1	0.7	0.6	0.5
Consumer lending rates								
Average	3.2	4.2	3.1	5.5	4.0			7.7
Standard deviation	0.7	0.9	0.8	0.6	0.9			1.3
Maximum	5.1	6.5	5.2	7.2	7.0			10.2
Minimum	2.1	2.6	1.4	4.2	2.3			4.4
Rates on short-term loans to enterprises								
Average	1.3	1.0	0.5	1.0	0.6	1.3	0.7	3.4
Standard deviation	0.6	0.2	0.6	0.2	0.8	0.5	0.3	1.1
Maximum	2.9	1.5	1.6	2.0	2.8	2.5	1.3	6.7
Minimum	0.4	0.4	–0.4	0.5	–1.8	–0.4	–0.1	1.9
Rates on long-term loans to enterprises								
Average		0.4	1.1	0.9	1.1	1.3		
Standard deviation		0.4	0.2	0.4	0.7	0.4		
Maximum		1.2	1.8	1.8	2.2	3.3		
Minimum		–0.3	0.5	0.1	–0.4	–0.5		
Current-account deposit rates								
Average	–2.0			–2.9		–2.7	–1.7	
Standard deviation	0.7			1.2		1.1	0.8	
Maximum	–1.0			–1.4		–1.3	–0.8	
Minimum	–3.8			–5.9		–6.0	–3.5	
Time deposit rates								
Average	–0.4	–0.1	–0.2	–0.5	–0.1	–0.9	–0.2	–1.1
Standard deviation	0.4	0.2	0.2	0.3	0.1	0.5	0.4	0.9
Maximum	0.6	0.2	0.2	0.1	0.2	–0.2	0.6	–0.1
Minimum	–1.5	–0.7	–0.6	–1.1	–0.3	–2.6	–1.1	–4.7

Spreads are based on bank rates and market rates of equivalent maturities and are sometimes negative due to a mismatch between the maturity of the loans and the corresponding market rate.

Table 8.8. Panel unit root tests on model variables applied to all countries

	Im, Pesaran and Shin (IPS) test		*Hadri test*	
	$Z^{a}_{t\ bar}$	*p-value*	Z_{τ}	*p-value*
H_0	*Non-stationarity*		*Stationarity*	
PCS indicator	–2.16	0.02	10.67	0.00
Bank interest rates				
Mortgage loans	0.98	0.84	18.78	0.00
Consumer loans	–0.89	0.19	16.59	0.00
Short-term loans to enterprises	–0.68	0.25	18.83	0.00
Long-term loans to enterprises	0.40	0.66	13.10	0.00
Current account deposits	1.64	0.95	13.86	0.00
Time deposits	–0.72	0.24	16.03	0.00
Market interest rates[a]				
Mortgage loans	0.04	0.52	17.08	0.00
Consumer loans	0.34	0.64	15.21	0.00
Short-term loans to enterprises	–0.68	0.25	17.23	0.00
Long-term loans to enterprises	0.94	0.83	13.39	0.00
Current account deposits	0.38	0.65	12.60	0.00
Time deposits	–1.56	0.06	16.46	0.00
PCS indicator times market interest rates[b]				
Mortgage loans	–2.16	0.01	15.76	0.00
Consumer loans	–1.88	0.03	12.64	0.00
Short-term loans to enterprises	–1.44	0.08	17.46	0.00
Long-term loans to enterprises	–1.38	0.08	13.74	0.00
Current account deposits	–1.60	0.06	12.65	0.00
Time deposits	–2.46	0.01	15.70	0.00

a Market rates are approximated according to Table 8.4
b The test statistics are explained in Section 8.4.2.

Table 8.9 Pedroni co-integration tests on the six long-run bank interest rate models

Bank interest rates	*Group mean panel cointegration tests*		
	ρ-statistic	*PP-statistic*	*ADF-statistic*
Mortgage loans	–3.19 (0.00)	–3.56 (0.00)	–0.07 (0.53)
Consumers loans	0.73 (0.77)	0.19 (0.57)	0.05 (0.52)
Short-term loans to enterprises	–5.79 (0.00)	–4.75 (0.00)	–1.50 (0.07)
Long-term loans to enterprises	–2.68 (0.00)	–2.91 (0.00)	–0.75 (0.22)
Current account deposits	1.14 (0.87)	1.29 (0.90)	0.66 (0.75)
Time deposits	–8.28 (0.00)	–7.08 (0.00)	–0.43 (0.33)

Note: The null hypothesis of this test assumes absence of co-integration; *p*-values in parentheses.

Table 8.9 shows the results for Pedroni's three panel co-integration tests as applied to the long-run models of the six bank rates.[25] For all bank rates except that on consumer loans and current-account deposits, the null hypothesis of no co-integration was rejected for two out of three tests, indicating a long-run equilibrium relationship between bank rates, market rates and the PCS indicator. For bank rates on consumer loans and current-account deposits, the null hypothesis of no co-integration cannot be rejected. Apparently, our sample is too short to detect a long-run relationship, also given the fact that changes in expected default rates may hide a stable long-run relationship.[26] A shortcoming for the interest rates on consumer loans might be that the consumer loan rate data are too highly aggregated. As many other country studies find evidence of co-integration,[27] and economic theory also expects it, we continue with the reservation that the results of the error correction models for consumer loans and current-account deposits have to be interpreted with caution.[28]

8.6. Empirical evidence on competition and the bank interest rate pass-through

In Section 8.5 the results of the IPS test on unit roots were mixed for the PCS indicator, while some interaction terms and the co-integration tests also yielded ambiguous results for consumer loans and current-account deposits. Therefore, as a first investigation into the impact of competition on the bank interest rate pass-through, we now analyse the effect of competition on the various bank loan interest rate spreads. We test the hypothesis that bank interest rate spreads are lower in more competitive markets using Equation (8.3). We also test whether the coefficient of competition, κ, is significantly negative. The results in Table 8.10 show that competition significantly reduces the bank rate spread for three out of four loan products, namely for mortgages, consumer loans and short-term loans to enterprises. No significant effect is found for rates on long-term loans to enterprises. The PCS indicator's coefficient shows that competition tends to keep bank loan rates more closely in line with the corresponding market rates (implying that they are lower), which confirms the first hypothesis.[29]

For the two deposit categories, stronger competition in the loan market causes the (negative) spread between bank and market rates to widen significantly. Hence, deposit rates are lower the stronger competition in the loan market is. Apparently, competition is heavier in the loan market than in the deposit markets, so that banks under competitive pressure compensate their decline in loan market income by lowering their deposit rates.

Table 8.11 presents the estimated long-run relationship of the error-correction model (ECM) presented in Section 8.4.1, in order to test the three hypotheses mentioned in that section.[30] When tested, one single EU-wide coefficient for market rates was rejected in favour of separate country-specific parameters for market rates. The ECM explains bank interest rates from the PCS indicator and the market rates, see Equation (8.2.a). It should be noted that the impact of market rates on bank interest rates is highly significant for all four rates considered and

Table 8.10. Effect of competition on the spreads between bank and market lending rates

	Mortgage loans		*Consumer loans*		*Short-term loans to enterprises*	
	coefficient	*z-value*	*coefficient*	*z-value*	*coefficient*	*z-value*
PCS indicator	–0.030	**–2.12	–0.075	***–3.03	–0.128	***–6.72
Constant	1.357	***5.54	5.818	***16.91	.736	***3.02
Country dummies[a]	$\chi^2(7)=498$		$\chi^2(5)=3095$		$\chi^2(7)=911$	
Monthly dummies[a]	$\chi^2(119)=693$		$\chi^2(119)=766$		$\chi^2(119)=223$	
R-squared, centred	0.687		0.907		0.793	
Number of observations	957		717		957	
	Long term loans to enterprises		*Current account (sight) deposits*		*Time deposits*	
	coefficient	*z-value*	*coefficient*	*z-value*	*coefficient*	*z-value*
PCS indicator	0.003	0.15	–0.154	***–8.26	–0.036	***–3.06
Constant	1.114	***4.26	–3.496	***–12.30	–0.655	***–2.80
Country dummies	$\chi^2(4)=240$		$\chi^2(3)=141$		$\chi^2(7)=640$	
Monthly dummies	$\chi^2(119)=1084$		$\chi^2(119)=1499$		$\chi^2(119)=389$	
R-squared, centred	0.670		0.832		0.691	
Number of observations	578		477		956	

Notes: Country dummies are included but not shown. Two and three asterisks indicate confidence levels of 95 per cent and 99 per cent, respectively. The z-value indicates whether the coefficient differs significantly from 0 under the normal distribution with mean zero and standard deviation one.

a Chi-squared distributed Wald tests on H_0 'all country dummy coefficients are zero' and 'all monthly time dummy coefficients are zero', respectively. These null hypotheses are rejected for all loan and deposit types.

in all eight euro-area countries. Moreover, in line with the existing literature, we find that the country-specific long-run pass-through coefficients (η_i) differ considerably across product categories (and across countries), with the eventual adjustment of bank interest rates to changes in market rates being strongest for mortgage loans, short-term loans to enterprises and time deposits.[31]

The first hypothesis to be tested with the ECM model is: loan interest rates are lower in more competitive loan markets than in less competitive loan markets. Table 8.11 shows that the effect of the combined terms with the PCS indicator of competition is (slightly) positive for all four loan products considered. But the chi-squared distributed Wald tests on H_0: $\zeta + \theta\ MR_{i,t} = 0$ also shows that the combined effects $\zeta + \theta\ MR_{i,t}$ are not significant at the 95 per cent confidence level. Note that the level of bank rates is significantly lower under competition (that is, $\zeta < 0$), but this effect is reduced by the cross term of market rates and indicator ($\theta\ MR_{i,t}\ PCS_{i,t}$). This outcome does not confirm our earlier finding of significantly lower loan market spreads under competition. Apparently, the simple spread model is a more successful tool for observing the competition effect than the more complicated ECM.[32]

Furthermore, we find that stronger loan market competition significantly reduces the interest rate on current-account deposits, which is the more important source of funding, while no significant effect is observed for time deposits. Our explanation is that loan market competition forces banks to reduce interest expenses on funding. For current-account deposits, this is roughly in line with our finding above of negative spreads on deposits that widen amid stronger loan market competition. The effects of the combined terms on the PCS competition indicator are also not significant regarding the deposit rates.

The second hypothesis applied to the ECM model is: in more competitive markets, bank interest rates show stronger long-run responses to the corresponding market rates than in less competitive markets. Our results suggest that all four bank loan rates do indeed respond significantly more strongly to market rates when competition is high, see the coefficient θ of the PCS indicator times the market rate term. Further, we find that the income loss of stronger competition in the loan market has been compensated by lower interest rates on current accounts.[33]Thus we observe that competition does make for stronger long-run loan bank rate responses to corresponding market rates, making for more rapid pass-through. Therefore, the second hypothesis has been accepted.

The third hypothesis related to the ECM model is: in the short run, more competitive markets adjust more quickly to changes in market interest rates than less competitive markets. To test this hypothesis, we estimate Equation (8.2.b). The results in Table 8.12 indicate that the immediate responses of banks' loans rates to changes in market rates do tend to be stronger in more competitive markets (see the ξ coefficient of the product term of changes in market rates and the PCS indicator, which is positive for all loan types in Table 8.12).[34] However, this effect is statistically significant only for short-term loans to enterprises, and then only at the 10 per cent level. With respect to bank deposit rates, it is remarkable that stronger competition on the loan market reduces (instead of increasing) the response of the current-account deposit rate to market rates. This would point to the fact that banks are price takers in the loan market and price makers in

Table 8.11 Estimates of the long-run models for the six bank interest rates

	Mortgage loans		*Consumer loans*		*Short-term loans to enterprises*	
	coefficient	*z-value*	*coefficient*	*z-value*	*coefficient*	*z-value*
PCS indicator (ζ)	–0.198	***–3.32	–0. 196	**–2.39	–0.153	**–3.39
Market rate AT (η)	0.843	***8.02	0.824	***6.15	0.937	***8.76
Market rate BE	0.913	***12.26	1.000	***5.98	0.892	***23.05
Market rate DE	0.923	***14.88	0.312	**2.41	0.325	***6.22
Market rate ES	0.777	***10.89	0.785	***7.63	0.725	***10.90
Market rate FR	0.989	***12.85	1.093	***13.38	0.877	***13.04
Market rate IT	0.870	***16.07			0.807	***16.90
Market rate NL	0.784	***18.11			0.879	***20.11
Market rate PT	1.274	***24.63	1.336	***23.06	1.344	***37.41
Market rate*PCS ind. (θ)	0.053	***4.29	0.057	***3.21	0.039	***3.47
Constant	1.951	***9.74	5.679	***11.21	2.813	***13.62
R-squared, centred	0.940		0.927		0.952	
Number of observations	957		717		957	
$\zeta + \theta\, MR_{i,t}$	0.034		0.055		0.002	
$\chi^2\ H_0: \zeta + \theta\, MR_{i,t} = 0$[a]	2.92, *p*-value = 0.09		2.39, *p*-value = 0.12		0.01, *p*-value = 0.92	

	Long-term loans to enterprises		Current account (sight) deposits		Time deposits	
	coefficient	*z-value*	*coefficient*	*z-value*	*coefficient*	*z-value*
PCS indicator (ζ)	–0.181	***–3.59	–0.146	***–5.75	–0.001	–0.60
Market rateAT (η)			0.063	***2.28	0.616	***10.17
Market rate BE	0.808	***16.79			0.921	***39.45
Market rate DE	0.615	***11.48			0.894	***33.03
Market rate ES	0.691	***10.89	0.259	***6.75	0.925	***26.99
Market rate FR	0.982	***14.42			0.997	***137.37
Market rate IT	0.745	***18.84	0.433	***18.09	0.856	***26.99
Market rate NL			0.083	***2.19	0.831	***12.41
Market rate PT					0.798	***38.33
Market rate*PCS-ind. (θ)	0.046	***4.48	0.037	***5.86	–0.015	–0.60
Constant	2.591	***11.58	1.457	***10.43	0.302	**3.15
R-squared, centred	0.956		0.966		0.972	
Number of observations	578		477		956	
$\zeta + \theta\, MR_{i,t}$	0.028		0.005		–0.024	
$\chi^2\ H_0: \zeta + \theta\, MR_{i,t} = 0$[a]	2.26, *p*-value=0.13		0.53, *p*-value=0.47		4.29, *p*-value =0.04	

Notes: One, two and three asterisks indicate levels of confidence of 90 per cent, 95 per cent and 99 per cent, respectively. Country dummies are included but not shown.

a Chi-squared distributed Wald tests on $H_0: \zeta + \theta\, MR_{i,t} = 0$. The null hypothesis is not rejected for any loan type.

Table 8.12 The short-term ECM model of six bank interest rates[a]

	Mortgage loans		*Consumer loans*		*Short-term loans to enterprises*	
	coefficient	*z-value*	*coefficient*	*z-value*	*coefficient*	*z-value*
ΔMarket rate AT (μ)	0.227	***3.15	0.203	*1.84	0.275	***3.41
ΔMarket rate BE	0.207	*1.73	0.358	1.32	0.408	***2.49
ΔMarket rate DE	0.511	***4.33	–0.267	–1.30	0.159	1.20
ΔMarket rate ES	0.217	*1.75	0.041	0.10	0.573	***3.36
ΔMarket rate FR	–0.025	–0.58	–0.005	–0.09	0.079	0.73
ΔMarket rateIT	0.156	1.11			0.066	0.42
ΔMarket rate NL	0.262	***2.79			0.464	***3.01
ΔMarket rate PT	0.173	*1.88	0.001	0.00	0.159	0.87
ΔMarket rate*PCS-ind. (ξ)	0.020	0.86	0.071	1.52	0.050	*1.66
Residual AT (–1) (λ)	–0.005	***–3.10	–0.004	***–2.89	–0.005	***–3.00
ResidualBE (–1)	–0.007	**–2.20	–0.003	–1.09	–0.005	–1.52
Residual DE (–1)	–0.003	–1.56	–0.003	**–2.07	–0.001	–0.23
Residual ES (–1)	–0.006	***–2.80	–0.003	–0.86	–0.000	–0.03
Residual FR (–1)	–0.006	***–3.45	–0.004	***–3.25	–0.003	–0.44
Residual IT (–1)	–0.006	**–1.96			–0.004	*–1.64
Residual NL (–1)	–0.004	–1.63			–0.000	–0.10
Residual PT (–1)	–0.009	***–3.89	–0.006	–1.50	–0.011	**–2.28
R^2 centred	0.19		0.03		0.19	
Number of observations	949		711		949	

	Long-term loans to enterprises		*Current account deposits*		*Time deposits*	
	coefficient	*z-value*	*coefficient*	*z-value*	*coefficient*	*z-value*
ΔMarket rate AT (μ)			0.107	***3.05	0.229	***2.90
ΔMarket rate BE	0.987	***6.97			0.532	***6.02
ΔMarket rate DE	0.657	***3.56			0.587	***6.27
ΔMarket rate ES	0.994	***3.67	0.374	***3.90	0.344	**2.09
ΔMarket rate FR	0.162	1.47			0.972	***38.82
ΔMarket rate IT	0.744	***3.34	0.312	***3.68	0.146	1.28
ΔMarket rate NL			0.099	**2.45	0.463	***4.95
ΔMarket rate PT					0.281	***3.37
ΔMarket rate*PCS-ind. (ξ)	0.070	1.41	–0.033	**–2.47	0.020	0.92
Residual AT (–1) (λ)			–0.004	**–2.16	–0.004	*–1.69
ResidualBE (–1)	0.001	0.31			–0.004	–1.58
Residual DE (–1)	–0.001	–0.80			–0.001	–0.64
Residual ES (–1)	–0.005	–1.51	–0.010	**–2.13	–0.006	**–2.03
Residual FR (–1)	–0.004	–1.36			0.000	0.24
Residual IT (–1)	–0.004	–1.33	–0.007	–1.41	–0.009	**–2.33
Residual NL (–1)			–0.003	**–2.18	–0.005	–1.46
Residual PT (–1)					–0.009	***–3.39
R^2 centred	0.27		0.18		0.63	
Number of observations	573		473		948	

Note: One, two and three asterisks indicate a level of confidence of, respectively, 90 per cent, 95 per cent and 99 per cent.
a See Equation (8.2.b).

the deposit market. All in all, we have little if any evidence supporting the third hypothesis.

8.7. Conclusions

This chapter analyses the effects of competition on bank lending rates in four loan markets and on two types of deposit rates. We measure competition by a novel approach, named the PCS indicator, which allows the estimation of competition on separate submarkets for loans. Our results from a simple interest rate spread model show that across eight euro-area countries, bank interest rate spreads on mortgage loans, consumer loans and short-term loans to enterprises are significantly lower in more competitive markets. This result implies that bank loan rates are lower under stronger competition. This may improve social welfare, but it may also result in more risky behaviour by the banks, causing more financial instability and less social welfare. Furthermore, banks act as price makers in the deposit market and as price takers in the loan market. Stronger loan market competition results in lower offered deposit rates, at the cost of social welfare. However, these results are not confirmed by our estimates with a more comprehensive, but also more complicated, error-correction model.

Furthermore, empirical evidence for all loan categories considered suggests that the response of banks' long-run loan interest rates to corresponding market rates is stronger in more competitive than in less competitive loan markets. Finally, we observe that competition in loan markets does not significantly reinforce the immediate response of bank interest rates to changes in corresponding market rates. Summarizing, these results show the existence of evidence that stronger loan market competition reduces bank loan rates while changes in market rates are transmitted more strongly to bank rates. These findings underline the substantial impact of bank competition on the monetary policy transmission mechanism. More loan market competition strengthens monetary policy transmission in the euro area.

Notes

1 Based on Leuvensteijn, M. van, C. Kok Sørensen, J.A. Bikker, A.A.R.J.M. van Rixtel (2013) Impact of bank competition on the interest rate pass-through in the euro area, *Applied Economics* 45, 1359–1380.
2 Except Kok Sørensen and Werner (2006), who used a nearly identical dataset.
3 For other euro area countries we have insufficient data to estimate the PCS indicator.
4 Enterprises comprise the entire population of non-financial corporations.
5 Of course, competition is not the only factor determining the level of bank interest rates. Factors such as credit and interest rate risk, banks' degree of risk aversion, operating costs and efficiency are also likely to impact on bank margins. See, for example, Maudos and Fernández de Guevara (2004).
6 See, for example, Neuwark and Sharpe (1992) and Mester and Saunders (1995) for empirical evidence of asymmetric interest rate pass-through effects among US banks.

7 In addition to bank competition, switching costs and other interest rate adjustment costs, bank rate rigidity may also be due to credit risk factors. For example, in a situation of credit rationing banks may decide to leave lending rates unchanged and to limit the supply of loans instead; see, for example, Winker (1999). Banks may also choose to provide their borrowers with 'implicit interest rate insurance' by smoothing bank loan rates over the cycle; see Berger and Udell (1992). Finally, sometimes banks give customers an interest rate option for a given period. These banks have to recoup the costs of their options which may reduce the speed of the interest rate pass-through for outstanding borrowers.

8 Sander and Kleimeier (2002, 2004) differ from other studies in that they also model the severity of the interest rate shock, rather than merely its direction. This approach aims to take into account menu cost arguments implying that banks tend to pass on changes in market rates of a minimum size only.

9 The few existing empirical studies based on the PCS indicator have all used a log-linear relationship. See, for example, Chapter 9.

10 For other arguments against the HHI, see Sections 6.2, 7.3 and 8.1.

11 See Chapter 7 which uses a similar approach.

12 Generalized Moment Method (GMM) is used to correct for endogeneity between market shares and marginal costs using different moment conditions.

13 Most likely, the favourable result for Germany hinges in part on the special structure of its banking system, being built on three pillars, i.e. commercial banks, publicly-owned savings banks and cooperative banks (see Hackethal, 2004).

14 In order to avoid spurious results, see Granger and Newbold (1974).

15 An error correction model is a dynamical system in which the deviation of the current state from its long-run relationship will be fed into its short-run dynamics. This provides a coherent framework for the analysis of interest rate dynamics.

16 See, for example, Mojon (2001), De Bondt (2002, 2005), Sander and Kleimeier (2004), and Kok Sørensen and Werner (2006).

17 Viz ., four types of loan products (mortgage loans, consumer loans and short- and long-term loans to enterprises) and two types of deposits (time deposits and current-account deposits).

18 As the model of interest rates is based on monthly data, while we have annual estimates of the PCS indicator, we construct monthly competition estimates – $PCS_{i,t}$ in absolute terms as follows. We place the annual PCS indicator estimate in June of the respective year and then interpolate on a monthly basis between these values using 12-month moving averages.

19 Note that competition causes a downward shift in the level of bank interest rates (that is, $\zeta < 0$) as well as a change in the relationship between market rates and bank rates (expressed by $\theta\, MR_{i,t}$).

20 Unit root tests analyse whether a time series variable is non-stationary over time. For a survey of panel unit root tests, see Banerjee (1999). For a more detailed description and application to a similar set of data, see also Kok Sørensen and Werner (2006).

21 In the panel versions of the tests the alternative hypothesis assumes a root which is less than one, but is identical across the countries. Hence, the group mean versions allow for stronger heterogeneity. We focus on the test's group mean version.

22 For some bank products in some countries, it is not possible (due to insufficient data availability) to extend interest rate series all the way back to 1994. Therefore, unbalanced samples were used for some bank products.

23 The two series were linked in January 2003 with a parallel level shift of the series prior to this date. The level shift was based on the average monthly difference between the NRIR and MIR series for the period from January to September 2003 for which observations for both definitions were available. In contrast to Kok Sørensen and Werner (2006), we use new business weights (applying monthly averages observed in the January 2003 toJune 2004 period to smooth out undue volatility) to aggregate the

MIR categories to the NRIR. We believe this captures the differences across countries more precisely in terms of initial rate fixation periods and also corresponds better to the new business rate nature of the NRIR statistics.

24 The market rates have been chosen to best match bank interest rates on the basis of information from the Methodological Notes for the NRIR statistics and from the volume weights of the MIR statistics.

25 P-values of the various test statistics were derived using the standard normal distribution, which is a valid assumption for co-integration tests; see Pedroni (1999).

26 For six countries, we have consumer loan rates available only for the twelve months following January 2003.

27 E.g. US (indirectly): Berger and Hannan (1991), Mester and Saunders (1995); euro studies: De Bondt (2005); Sander and Kleimeier (2004); UK: Heffernan (1997), Hofmann and Mizen (2004); Belgium: De Graeve, De Jonghe, and Vander Vennet (2007); Ireland: Bredin et al. (2002).

28 Estimations in first differences of bank consumer loan rates reveal that competition does not have a significant effect on changes in lending rates, in line with the results of Table 8.12.

29 A re-estimation of Equation (8.3) with the distance to default for, respectively, mortgage, consumer loans and loans to firms using ECB data suggests no substantial change in the parameter of the PCS-indicator. This lack of change appears for each of the four types of loans. Unfortunately, a rising level of defaults tends to push lending rates down instead of up (as one would expect). Apparently, this indicates an under-pricing of default risk in the 1999–2002 period, see for instance Pavlov and Wachter (2006). Inclusion of GDP to capture the business cycle did not change this result. Hence, inclusion of risk does not improve (nor does it significantly change) our relationship between competition and the interest rate pass-through.

30 We use Newey and West's kernel-based heteroskedastic and autocorrelation consistent (HAC) variance estimations to correct for heteroskedasticity and autocorrelation, with the bandwidth set on two periods.

31 See also Mojon (2001), De Bondt (2005) and Kok Sørensen and Werner (2006).

32 Re-estimation with a risk measure did not affect the estimation results of the ECM, see note 29.

33 As mentioned in Section 8.5, the estimated long-run relationship between, on the one hand, interest rates on consumer loans and current-account deposits and, on the other hand, their corresponding market rates may be spurious owing to lack of a statistically significant co-integration relationships.

34 The null hypotheses of single EU-wide parameters for market interest rates and residuals in the short-run ECM model were rejected for most loan categories in favour of separate country-specific parameters.

References

Banerjee, A. (1999) Panel data unit roots and cointegration: an overview, *Oxford Bulletin of Economics and Statistics*, Special Issue, 607–629.

Berger, A.N., and T.H. Hannan (1991) The rigidity of prices: evidence from the banking industry, *American Economic Review* 81 (4), 938–945.

Berger, A., and G. Udell (1992) Some evidence on the empirical significance of credit rationing, *Journal of Political Economy* 100, 1047–1077.

Boone, J., and M. van Leuvensteijn (2010) Measuring competition using the profit elasticity: American sugar industry, 1890–1914, CEPR Discussion paper, no. 8159.

Borio, C., and W. Fritz (1995) The response of short-term bank lending rates to policy rates: a cross-country perspective, BIS Working Paper No. 27, May.

Bredin, D., and G. O'Reilly (2004) An analysis of the transmission mechanism of monetary policy in Ireland, *Applied Economics* 36, 49–58.

Bredin, D., T. Fitzpatrick, and G. O'Reilly (2002) Retail interest rate pass-through: the Irish experience, *Economic and Social Review* 33 (2), 223–246.

Corvoisier, S., and R. Gropp (2002) Bank concentration and retail interest rates, *Journal of Banking & Finance* 26, 2155–2189.

Cottarelli, C., and A. Kourelis (1994) Financial structure, bank lending rates and the transmission of monetary policy, IMF Staff Paper no. 42, 670–700.

Cottarelli, C., G. Ferri, and A. Generale (1995), Bank lending rates and financial structure in Italy: A case study, IMF Working Paper no. 38 (April).

De Bondt, G.J. (2002) Retail bank interest rate pass-through: new evidence at the euro area level, ECB Working Paper Series No. 136.

De Bondt, G.J. (2005) Interest rate pass-through: empirical results for the euro area, *German Economic Review* 6, 37–78.

De Graeve, F., O. De Jonghe, and R. Vander Vennet (2007) Competition, transmission and bank pricing policies: Evidence from Belgian loan and deposit markets, *Journal of Banking & Finance* 31, 259–278.

ECB (2006) Differences in MFI interest rates across Euro Area countries, September, Frankfurt.

Genesove D., and Mullin, W.P. (1998) Testing static oligopoly models: Conduct and cost in the sugar industry, 1890–1914, *Rand Journal of Economics* 29, 355–377.

Granger, C.W.J., and P. Newbold (1974) Spurious regressions in econometrics, *Journal of Econometrics* 2: 111–120

Gropp, R., C. Kok Sørensen, and J. Lichtenberger (2007) The dynamics of bank spreads and financial structure, European Central Bank Working Paper Series No. 714.

Gual, J. (1999) Deregulation, integration and market structure in European banking, *Journal of the Japanese and International Economies* 13, 372–396.

Hackethal, A. (2004) German banks and banking structure, in: J.P. Krahnen and R.H. Schmidt (eds), *The German Financial System*, Oxford University Press, 71–105.

Hadri, K. (2000) Testing for stationary in heterogeneous panel data, *Econometrics Journal*, 3, 148–161.

Hayashi, F. (2000) *Econometrics*, Princeton University Press.

Heffernan, S.A. (1997) Modelling British interest rate adjustment: An error-correction approach, *Economica* 64, 211–231.

Heinemann, F., and Schüler, M. (2002) Integration benefits on EU retail credit markets – Evidence from interest rate pass-through, ZEW, mimeo.

Hofmann, B., and P. Mizen, (2004) Interest rate pass-through and monetary transmission: Evidence from individual financial institutions' retail rates, *Economica* 71 (2), 99–123.

Im, K.S., M.H. Pesaran, and Shin, Y. (2003) Testing for unit roots in heterogeneous Panels, *Journal of Econometrics*, 115, 53–74.

Jorgenson, D.W. (1986) Econometric methods for modelling producer behavior, in E. Grilliches and M. Intrilligator (eds), *Handbook for Econometrics*, Vol. III, The Netherlands, Elsevier Science Publishers.

Klein, M. (1971) A theory of the banking firm, *Journal of Money, Credit, and Banking* 3, 205–218.

Kok Sørensen, C., and T. Werner (2006) Bank interest rate pass-through in the euro area: a cross-country comparison, ECB Working Paper Series No. 580.

Kuan-Min, W., and T. Thanh-Binh Nguyen (2010), Asymmetric pass-through and risk of interest rates: an empirical exploration of Taiwan and Hong Kong, *Applied Economics* 42, 659–670.

Lago-González, R., and V. Salas-Fumás (2005) Market power and bank interest rate adjustments, Banco de España Working Paper no. 0539.

Maudos, J., and J. Fernández de Guevara (2004) Factors explaining the interest rate margin in the banking sectors of the European Union, *Journal of Banking & Finance* 28, 2259–2281.

Mester, L.J., and A. Saunders (1995) When does the prime rate change?, *Journal of Banking & Finance* 19, 743–764.

Mojon, B. (2001) Financial structure and the interest rate channel of ECB monetary policy, *Economie et Provision* 147, 89–115.

Monti, M. (1972) Deposit, credit, and interest rate determination under alternative bank objectives, in G.P. Szego and K. Shell (eds), *Mathematical Methods in Investment and Finance*, Amsterdam, North-Holland.

Neuwark, D., and S. Sharpe (1992) Market structure and the nature of price rigidity: evidence from the market of consumer deposits, *Quarterly Journal of Economics* 107, 657–680.

Pavlov, A., and S.M. Wachter (2006) The inevitability of marketwide underpricing of mortgage default risk, *Real Estate Economics, American Real Estate and Urban Economics Association* 34, 479–496.

Pedroni, P. (1999) Critical values for cointegration tests in heterogeneous panels with multiple regressors, *Oxford Bulletin of Economics and Statistics*, Special Issue, 653–670.

Pedroni, P. (2004) Panel cointegration: asymptotic and finite sample properties of pooled time series tests with an application to the PPP hypothesis, *Econometric Hypothesis*, 20, 597–625.

Sander, H., and S. Kleimeier (2002) Asymmetric adjustment of commercial bank interest rates in the euro area: an empirical investigation into interest rate pass-through, *Kredit und Kapital* 35, 161–192.

Sander, H., and S. Kleimeier (2004) Convergence in euro zone retail banking?, *Journal of International Money and Finance* 23, 461–492.

Scholnick, B. (1996) Asymmetric adjustment of commercial bank interest rates: Evidence from Malaysia and Singapore, *Journal of International Money and Finance* 15, 485–496.

Vives, X. (2010), Competition and stability in banking, CEPR Policy Insight No. 50.

Weth, M.A. (2002) The pass-through from market interest rates to bank lending rates in Germany, Deutsche Bundesbank Discussion Paper 11/02.

Winker, P. (1999) Sluggish adjustment of interest rates and credit rationing: an application of unit root testing and error correction modelling, *Applied Economics* 31, 267–277.

9 Competition in the life insurance industry[1]

Jacob A. Bikker and Michiel van Leuvensteijn

The lack of available prices in the Dutch life insurance industry makes competition an elusive concept that defies direct observation. Therefore, this chapter investigates competition by analysing several factors which may affect the competitive nature of a market and various indirect measurement approaches. After discussing various supply and demand factors which may constitute a so-called tight oligopoly, we establish the existence of scale economies and the importance of cost X-inefficiency, since severe competition would force firms to exploit available scale economies and to reduce X-inefficiencies. Both scale economies and X-inefficiencies turn out to be substantial, although more or less comparable to those found for insurers in other countries and for other financial institutions. Further, we measure the effects of competition, applying the PCS indicator. This indicator points to moderate competition in comparison to other sectors in the Netherlands. Further investigations of submarkets should reveal where policy measures in order to promote competition might be appropriate.

9.1. Introduction

This chapter investigates efficiency and competitive behaviour on the Dutch life insurance market. In the Netherlands, the life insurance sector is important, with a business volume of €22 billion in terms of annual premiums paid, invested assets of €337 billion and insured capital of €990 billion at end–2010.[2] This market provides important financial products, such as endowment insurance, annuities, term insurance and burial funds, of often sizeable value for consumers. The financial planning of many households depends on the proper functioning of this market. The complexity of the products and dependency on future investment returns make many life insurance products rather opaque. Therefore, competition and efficiency in this sector are important issues, both from the point of view of consumers as well as that of supervisors whose duty it is to protect the interests of consumers.

Most life insurance policies have a long life span, which makes consumers sensitive to the sustainability of the respective firms. Life insurance firms need to remain in a financially sound condition over decades in order to be able to pay out the promised benefits. The sector has a safety net arrangement in case a life insurer fails, but that does not cover all risks and excludes policies of the largest ten firms. Without sufficient profitability it could be questionable whether life insurers are able to face unfavourable developments such as a long-lasting decline of long-term interest rates. Obviously, there may be a complex trade-off between increased competition with a short-run advantage for consumers of low premiums, but possibly the drawback of higher long-run risk with respect to the insurance benefits. In practice, the likelihood that an insurer in the Netherlands fails appears to be rather limited with only one bankruptcy in the last twenty years. Obviously, improvement of efficiency would benefit all stakeholders, both in the short and the long run. Also the impact of competition on this trade-off between short and long-term interests makes it worthwhile to further investigate competition in this market.

Life insurance firms sell different products using various distribution channels, thereby creating several submarkets. The degree of competition may vary across these submarkets. For instance, submarkets where parties bargain on collective contracts (mainly pension schemes provided by employers) and submarkets for direct writers are expected to be more competitive than submarkets where insurance agents sell products to uninformed but trusting customers. Lack of sufficient data on prices of life insurance products, market shares of products and distribution channels makes it impossible to drill down to competition on submarkets.

Lack of data also prohibits us from measuring competition among life insurers *directly* (for instance, by a price-cost margin), even for the overall life insurance market. One qualitative way to investigate this market is to work out what its structural features are, particularly those related to its competitive nature. On the supply side, we find that the market power of insurance firms is limited due to their plurality and that ample entry opportunities exist, all of which contributes to sound competitive conditions. But on the demand side, we observe that consumer power is limited, particularly due to the opaque nature of many life insurance products, and that there are few substitution possibilities for life insurance policies, which could hamper increased competition. Combining these various insights, we have reasons to analyse the competitive nature of this market further.

An often-used indirect, quantitative measure of competition is efficiency. Increased competition is assumed to force firms to operate more efficiently, so that high efficiency may indicate the existence of competition and vice versa. We distinguish between various types of efficiency, particularly scale efficiency and X-efficiency. Scale economies are related to output volumes, whereas cost X-efficiency reflects managerial ability to drive down production costs, controlled for output volumes and input price levels. There are various methods to measure scale economies and X-efficiency.[3] We use a translog cost function to reveal the existence of scale economies, and a stochastic cost frontier model to measure X-efficiency. Large unemployed scale economies may raise questions about the competitive pressure in the market. Note that the existence of scale efficiency is also important for the potential entry of new firms, an important determinant of competition. Strong scale effects would put new firms at a disadvantage.

A straightforward measure of competition is the profit margin. Supernormal profits would indicate insufficient competition. We observe profits of Dutch life insurers over time and compare them with profits of foreign peers.

Another indirect measure of competition is the so-called PCS indicator. This approach is based on the notion that competition rewards efficiency and punishes inefficiency. In competitive markets, efficient firms perform better – in terms of market share and hence profit – than inefficient firms. The PCS indicator measures the extent to which efficiency differences between firms are translated into performance differences. The more competitive a market is, the stronger is the relationship between efficiency differences and performance differences. The PCS indicator is usually measured over time, yielding a picture of the development of competition. Further, the level of the PCS indicator for life insurance can be compared with levels elsewhere in the services sector, to assess the relative competitiveness of the life insurance market.

Our chapter is part of a larger research project on competition in the life insurance industry, see CPB (2005). Other chapters of that report go into more detail regarding barriers to competition, product choice and the role of financial advisers. This chapter aims to measure competitive behaviour in and the performance of the entire Dutch life insurance market. The current chapter is complementary to the detailed studies in the following sense; whatever goes on in the much-discussed financial advice part of the business, the current chapter verifies what can be said about competition on the market on an aggregate level. Any problems (or lack of problems) should ultimately show up in aggregate indicators of competition. Since we use four different empirical aggregate indicators (average profit margins, scale economies, X-inefficiencies and the PCS indicator), we will obtain a reasonably accurate picture of competition in this market.

The outline of the chapter is as follows. Section 9.2 provides a brief and general explanation of the production of life insurance firms. Section 9.3 investigates the competitive structure of demand and supply sides of the Dutch life insurance market. Section 9.4 measures scale economies based on the so-called translog cost function, while the next section introduces the measurement of X-efficiency. Section 9.6 discusses the PCS indicator. Section 9.7 describes the data used and Section 9.8 presents the empirical results of the various indirect measures of competition. The last section sums up and draws conclusions.

9.2. The production of life insurances

The core business of insurance firms is to sell protection against risks.[4] There are two quite different types of insurance products: life insurance and non-life or property and casualty (P&C) insurance.[5] Life insurance covers deviations in the timing and size of predetermined cash flows due to (non-)accidental death or disability. While some life insurance products pay out only in the incident of death (term insurance and burial funds), others do so at the end of a term or a number of terms (endowment insurance).[6] A typical annuity policy pays an annual amount starting on a given date (if a specific person is alive) and continuing until that person passes away. The benefits of insurance can be guaranteed beforehand so that the insurance firm bears the risk that invested premiums may not cover the promised payments. Such guaranteed benefits may be accompanied by some kind of profit sharing, e.g. depending on indices of bonds or shares. The benefits of insurance can also be linked to capital market investments, e.g. a basket of shares, so that the insurance firm bears no investment risk at all. Such policies are usually referred to as unit-linked policies. We also observe mixed products, e.g. unit linked policies with guaranteed minimum investment returns.

A major feature of life insurance is its long-term character, often continuing for decades. Therefore, policyholders need to trust their life insurance company, making insurers very sensitive to their reputation. Life insurers need to hold large reserves to cover their calculated insurance liabilities. These reserves are financed by – annual or single – insurance premiums and invested mainly on the capital market. The major risk of life insurers concerns mismatches between liabilities and assets. Idiosyncratic life risk is negligible as it can be well diversified. Systematic life risk, however, such as increasing life expectancy, can also pose a threat to life insurers. Yet their major risk will always be investment risk. The main services which life insurance firms provide to their customers are life (and disability) risk pooling and financial intermediation. Significant expenditures include sales expenses, whether in the form of direct sales costs or fees paid to insurance agencies, administrative costs, investment management and product development.

In the Netherlands, the insurance product market is heavily influenced by tax privileges. In the past, endowment-insurance allowances, including any related investment income, used to be tax-exempt, up to certain limits, provided that certain none-too-restrictive conditions were met. Annuity premiums were tax deductible, but annuity allowances were taxed. Again this implies that investment income was enjoyed tax-free while consumers could often also benefit from lower marginal tax rates after retirement. In 2001, a major tax revision reduced the tax benefits for all new policies, while the rights of existing policies were respected.[7] The tax reduction was made public in earlier years, so that consumers could bring forward their spending on annuities and insurers were eager to sell. Endowment insurance policies became subject to wealth tax and income tax exemption limits were reduced. At the same time, both the standard deduction for annuity premiums and the permission for individuals to deduct annuity premiums to repair pension shortfalls were also reduced. The reduced subsidy on annuities, in particular, has had a great impact on volumes. In 2003, the standard deduction for annuity premiums was abolished entirely, whereas the permission to do so on an individual basis was limited even further. Finally, in 2008, tax reduction on savings for pensions and mortgage redemptions was extended to bank savings plans ('banksparen'), increasing competition between life insurers and banks.

9.3. The competitive structure of the Dutch life insurance market

This section briefly discusses structural characteristics of the life insurance market that may affect competition.[8] The diagnostic framework of Chapter 2 enables an assessment of whether a market structure constitutes a tight oligopoly. This is an oligopoly which facilitates the realization of supernormal profits over a substantial period of time, where 'facilitate' reflects that the probability of supernormal profits being observed is higher than in a more competitive market; 'supernormal profits' exceed a market conform rate of risk-adjusted return on capital, and a 'substantial period of time' reflects that oligopolies will be stable for a number of years.

9.3.1. Supply-side factors

The diagnostic framework of Chapter 2 contains a list of coordinated and unilateral factors that increase the probability of a tight oligopoly. Coordinated factors refer to explicit and tacit collusion, while unilateral factors denote actions undertaken by individual firms without any form of coordination with other firms. Frequent interaction, transparency and symmetry (in terms of equal cost structures) are beneficial to a tight oligopoly since they make it easier for firms to coordinate their actions and to detect and punish deviations from the (explicitly or tacitly) agreed line of behaviour. Heterogeneous products make it easier for firms to raise prices independently of competitors, as consumers are less likely to switch to another firm in response to price differences. Structural links between firms such as cross-ownerships would give firms a stake in each other's performance, thus softening competition.[9] Information about risks plays a crucial role in markets for financial products. In the case of life insurance, adverse selection may play a role when consumers have more information regarding their life expectancy than insurance companies. Adverse selection may lead to higher price-costs margins.

Economic theory indicates that a high concentration and high entry barriers are conducive to the realization of supernormal profits. An indicator of market concentration or the number of firms, the first determinant of competition, is the Herfindahl–Hirschman index (HHI).[10] Over 2006–2011 we calculate an average HHI index value of 1,216 for the Dutch life insurance industry (see Table 9.1), which is far below any commonly accepted critical value. This low figure also reflects the large number of Dutch life insurance firms, which, over the respective years, declined from more than ninety to fifty. These figures are not unusual for large countries such as Australia, Canada and Japan, while Germany, the UK and the US have considerably lower ratios. However, one should keep in mind that, by definition, such ratios are substantially higher in smaller markets or countries. We conclude that insurance market concentration in the Netherlands is moderate, although in market segments, such as collective contracts, concentration may be substantial (CPB, 2005).

The second factor determining competition is the set of barriers to entry. Bikker and van Leuvensteijn (2008) show that the number of entrants as a percentage of the total sample of Dutch insurance firms varied from 2 per cent in 1991 to 8 per

Table 9.1 HHI concentration indices based on gross premiums

	2002	*2003*	*2004*	*2005*	*2006*	*2007*	*2008*	*2009*	*2010*	*2011*	*Averages*
Austria	740	782	811	808	778	1322	1287	726	698	660	861
Belgium	1465	1428	1530	1699	1880	1878	1517	1744	1444	1799	1638
Bulgaria						1453	1306	1197	1102	1245	1261
Czech Republic				1327	1298	1321	1550	1312	1141	1352	1329
Denmark	1132	1050	956	942	822	790	680	681	639	834	834
France				538	555	488	414	422	438	680	471
Germany	317	297	282	331	401	311	286	389	394	343	343
Italy	2198	1889	1599	582	601	592	521	569	536	978	978
Netherlands				1298	979	1352	1274	1143	1287	1261	1216
Switzerland	998	981	1055	1145	1650	1635	1403	1219	1158	1274	1274
UK	1017	1095	625	693	826	739	814	1051	1041	1497	838
Australia	2846	2000	1433	1520	1665	1660	1418	1470	1503	2110	1478
US	130	128	137	158	173	167	171	167	171	179	145
Canada	9117	8903	8783	5487	4273	3216	3313	3734	2629	874	4121
Japan	1106	964	1083	984	885	691	929	830	876	847	809

Sources: ISIS (data for individual life insurers) and Insurance Europe (for country totals). We have compared gross premiums (GP) from ISIS with GP from 'Insurance Europe' and have deleted concentration indices if the coverage ratio did not range between 67 per cent and 150 per cent.

cent in 1997. These numbers were relatively high compared with countries such as Canada, Germany and the UK, where the degree of entry varied between 1 and 4 per cent. This suggests that entry opportunities in the Dutch life insurance market seemed to be quite large compared with other countries. More recent figures on entries are not available.

9.3.2. Demand-side factors

Demand-side factors also affect the intensity of competition, see Chapter 2. The elasticity of residual demand determines how attractive it is for a firm to unilaterally change its prices. High search and switching costs contribute to low firm-level demand elasticity. Stable, predictable demand makes it easier for firms to collude in order to keep prices high, as it makes cheating by one or more firms easier to detect than amid fluctuating demand.

In practice, the elasticity of residual demand for life insurance policies is limited, due to the absence of perfect substitutes. Investment funds or bank savings could in principle be an alternative for old-age savings (such as annuities), but lack the risk-pooling element, which is essential for life insurance policies. Moreover, annuities generally enjoy a more favourable status due to the tax deductibility of premiums (particularly in the Netherlands, although less since 2001; since 2008, tax reduction is also granted to bank savings for pensions and mortgage redemptions, the so-called 'banksparen'), which is another reason why alternatives are less attractive. Endowment insurance policies are often linked to mortgage loans, under constructs where the importance of risk-pooling is less dominant and may diverge across policyholders.

High switching costs are typical for life insurance policies, since contracts are often of a long-term nature and early termination of contracts is costly because it involves disinvestments and compensation by the client of the company of not-yet-paid acquisition costs, which are of front-loading nature.[11]

Search costs for life insurance products are high as these products are complicated and the market is opaque. They could be alleviated if searching could be entrusted to insurance agents, which would help consumers to avoid errors in their product choice. Moreover, it would make the market more competitive by raising the elasticity of demand. However, the Dutch market for financial advice may not function properly (CPB, 2005).[12] In particular, due to the incentive structure in this market (notably the use of commissions) coupled with inexperienced consumers, insurance agents may give advice that is not in the best interest of consumers. Since 2013, the incentive structure has changed, now that commissions have been banned and consumers pay the agents for independent advice.

Consumer power is weaker as the market is less transparent. Strong brand names are indicators of non-transparency, as confidence in a well-known brand may replace price comparisons or personal judgement. Another indicator is the degree to which buyers organize themselves, for instance, to be informed and to reduce the opacity of the market. The major consumer organization in the

Netherlands, many Internet sites[13] and other sources such as the *Money View* magazine, compare prices and inform consumers continuously on life insurance policy terms and prices in order to enable them to make comparisons and well-founded choices. For a minority of consumers this is sufficient to take out a life insurance policy as direct writers or at banks or post offices. However, as products remain complicated and come in many different flavours (in terms of duration, and so on), the majority of consumers are unable to take out policies independently, or are unwilling to make the effort, and call in the services of insurance agents. A third indicator is the degree to which consumers can take out life insurance policies collectively. Collective contracts are usually based on thorough comparisons of conditions and prices by experts, are often negotiated via a common employer and contribute substantially to consumer power but, of course, many people are unable to take advantage of this empowering option. All in all, we conclude that buyer power is low amid an opaque life insurance market, but that this problem has been reduced in part by various types of cooperation in favour of consumers.

9.3.3. Conclusions

The supply-side characteristics of the market for life insurance suggest limited supplier power: the number of firms is quite large, the level of concentration is not particularly high and entry is relatively easy. However, on the demand side we find factors such as high search and switching costs, few substitution options (at least until 2008, when 'banksparen' was introduced), limited consumer power due to the opaque nature of life insurance products and substantial product differentiation. The demand-side conditions may impair the competitive nature of the life insurance market and call for further analysis

9.4. Measuring scale economies

In the present market, we expect that scale economies would be reduced under heavier competition.[14] The existence of non-exhausted scale economies is an indication that the potential to reduce costs has not been employed in full and thus can be seen as an indirect indicator of (lack of) competition. This is the first reason why we investigate scale economies in this chapter. Another reason is that we will correct for (potential) distortion by possible scale economies in a subsequent analysis based on the PCS indicator. This correction can be carried out using the estimation results of this section.

We measure scale economies using a translog cost function (TCF). The measurement and analysis of differences in life insurance cost levels is based on the assumption that the technology of an individual life insurer can be described by a production function which links the various types of life insurer output to input factor prices, such as wages (management), acquisition fees and so on. Under proper conditions, a dual cost function can be derived, using output levels and factor prices as arguments. In line with most of the literature, we use the translog function to describe costs. Christensen et al. (1973) proposed the TCF as a second-order Taylor expansion, usually around the mean, of a generic function with all variables appearing as logarithms. This TCF is a flexible functional form that has proved to be an effective tool for the empirical assessment of efficiency. For theoretical underpinning and an overview of applications in the literature, see Bikker et al. (2006). The TCF reads as follows:

$$\ln c_{it} = a + \sum_j \beta_j \ln x_{ijt} + \sum_j \sum_k \gamma_{jk} \ln x_{ijt} \ln x_{ikt} + v_{it} \qquad (9.1)$$

where the dependent variable c_{it} is the cost of production of the *i*th firm ($i = 1, \ldots, N$) in year *t* ($t = 1, \ldots, T$). The explanatory variables x_{ijt} represent output or output components ($j, k = 1, \ldots, m$) and input prices ($j, k = m + 1, \ldots, M$). The two sum terms constitute the multiproduct TCF: the linear terms on the one hand and the squares and cross terms on the other, each accompanied by their respective unknown parameters β_j and γ_{jk}. v_{it} is the error term.

A number of additional calculations need to be executed to be able to understand the coefficients of the TCF in Equation (9.1) and to draw conclusions from them. For these calculations, the insurance firm-year observations are divided into a number of size classes, based on the related value of premium income. The marginal costs of output category *j* (for $j = 1, \ldots, m$) for size class *q* in units of the currency, $mc_{j,q}$, is defined as:

$$mc_{j,q} = \partial c / \partial x_j = (c_q / x_{j,q})\, \partial \ln c / \partial \ln x_j \qquad (9.2)$$

where $x_{j,q}$ and c_q are averages for size class *q* of the variables. It is important to check whether marginal resource costs are positive at all average output levels in each size class. Otherwise, from the point of view of economic theory, the estimates would not make sense. Scale economies indicate the amount by which operating costs go up when all output levels increase proportionately. We define scale economies as:[15]

$$SE = \sum_{j=1}^{m} \partial \ln c / \partial \ln x_j \qquad (9.3)$$

where $SE < 1$ corresponds to economies of scale, that is, a less than proportionate increase in cost when output levels are raised, whereas $SE > 1$ indicates diseconomies of scale.

The literature provides various examples of diseconomies-of-scale measurement. Fecher et al. (1991) applied translog cost functions to estimate scale economies in the French insurance industry. They find increasing returns to scale. However, it is unclear whether this effect is significant; a 1 per cent increase of production increases costs by only 0.85 per cent. Grace and Timme (1992) examined cost economies in the US life insurance industry and find strong and significant scale economies. Depending on the type and size of firm, an increase of production by 1 per cent will increase costs by 0.73 to 0.96 per cent.

This chapter applies two versions of the TCF. The first is used to estimate the scale effects and marginal cost that will, in turn, be taken as input for the PCS indicator model. In this version, production is proxied by *one* variable, namely premium income. Particularly for marginal costs, it is necessary to use a single measure of production, even at some expense to accuracy (see Section 9.1). The second version is the stochastic cost approach model discussed in the next section, which is used to estimate X-inefficiencies. Here it is essential that the multi-product character of life insurance is recognized, so a set of five variables has been used to approximate production.

9.5. Measuring X-inefficiency

It is expected that increased competition will force insurance firms to drive down their X-inefficiency. Therefore, X-efficiency is often used as an indirect measure of competition. X-efficiency reflects managerial ability to drive down production costs, controlled for output volumes and input price levels. X-efficiency of firm *i* is defined as the difference in costs between that firm and the best practice firms of similar size and input prices (Leibenstein, 1966). Errors, lags between the adoption of the production plan and its implementation, human inertia, distorted communications and uncertainty cause deviation between firms' performance and the efficient frontier formed by the best-practice life insurers with the lowest costs, controlled for output volumes and input price levels.

Various approaches are available to estimate X-inefficiency (see, for example, Lozano-Vivas, 1998). All methods involve determining an efficient frontier on the basis of observed (sets of) minimum values rather than presupposing certain technologically determined minima. Each method, however, uses different assumptions and may result in diverging estimates of inefficiency. In the case of banks, Berger and Humphrey (1997) report a roughly equal split between studies applying non-parametric and parametric techniques. The number of efficiency studies for life insurers is small compared with that for banks. For a survey, see Cummins and Weiss (2000) and Bikker et al. (2006). *Non-parametric* approaches, such as data envelopment analysis (DEA) and free disposable hull (FDH) analysis, have the practical advantage that no functional form needs to be specified. At the same time, however, they do not allow random error terms, so that specification errors, missing variables and so on, if they occur, may be wrongly measured as inefficiency, raising the inefficiency estimate. The results of the DEA method are also sensitive to the number of constraints specified. An even greater disadvantage of these techniques is that they generally ignore prices and can, therefore, account only for technical, not for economic inefficiency.

One of the *parametric* methods is the stochastic frontier approach, which assumes that the error term is the sum of a model error and an inefficiency term. These two components can be distinguished by making one or more assumptions about the asymmetry of the distribution of the inefficiency term. Although such assumptions are not very restrictive, they are nevertheless criticized for being somewhat arbitrary. A flexible alternative for panel data is the distribution-free approach, which avoids assumptions regarding the distribution of the inefficiency term, but supposes that the error term for each life insurance company over time is zero. Hence, the average predicted error of a firm is its estimated inefficiency. The assumption under this approach of – on average – zero random error terms for each company is a very strong one, and hence a drawback. Moreover, shifts in time remain unidentified. Finally, the thick frontier method does not compare single life insurers with the best-practice life insurers on the frontier, but produces an inefficiency measure for the whole sample. The 25th percentile of the life insurer cost distribution is taken as the 'thick' frontier and the range between the 25th and 75th percentiles as inefficiency. This approach avoids the influence of outliers, but at the same time assumes that all errors of the 25th percentile reflect only random error terms, not inefficiency.

All approaches have their pros and cons. All in all, the widely used stochastic frontier approach is selected for use in this chapter as being the least biased in principle. Berger and Mester (1997) have found that the efficiency estimates are fairly robust to differences in methodology, which fortunately makes the choice of efficiency measurement approach less critical.

The stochastic cost frontier (SCF) function[16] elaborates on the TCF, splitting the error term into two components, one to account for random effects due to the model specification and another to account for cost X-inefficiencies:

$$\ln c_{it} = a + \sum_j \beta_j \ln x_{ijt} + \sum_j \sum_k \gamma_{jk} \ln x_{ijt} \ln x_{ikt} + v_{it} + u_{it} \tag{9.4}$$

The sub-indices refer to firms i and time t. The v_{it} terms represent the random error terms of the TCF, which are assumed to be identically and independently $N(0,\sigma_v^2)$ distributed and the u_{it} terms are *non-negative* random variables which describe cost inefficiency and are assumed to be identically and independently half-normally ($|N(0,\sigma_u^2)|$) distributed and to be independent from the v_{it}. In other words, the density function of the u_{it} is (twice) the positive half of the normal density function.

The cost efficiency of a life insurer relative to the cost frontier estimated by Equation (9.4) is calculated as follows. X is the matrix containing the explanatory variables. Cost efficiency is defined as:[17]

$$EFF_{it} = E(c_{it} \mid u_{it} = 0, X) / E(c_{it} \mid u_{it}, X) = 1/\exp(u_{it}) \tag{9.5}$$

In other words, efficiency is the ratio of expected costs on the frontier (where production would be completely efficient, or $u_{it} = 0$) to expected costs, conditional upon the observed degree of inefficiency.[18] The numerator and denominator are both conditional upon X, the given level of output components and input prices. Values of EFF_{it} range from 0 to 1. We define inefficiency as $INEFF = 1 - EFF$.[19]

The SCF model encompasses the TCF in cases where the inefficiencies u_{it} can be ignored. A test on the restriction which reduces the former to the latter is available after reparameterization of the model of Equation (9.4) by replacing σ_v^2 and σ_u^2 by, respectively, $s^2 = \sigma_v^2 + \sigma_u^2$ and $\lambda = \sigma_u^2/(\sigma_v^2 + \sigma_u^2)$, see Battese and Corra (1977). The λ parameter can be employed to test whether an SCF model is necessary at all. Acceptance of the null hypothesis $\lambda = 0$ would imply that $\sigma_u = 0$ and hence that the term u_{it} may be removed from the model, so that Equation (9.4) narrows down to the TCF of Equation (9.1).

An extensive body of literature is devoted to the measurement of X-efficiency in the life insurance markets, see Bikker et al. (2006) for an overview. Most studies estimate efficiency on a single country base, using different methods to measure scale economies and X-efficiency. Furthermore, the studies employ diverging definitions for output, input factors and input factor prices. The key results of the insurance economies studies are that scale economies exist, that scope economies are small, rare or even negative and that average X-inefficiencies vary from low levels around 10 per cent to high levels up to above 50 per cent, generally with large dispersion of inefficiency for individual firms. The studies present mixed results with respect to the relationship between size and inefficiency. The stochastic cost frontier approach is generally seen as more reliable than the non-parametric methods, which appear to provide diverging levels and rankings of inefficiencies.

9.6. The PCS indicator of competition

The PCS approach is based on the idea that competition rewards efficiency. In general, an efficient firm will capture a larger market share and hence realize higher profits than a less efficient one. Crucial for the PCS indicator approach is that this effect will be stronger the more competitive the market is. This leads to the following empirical model:

$$\pi_{it}/\pi_{jt} = \alpha + \beta_t\,(mc_{it}/mc_{jt}) + \gamma\,\tau_t + \varepsilon_{it} \tag{9.6}$$

where α, β_t and γ are parameters and π_{it} denotes the profit of firm *i* in year *t*. Relative profits π_{it}/π_{jt} are defined for any pair of firms and depend, among other things, on the relative marginal costs of the respective firms, mc_{it}/mc_{jt}. The variable τ_t is a time trend and ε_{it} an error term. The parameter of interest is β_t. It is expected to have a negative sign, because relatively efficient firms make higher profits. In what follows we will refer to β_t as the PCS indicator. The PCS indicator shows that when profit differences are increasingly determined by marginal cost differences, this indicates increased competition. The PCS indicator can be used to answer two types of questions. The first type focuses on the time dimension of β_t 'how does competition evolve over time?' while the second type looks at the potential cross-section nature of Equation (9.6) 'how does competition in the life insurance market compare with competition in other service sectors?' Since measurement errors are less likely to vary over time than over industries, the former interpretation is more robust than the latter. For this reason, this indicator focuses on the *change* in β_t over time within a given sector. Comparisons of β_t across sectors are possible, but unobserved sector-specific factors may affect β_t. An advantage of the PCS indicator is that it is linked more directly to competition than are measures such as scale economies and X-inefficiency, or frequently used (both theoretically and empirically) but often misleading measures such as the concentration index.[20] The PCS indicator requires data of fairly homogeneous products. Although some heterogeneity in life insurance products exists, its degree of homogeneity is high compared with similar studies using the PCS indicator (e.g. Creusen et al., 2005).

We are not aware of any empirical application of the PCS model to the life insurance industry. Boone and Weigand in CPB (2000) and Boone (2004) have applied their model on data from different manufacturing industries. Both papers approximate a firm's marginal costs by the ratio of variable costs to revenues, as marginal costs cannot be observed directly. CPB (2000) uses the *relative* values of profits and the ratio of variable cost to revenues, whereas Boone et al. (2004) consider the *absolute* values. To obtain a comparable scale for the dependent variable (relative profits) and the independent variable (relative marginal costs) and to avoid too strong effects of outliers on the estimated slope, both these variables are expressed in logarithms. Consequently, all observations of companies making losses (i.e. negative profits) have been deleted, introducing a bias in the sample towards profitable firms. PCS realizes that this introduces a focus towards profitable firms, but states that the competitive effect of loss-making firms is still present in the behaviour and results of the other firms in the sample.[21]

Finally, we adjust the PCS model also by replacing often-used proxies for marginal costs, such as average variable cost, by a model-based estimate of the marginal cost itself. We are able to do so using the translog cost function from Section 9.4. Moreover, this enables us to correct the marginal cost for the effects of scale economies. The correction is based on an auxiliary regression where marginal costs are explained by a quadratic function of production. The residuals of this auxiliary regression are used as adjusted marginal costs.

9.7. Description of the data

This chapter uses data of the former Pensions and Insurance Supervisory Authority of the Netherlands, which in 2004 merged with De Nederlandsche Bank. The data were reported by Dutch life insurance companies over 1995–2003 in the context of supervision and consists of 867 firm-year observations. In our dataset, the number of active companies in the Netherlands was 84 in 2003 and 105 in 1998. In 2003, 40 insurers were independent and 46 were owned by 16 holding companies. Most of the latter 46 subsidiary companies operated entirely or highly independently and thus competed against siblings as well. In a few cases, subsidiary companies were more integrated, so less independent from their holding companies. However, as they focused on different product types, used different distribution channels or operated in different regions, the question whether they competed with one another is less relevant. We conclude that the aggregation of insurers at the holding company level would be less appropriate.

The average size of a life insurance company in terms of total assets on its balance sheet is around €2.5 billion (see Table 9.2). Such an imaginary average firm has around half a million policies in its portfolio, insures a total endowment capital of €7 billion and has current and future annual rents worth almost €400 million. Profits are defined as technical results, so that profits on investments are included, and are taken before tax. Profits of the average firm amount to 5.5 per cent of their premium income. The average firm uses 5 per cent of its gross premiums for reinsurance. Roughly 63 per cent of premiums are from individual contracts, the remainder are of a collective nature. More than half of the insurance firms have no collective contracts at all. Two-thirds of the contracts are based on

Table 9.2 Description of the data on Dutch insurance firms (1995–2003)

	Median	*Mean*		*Standard deviation*
		Weighted[a]	*Unweighted*	
Total assets (in million €)	521.5	–	2,472.5	6,991.6
Annual premiums (in million €)	66.0	–	247.7	588.8
Annual costs, total (in million €)	18.2	–	32.8	63.2
Annual profits (in million €)	2.6	–	15.7	47.6
Total endowment capital (in million €)	2,229	–	7,376	13,483
Amount of annuity rent[b] (in million €)	9	–	387	1,397
Total unit-linked capital (in million €)	67	–	246	589
Number of policies (in 1000 €)	168.7	–	522.4	973.6
Profit/premiums	0.047	0.078	0.055	0.25
Reinsurance ratio	0.013	0.034	0.050	0.11
Acquisition costs/total costs	0.53	0.34	0.53	1.86
Individual contracts ratio	1.00	0.63	0.90	0.21
Periodic payments ratio	0.72	0.52	0.67	0.27
Unit-linked funds ratio	0.25	0.44	0.33	0.32
Endowment premium ratio	0.93	0.57	0.82	0.26
Acquisition costs/premium	0.09	0.06	0.16	0.29
Management costs/premium	0.18	0.13	0.23	0.22
Number of observations per year				
1995	94		2000	94
1996[c]	103		2001	93
1997	104		2002	89
1998	105		2003	84
1999	101		Total	867

a These ratios are weighted averages where the weights are the size of insurance firms. Note that the weighted average of 'profit/premiums' is also equal to total profits divided by total premiums
b Annual payment
c Ten new entrees in 1996 and one termination.

periodic payments. Annual premiums reflect both old and new contracts. Because 48 per cent of the premiums paid, on average, are of the lump sum type, whereas 15 per cent of periodic premiums also refer to new policies, some 63 per cent of annual premiums stem from new business. Note that cost and profit figures are also based on a mixture of new and old business. Balance-sheet and profit-and-loss data for new policies only are not available. So-called unit-linked fund policies, where policyholders bear the investment risk on their own deposits (that is, premiums minus costs), have become more popular; 44 per cent of premiums relate to this type of policy. Endowment insurance is the major product category, responsible for 57 per cent of all premiums collected. This type of insurance policy is often sold in combination with a mortgage loan. The total costs are around 13 per cent of total premium income, half of which consists of acquisition (or sales) costs. The medians and the differences between weighted and unweighted averages reflect skewness in the (size) distributions. Larger firms tend to have higher profit margins and relatively lower acquisition costs, lower management costs, fewer individual contracts, fewer periodic payments, more unit-linked funds policies and fewer endowment policies.

9.8. Empirical results

9.8.1. Scale economies

This section estimates scale economies using the translog cost function (TCF). In a later section, the TCF is used also to calculate marginal costs (see Section 9.4). For these two purposes, the TCF explains the insurance company's cost by (only) one measure of production, namely premiums. As both scale effects and marginal costs are obtained from the first derivatives of the TCF to production, we will disregard other production measures here. Generally, inclusion of more measures of production components or proxies is common practice in the case of multi-product firms, and has indeed been applied in the X-efficiency models in Sections 9.8.2 and 9.8.3.

In the literature, measuring output in the life insurance industry is much debated. Where in many other industries, output is equal to the value added, we cannot calculate this figure for insurers, due to conceptual problems.[22] Most studies on the life insurance industry use premium income as output measure. Hirschhorn and Geehan (1977) view the production of contracts as the main activity of a life insurance company. Premiums collected directly concern the technical activity of an insurance company. The ability of an insurance company to market products, to select clients and to accept risks are reflected by premiums. However, premiums do not reflect financial activities properly, as e.g. asset management represented by return on investments is ignored.[23] Despite shortcomings, this section also uses premium income as the output measure.

As our model reads in logarithms, we cannot use observations where one or more of the variables have a zero or negative value. Insurance firms may employ various sales channels: own sales organizations, tied and multiple insurance agencies, and other channels, such as banks, post offices, etc. We have to drop observations of firms that do not use insurance agencies and report zero acquisition costs. In this sense, we clearly are left with a sub-sample of firms.

Table 9.3 presents the TCF estimates. We assume that costs are explained by production (in terms of total premiums), reinsurance and acquisition (proxies of prices of reinsurance and acquisition fees),[24] so that these variables also emerge as squares and in cross terms. To test this basic model for robustness, we also add

Table 9.3 Estimation results of the translog cost function[a]

Dependent variable: total costs	*Basic model*		*Extended model*	
Explanatory variables:	*Coefficient*	*t-value*[b]	*Coefficient*	*t-value*[b]
Premium income (production)	0.50	**5.5	0.16	1.3
Reinsurance ratio	0.26	**2.6	0.13	0.9
Acquisition ratio	–0.18	–1.3	0.05	0.2
Premium income^2	0.01	**2.6	0.03	**4.9
Reinsurance ratio^2	0.04	0.6	0.01	0.9
Acquisition ratio^2	–0.03	*–1.9	–0.02	–0.7
Premium income * reinsurance ratio	–0.03	**–3.0	–0.01	–1.1
Premium income * acquisition ratio	0.03	*1.7	0.02	0.9
Reinsurance ratio * acquisition ratio	0.01	0.9	0.06	**2.5
Individual premiums ratio			–0.09	–0.7
Periodic premium ratio			0.27	**7.9
Unit-linked fund ratio			–0.05	**–3.1
Endowment insurance ratio			0.15	*2.1
Intercept	2.24	**4.4	4.10	**5.5
Adjusted R^2	0.89		0.89	
No. of observations	607		456	
Economies of scale	0.82		0.79	
Idem, small firms (25%)	0.72		0.58	
Idem, small to medium-sized firms (50%)	0.77		0.68	
Idem, medium-sized to larger firms (75%)	0.80		0.74	
Idem, large firms (100%)	0.87		0.90	

a All terms are expressed in logarithms
b One and two asterisks indicate a level of confidence of 95 per cent and 99 per cent, respectively.

four control variables in an extended version of the model. Periodic premium policies go with additional administrative costs, whereas unit-linked fund policies save costs. The bottom lines of Table 9.3 show that life insurance companies, on average, enjoy scale economies of 18 per cent. Correcting for differences in the product mix or the share of unit-linked funds and so on does not change the results in qualitative terms. We also calculated average scale economies for various size classes with size measured as the companies' premium income. Scale economies appear to be larger for the smaller size classes. According to the extended model, small firms – in the lower 25 percentile class – may realize average scale economies of 42 per cent, whereas large firms – in the upper 25 percentile class – enjoy just 10 per cent economies of scale. Decreasing scale economies with firm size have also been found by Fecher et al. (1993) for the French life insurance industry. The comparison between the basic model and the extended model makes clear that the average scale economies per size class depend (only) slightly on the model specification. Although the average economies of scale for both models are rather similar, the dependency of the scale economies on size classes in the basic model is less than in the extended model.

The optimal production volume in terms of gross premium is defined as the volume where an additional increase would no longer diminish marginal costs, so that the derivative of marginal costs is zero. According to the basic model, the optimal size can be calculated as far above the size of all existing life insurance firms.[25] This implies that (almost) all firms are in the (upper) left-hand part of the well-known U-shaped average cost curve. The scale economies suggest that consolidation in the Dutch insurance markets is still far from its optimal level, but of course, diseconomies of conglomeration and mistakes in post-merger integration can outweigh scale economies.

The TCF estimates make clear that average scale economies of around 20 per cent are an important feature of the Dutch life insurance industry. These scale economies are generally higher than those found for banks in the Netherlands (e.g. Bos and Kolari, 2005) and elsewhere (e.g. Berger et al., 1993), but not uncommon in other sectors. Similar figures were found in other countries. Fecher et al. (1991) find 15 per cent for France and Grace and Timme (1992) observe 4 to 27 per cent for the US, depending on firm type and size. The existence of substantial scale economies might indicate a moderate degree of competition, where firms have not been forced to employ all possible scale economies.

9.8.2. Cost X-inefficiency

In this section we apply the stochastic cost frontier model (9.5) to data on Dutch insurance firms. Costs are defined as total operating expenses, which consist of two components, acquisition costs and other costs. The latter include management costs, salaries, depreciation on capital equipment, and so on. A further breakdown of 'other costs' would be highly welcome, but is regrettably unavailable. The price of the two input factors, acquisition costs and other costs, has been estimated as the ratio of the respective costs and total assets. Such a proxy is fairly common in the efficiency model literature, in the absence of a better alternative.

As said, the definition of production of life insurance firms is a complicated issue. Insurance firms produce a bundle of services to their policy holders. In particular, for life insurances services may be provided over a long period. Given the available data, we have selected the following five proxies of services to policyholders, together constituting the multiple products of insurance firms: (1) annual premium income. This variable proxies the production related to new and current policies. A drawback of this variable might be that premiums are made up of the pure cost price plus a profit margin. But it is the only available measure of new policies; (2) the total number of outstanding policies. This variable approximates the services provided under all existing policies, hence the stock instead of the flow. In particular, it reflects services supplied in respect of all policies, irrespective of their size; (3) the sum total of insured capital; (4) the sum total of insured annuities. Endowment insurances and annuity policies are different products. The two variables reflect the different services which are provided to the respective groups of policyholders; and (5) unit-linked policies. There are two types of policy regarding the risk on the investments concerned. The risk may be borne either by the insurance firms or by the policy holders. The latter type of policy is also known as 'unit-linked'. As the insurance firm provides different services in respect of these two types of policy, we include the variable 'unit-linked policies'. Note that these five production factors do not describe the production of separate services, but aspects of the production. For example, a unit-linked policy may be of either an endowment insurance type or an annuity type, so that two variables describe four different types of services.

The five production measures and the two input prices also appear as squares and cross terms in the translog cost function, making a total of 35 explanatory variables. Such models have proved to provide a close approximation to the complex multiproduct output of financial institutions, resulting in an adequate explanation of cost, conditional on production volume and input factor prices. In our sample, this model explains 94.0 per cent of the variation in the (logarithm of) cost.[26]

The set of suitable (non-zero) data regards 105 licensed life insurance firms in the Netherlands over the 1995–2003 period and contains a total of 689 firm-year observations. This panel dataset includes new entries, taken-over firms and merged companies and, hence, is unbalanced.

Table 9.A.1 in Appendix 9.I provides the full set of estimation results (see cost column). Due to the nonlinear nature of the TCF it is difficult to interpret the coefficients of the individual explanatory variables. As indicated by γ, 91 per cent of the variation in the stochastic terms (σ^2) of the cost model is attributed to the inefficiency term. A test on the hypothesis that inefficiency can be ignored ($\gamma = 0$) is rejected strongly. The essential results are the cost efficiency values calculated according to Equation (9.5). Table 9.4 provides average values of cost X-efficiency per year and for the total sample (see cost column).

The average cost X-*efficiency* is 72 per cent, so that the *inefficiency* averages 28 per cent. This implies that on average, insurers' costs are 28 per cent higher than at the best-practice firms, conditional on production composition, production scale and input prices. The average cost X-efficiencies fluctuate irregularly over time, so that no clear time trends are discernible. The inefficiencies are assumed to reflect managerial shortcomings in making optimal decisions in the composition of output factors and the use of input factors. A possible reduction of cost by at least one quarter does not seem plausible in a competitive market. However, it should be remembered that these inefficiency figures set an upper bound to the measured inefficiencies, as they may partly be the result of imperfect measurements of production and input factor prices. Particularly in services, which includes the financial sector, production is difficult to measure, while our dataset also suffers from none-too-exact information on input prices. Instead of drawing

Table 9.4 Average cost X-efficiency in 1995–2003

Year	*Cost X-efficiency*
1995	0.716
1996	0.727
1997	0.741
1998	0.724
1999	0.725
2000	0.710
2001	0.729
2002	0.728
2003	0.718
Total	0.724

Table 9.5 Average cost X-efficiency over size classes

Size class	*Cost*	*Average size (× €1000)*
1	0.747	13,261
2	0.763	94,904
3	0.731	277,937
4	0.693	548,474
5	0.696	936,795
6	0.701	2,107,749
7	0.742	14,479,608
Total average	0.724	2,447,891
Median		519,970

strong conclusions regarding competition, it is better to compare the results with benchmarks. Any comparison should be made with caution, as estimation results are generally based on varying estimation techniques, different insurance production models and diverging empirical specifications. In the literature, the insurance inefficiency figures in other countries range from 10 to 65 per cent. This implies that our inefficiencies are nothing out of the ordinary and even on the low side. They are similar to the inefficiencies that have generally been found in the banking literature which spread – widely – around a 20 per cent mean value (Berger and Humphrey, 1997; Altunbas et al., 2000; Hauner, 2005; Kasman and Yildirim, 2006). Bikker (2004, page 218) reports an average X-inefficiency for Dutch banks in 1997 of 26 per cent, remarkably similar to the figure for insurance firms.

Table 9.5 shows average cost X-efficiency for seven size classes. Here we observe a clear U-curve for cost efficiency: higher efficiency for small insurance firms, lower efficiency for medium-sized companies and resurging efficiency for larger firms. A possible explanation could be that smaller firms generally profit from their orderly structure and neatly arranged composition of products, so that differences in managerial inability across smaller firms are limited (as has also been found for banks, see Bikker, 2004, pp. 209ff.). The largest firms operate more on competitive submarkets such as pensions and on the more competitive international markets, which have forced them to become more efficient.

9.8.3. Profitability

A straightforward measure of competition is the profit margin. Supernormal profits would indicate insufficient competition. A traditional measure of profitability is the price-cost margin.[27] We cannot calculate the price-cost margin for life insurance companies, as we do not know the output prices and market shares of all insurance products per firm. However, we are able to calculate the average profit margin, defined as the ratio of profits before taxes and gross premium written. Using figures on consolidated life insurance firms from the ISIS dataset, we compare the Netherlands with some major European economies (see Table 9.6).[28] We are aware that profits could be influenced by differences in accounting rules,

Table 9.6 Average profit margins of life insurance firms in various countries (%) [a]

	ISIS[b]					*DNB*
	Germany	*France*	*UK*	*Italy*	*The Netherlands*	*The Netherlands*
1995	0.02	—	0.05	—	—	—
1996	0.02	0.03	0.06	—	0.15	0.13
1997	0.02	0.02	0.08	0.07	0.16	0.13
1998	0.02	0.03	0.09	0.03	0.16	0.13
1999	0.02	0.04	0.06	0.02	0.16	0.15
2000	0.02	0.04	0.05	0.05	0.14	0.15
2001	0.01	0.04	0.04	0.02	0.14	0.13
2002	0.02	0.02	0.02	0.01	0.02	0.02
2003	0.03	0.04	0.03	0.02	0.05	0.03
2004	0.03	0.03	0.06	0.03	0.14	0.13
2005	0.04	0.03	0.16	0.04	0.19	0.18
2006	0.03	0.02	0.19	0.07	0.24	0.18
2007	0.03	0.04	0.09	0.07	0.46	0.27
2008	0.00	0.03	–0.12	–0.01	–0.25	–0.27
2009	0.02	0.04	0.14	0.05	0.04	0.11
2010	0.02	0.04	0.15	0.03	0.12	0.01
2011	0.02	0.02	0.08	0.00	0.11	–0.06
2012	0.03	0.07	0.09	0.11	–0.04	0.01
Average	0.02	0.03	0.07	0.03	0.12	0.09

a Weighted averages.
Sources: Own calculations based on ISIS (first columns) and DNB (last column).

products, distribution channels, maturity or other characteristics of the markets.[29] However, we draw some conclusions from the remarkable profit margins in the Netherlands (around 9 per cent) compared with those in other EU countries like France, Germany, Italy and the UK, with respective profit margins of around 7 per cent, 2 per cent, 5 per cent and 4 per cent. The higher profits in the Netherlands suggest less competition than in the other countries.[30] The Dutch profit margins may be exaggerated, because the ISIS dataset includes fewer small life insurance companies, but this also holds for the other countries.

We also have data published by De Nederlandsche Bank (DNB, the Dutch insurance supervisor), which include all licensed firms and refer to domestic activities only. These figures also point to high Dutch profit margins of around 7 per cent. Of course, these figures largely reflect profit margins on past production, as profit stems from the existing portfolio of policies and not only from new business.[31] Sources at hand of specialized on-site supervisors indicate that profit margins on domestic production have declined strongly in recent years. Where Table 9.6 concludes that competition in the Dutch market was weak in the past, this has probably changed in recent years.

9.8.4. The PCS indicator

Table 9.7 presents estimates of the PCS indicator, based on an extended version of Equation (9.6) with profits and marginal costs in logarithms. Marginal costs are represented in three ways: average variable cost, defined as management costs as share of the total premium as suggested in Boone (2004) and Creusen et al. (2004), marginal cost, derived from the translog cost function of Section 9.8.1, and adjusted marginal costs, i.e. marginal costs adjusted for scale economies (see Appendix 9.II).[32] Average variable costs have the advantage of being less complex, since they are not model based, but they are less accurate because we cannot distinguish between variable and fixed costs. In practice, average variable costs are commonly proxied by average costs. We prefer the marginal cost derived from a translog cost function, as this is the most accurate measure. Adjusted marginal costs allow one to distinguish between the effects of two components of marginal cost, namely scale economies and X-efficiency.

Following Chapter 3, Boone (2004) and Creusen et al. (2004), we also introduce so-called fixed effects, that is, a dummy variable for each insurance firm (coefficients of the dummies are not reported here).[33] The advantage is that these fixed effects pick up all insurance company-specific characteristics, including scale, that are not captured by the other variables, so that part of the disturbances is eliminated. Around 10 per cent of the variance in the error term of the model without fixed effects (unexplained variance: σ_u^2) can be explained by these fixed effects (explained variance: σ_e^2) when they are introduced, where ρ is equal to $\sigma_u^2/(\sigma_u^2+\sigma_e^2)$. With respect to the control variables, we find a systematic, significantly positive contribution of individual policyholders to profits. The other control variables, periodic payments policies, unit-linked policies and endowment policies, do not affect profits.

Table 9.7 Fixed effects estimates of the PCS model for profits[a]

	Average variable cost		*Marginal cost*		*Adjusted marginal cost*[b]	
	Coefficient	*t-value*[c]	*Coefficient*	*t-value*[c]	*Coefficient*	*t-value*[c]
Respectively average variable and marginal cost, in 1995 (β)	–0.52	**–2.7	–0.53	**–2.5	–0.32	–1.4
Idem, 1996	–0.42	*–2.2	–0.38	*–1.8	–0.20	–0.9
Idem, 1997	–0.43	*–2.0	–0.32	–1.3	–0.05	–0.2
Idem, 1998	–0.69	**–3.2	–0.70	**–2.9	–0.23	–0.9
Idem, 1999	–0.34	*–1.7	–0.35	–1.5	–0.08	–0.3
Idem, 2000	–0.43	*–2.1	–0.38	–1.5	–0.10	–0.4
Idem, 2001	–0.55	**–2.7	–0.42	*–1.7	–0.15	–0.6
Idem, 2002	–0.17	–0.9	0.14	–0.5	0.39	1.3
Idem, 2003	–0.37	*–1.7	–0.18	–0.7	0.35	1.2
Individual premiums ratio	1.71	**3.0	1.46	**2.4	1.42	*2.3
Periodic payments ratio	0.34	0.9	0.26	0.6	0.14	0.4
Unit-linked funds ratio	0.22	0.6	0.34	0.8	0.34	0.8
Endowment insurance ratio	–0.27	–0.4	–0.25	–0.3	–0.52	–0.7
Intercept	6.76	**8.1	7.48	**7.4	8.15	**11.5
σ_u	2.01		1.97		0.25	
σ_e	0.66		0.67		0.11	
ρ	0.90		0.89		0.84	
Overall R^2	0.01		0.01		0.00	
Within/between R^2	0.26	0.04	0.28	0.04	0.26	0.08
No. of observations (groups)	500	(89)	444	(85)	444	(85)

a Profits and marginal costs are in logarithms
b Adjusted for scale economies
c One and two asterisks indicate a level of confidence of 95 per cent and 99 per cent, respectively.

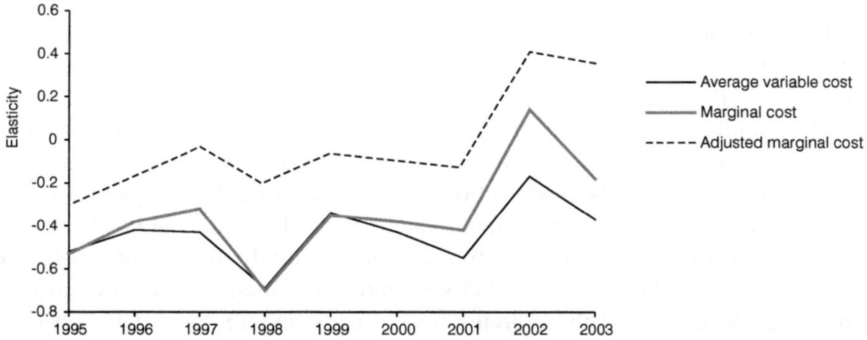

Figure 9.1 Effect of average variable costs and (adjusted) marginal costs on profits

As indicators of competition, the annual estimates of β are, of course, pivotal in the analysis. The first two columns of Table 9.7 present estimates of β based on average variable costs, which range from –0.2 to –0.7 and are significant in all years but one. The model-based marginal cost estimates are slightly higher but only significant in four out of nine years. Although the level of the indicator is difficult to interpret, its low degree of significance suggests moderate competition. When marginal costs are adjusted for scale economies, none of the betas are significant. This indicates that scale economies are an important component of the observed PCS indicator. Figure 9.1 shows that the coefficient β fluctuates somewhat over time in all three model versions. We observe an upward trend, indicating a (slight) decline in competition over the respective years. Average variable costs and model-based marginal costs result in similar estimates. The third measure of marginal costs renders a comparable pattern over time, but – due to the eliminated scale economies – at a higher level.

In order to assess whether our estimates for the PCS indicator are high or low, we compare them with estimates for other Dutch industries. Creusen et al. (2005) estimated the traditional PCS model for the manufacturing and service industries and found elasticities between average variable costs and profits of around, respectively, –5.7 and –2.5, for the years 1993–2001. The PCS indicator of the life insurance industry is around –0.45. As noted in Section 9.6, comparisons of the PCS indicator across sectors are problematic due to measurement errors caused, for example, by accounting differences regarding profits and losses. However, the absolute value of the PCS indicator of insurances appears to be much lower (closer to zero) than in other service industries. Moreover, estimations using exactly the same definition of profit as in Creusen et al. (2005) render the same conclusion.[34] All in all, this implies that the life insurance industry is less competitive than the manufacturing and (other) service industries.

Due to the logarithmic specification of the PCS model, all loss-making firms, including new entrants, have been ignored. This creates a potential bias because 20 per cent of our observations concerned loss-making companies. Estimations of the PCS indicator in a model with ratios instead of logarithms using the full sample results in a significantly more negative relationship between efficiency and profits. Solving this bias would add at most –0.5 to the PCS indicator. The conclusion remains that the PCS indicator for the life insurance industry is substantially lower than it is for other service industries. Furthermore, the PCS indicator is subject to the same deficiencies as the profit margin in Section 9.8.3, as it is based on the profitability of past business instead of on new production only. The next section solves these issues by analysing another performance indicator: market share. Note that similarly to what has been said above for profits, market shares will react more strongly to marginal costs, the more competitive the market is. Market shares are based on annual premiums and a significant part of these premiums, 55 per cent, are due to new policies. Therefore, market shares largely reflect the current business. Furthermore, using market shares, we can utilize information of the full sample, loss-making firms included.

9.8.5. Sensitivity analysis: the PCS indicator based on market shares

Although the indicator as originally formulated by PCS is based on relative profits, the idea behind it – namely that competition rewards efficiency – implies that we could also use the intermediate item 'relative market share' as our outcome variable. Therefore, as a check on the findings in the previous section, this section presents estimation results based on markets shares. Results are shown in Table 9.8. We find that average variable costs appear to have a significantly negative effect on market shares, see the first two columns. An increase of 1 per cent in this marginal cost measure causes a loss of around 0.45 per cent in market share. Note that this value is similar to the PCS indicator based on profits in Section 9.8.5.

If we consider changes in β_l over time, we observe larger negative values in the years just before the major fiscal policy change-over of 2001 with respect to annuities, as described in Section 9.2 (see also Figure 9.2). This indicates that competition has intensified somewhat in these years, probably with respect to annuities, which is in line which the observed increase in advertising and sales. In the subsequent years, we see that the effect of marginal costs on market shares decreases, pointing to weakening competition.

Considering the other estimation results in Table 9.8, it is clear that unit-linked policies appear to have been a major innovation when it comes to gaining market shares.[35] Collective contracts are also effective in gaining larger market shares. The year dummies are (almost) insignificant and, therefore, have not been shown in the table. When – as a second robustness test – the four control variables are dropped, we find similar results for β_l (not reported here). The main conclusion is that the central results – significant negative values for the β_l and a (negative) peak in the β_l just before the fiscal reform of 2001 – appear to be robust with respect to specification choices.

The two middle columns of Table 9.8 repeat the results for marginal cost instead of average variable cost. The values of β_l are similar in level and development over time and slightly less significant.[36] Apparently, average (variable) costs do

Table 9.8 Fixed effects estimates of the model for market shares[a]

	Average variable cost		Marginal cost		Adjusted marginal costs[b]	
	Coefficient	*t-value*[c]	*Coefficient*	*t-value*[c]	*Coefficient*	*t-value*[c]
Respectively, average variable and (adjusted) marginal cost, in 1995 (β_1)	–0.36	**–5.4	–0.37	**–7.0	–0.18	*–2.2
Idem, 1996	–0.45	**–7.3	–0.44	**–7.5	–0.26	**–3.4
Idem, 1997	–0.50	**–7.8	–0.48	**–7.1	–0.25	**–3.1
Idem, 1998	–0.47	**–6.8	–0.44	**–5.5	–0.19	*–2.1
Idem, 1999	–0.57	**–7.9	–0.56	**–7.2	–0.11	–1.1
Idem, 2000	–0.59	**–8.3	–0.59	**–5.9	–0.38	**–4.1
Idem, 2001	–0.48	**–6.6	–0.42	**–2.8	–0.23	*–2.3
Idem, 2002	–0.34	**–5.2	–0.34	*–2.2	–0.10	–1.0
Idem, 2003	–0.33	**–4.4	–0.28	*–1.9	0.02	0.2
Individual premiums ratio	0.62	**2.9	0.74	**3.0	0.66	**2.8
Periodic payments ratio	–0.71	**–5.3	–0.70	**–6.2	–0.82	**–5.7
Unit-linked funds ratio	0.45	**3.3	0.56	**4.3	0.59	**4.0
Endowment insurance ratio	0.63	**2.9	0.40	1.0	0.25	1.0
Intercept	–7.13	**25.7	–6.81	**21.5	–6.03	**–24.5
σ_u	2.11		1.86		1.95	
σ_e	0.30		0.29		0.31	
ρ	0.98		0.98		0.98	
Overall R^2	0.19		0.10		0.02	
Within/between R^2	0.30	0.17	0.28	0.11	0.19	0.01
Number of observations (groups)	651	(101)	581	(96)	581	(96)

a Market shares and marginal costs in logarithms
b Adjusted for scale economies
c One and two asterisks indicate a level of confidence of 95 per cent and 99 per cent, respectively.

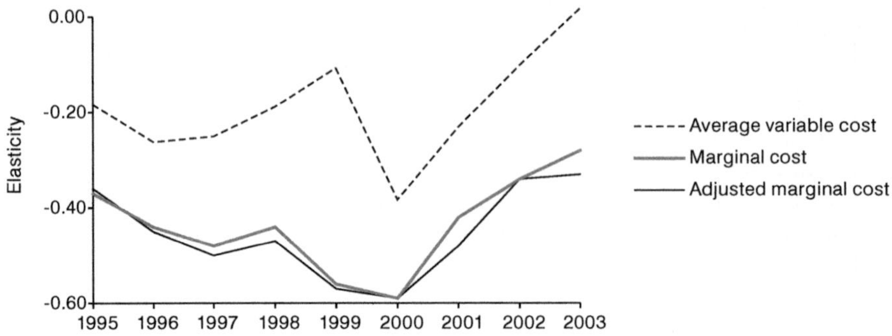

Figure 9.2 Effect of average variable costs and (adjusted) marginal costs on market shares

well as a proxy for marginal costs. The control variables have effects in line with earlier results.

Although the results presented above uniformly indicate that efficiency gains lead to larger market shares, this could also be fully or partly due to scale economies, as observed in Section 9.8.1. Large firms enjoy these scale economies which reduce marginal costs and work to increase market shares. To avoid possible distortion due to this kind of endogeneity, we correct the marginal costs (*mc*) for scale economies as set out in Appendix 9.II. This correction for scale economies yields the purest method for investigating the present relationship. The right-hand columns of Table 9.8 present the estimates for the market share model based on marginal cost adjusted for scale economies. As in the earlier model versions, we find that higher marginal cost tend to diminish a firm's market share and vice versa. However, the value of β_l and its level of significance are much lower now (i.e. around –0.2), apparently due to the fact that the positive contribution of scale economies has been eliminated (see also Figure 9.2). Note that this coefficient may also be affected by measurement errors. Nevertheless, if we estimate one single β_l for the whole period, this coefficient is significant (not reported). The control variable coefficients are similar to earlier results. The conclusion is that even after correcting for scale economies, efficiency gains still tend to increase market shares, although its contribution is smaller.

Figure 9.2 shows that the annual estimates of β in each of the three model versions indicate no upward or downward trend. Higher negative values of β are found in the years just before the major fiscal policy change-over of 2001 with respect to annuities, as described in Section 9.2. This indicates that competition has intensified somewhat in these years with respect to annuities, which account for some 30 per cent of the market. In the subsequent years, we see that the effect of marginal costs on market shares decreases, pointing to weaker competition. In these years, profit margins on annuities recovered (according to sector experts). Apparently, the level of competition changed somewhat over time.

9.9. Conclusions

This chapter analyses competition and efficiency in the Dutch life insurance market. As competition cannot be observed directly, we use five indicators to estimate competition in an indirect manner.

The first indicator is of a qualitative nature. We investigate the structure of the insurance market using the so-called tight oligopoly analysis, yielding diverging results. For the supply-side factors we find that supplier power is limited, due to the large number of insurance firms, and that ample entry possibilities exist, which in principle enable sound competition. On the demand side, however, we observe that consumer power is limited, particularly due to the opaque nature of many life insurance products, and that there are few alternatives to life insurance policies until 2008, when bank saving were given the same tax privileges, which may weaken competition. In short, the overall picture resulting from these considerations is mixed.

The second indicator is the scale efficiency level. A translog cost function has been applied to measure scale economies in the Dutch life insurance industry. Estimates indicate that scale economies exist and amount to 20 per cent on average, ranging from 10 per cent for large firms to 42 per cent for small firms. Such scale economies are substantial compared with what has been found in other countries and to what is usually found for other financial institutions such as banks. All existing insurance companies are far below the estimated (theoretical) optimal size, so that further consolidation in the Dutch life insurance market might be beneficial. Apparently, competitive pressure in the insurance market has so far been insufficient to force insurance firms to exploit these existing scale economies. Of course, consolidation could interfere with entry of new competitors.

The third indicator is the X-efficiency level. We find cost X-inefficiency estimates of around 25 per cent, on average, a magnitude which would not be expected in a market with increased competition. Incidentally, such inefficiencies are not uncommon for life insurance in other countries or other financial institutions.

The fourth indicator is the profit margin. We observe that the profit margins of Dutch life insurance firms have been high compared with those of their peers in other European countries. This could indicate relatively less competitive pressure in the Netherlands. However, this result mainly reflects the competitive situation in the past rather than in more recent years. Anecdotal evidence states that current profit margins in the domestic market are small, whereas, given the current low interest rates, the outlook for the (near) future is also not favourable.

The fifth indicator is the PCS indicator. Estimates of this indicator point to weak competition in the Dutch life insurance industry in comparison to indicator values in other service industries. All our empirical analyses are based on balance sheet and profit and loss data from both new and old business. Although the majority of annual premiums stems from new policies, the portfolio of policies is built up over the years. Hence, eventual improvement of competition shows up in these figures only with some delay, depending on the approach. However, annual estimates of the PCS indicator for the most recent years find a weakening rather than a strengthening of competition.

The evidence in this chapter does not allow us to draw strong conclusions on competition in the insurance market. The reason is that our analysis is on an aggregate level and disregards potentially relevant details with respect to e.g. product markets, distribution channels and tax treatment, due to lack of data. Yet, all five indicators point to a lack of competition.

Deliberations about possible policy measures to promote competition in the life insurance market should take into account the trade-off that exists between heavier competition, with the advantage of lower premiums and better services for consumers in the short run, and its downside, the possibility of a long-term deterioration in insurers' solvency, leading to less assured future insurance benefits. Furthermore, possible policy measures should be aimed at the right submarkets or distribution channels. Due to data limitations, our analyses could not distinguish between life insurers and independent insurance agents. Recent research has revealed that the financial advice market does not function properly and may hamper competition. This may be an important indication of where to start enforcing of competition.

Besides, it seems obvious that reduction of both X-inefficiency and scale inefficiency would be advantageous for all parties involved. Developments in information technology make further improvements in efficiency possible. Our empirical research suggests that consolidation might carry substantial cost savings. A comparison with other countries teaches that consolidation in foreign markets is far stronger. Apparently, the Dutch market is lagging in this respect. From that perspective and also given the observed potential savings, further consolidation would be sensible.

Appendix 9.I.: Estimation results

Table 9.A.1 provides a full set of estimation results.

Appendix 9.I.: Marginal costs adjusted for scale economies

Section 9.8.1 has confirmed the existence of substantial scale economies in the Dutch life insurance industry. To avoid possible distortion due to endogeneity, we correct the marginal costs (*mc*) for scale economies, based on a simple regression of *mc* on production, where *mc* occurs both in linear terms and squared, either as logarithms or in their natural form (the former for the market share model, the latter for the profit margin model). Table 9.A.2 shows that a 1 per cent increase in production reduces marginal costs by, on average, 0.15 per cent according to the log-based model and 0.17 per cent in the second model.[37] These figures are in line with the scale economies of Section 9.8.1. The residuals of these auxiliary equations are interpreted as marginal costs corrected for scale economies.

Table 9.A.1 Estimation results of the cost and profit X-efficiency models for insurance firms

Variables	*Coefficients*	*t-values*[a]
Intercept	4.020	**5.1
Premiums (1)	0.149	0.9
Unit-linked funds (2)	0.317	**4.5
Numbers of policies (3)	–0.178	–1.3
Endowment insurance (4)	0.305	**3.4
Amount of annual annuities (5)	0.267	**4.0
Price of acquisition (6)	0.181	1.5
Price of other cost (7)	1.630	**8.0
Squares (1)	–0.054	**–2.6
Squares (2)	0.000	0.0
Squares (3)	–0.005	–0.4
Squares (4)	0.013	**2.5
Squares (5)	0.004	1.5
Squares (6)	0.038	**5.3
Squares (7)	–0.058	**–4.0
Cross terms (1, 2)	0.039	**4.4
Cross terms (1, 3)	0.084	**3.4
Cross terms (1, 4)	–0.018	–1.3
Cross terms (1, 5)	0.014	1.0
Cross terms (1, 6)	0.025	1.2
Cross terms (1, 7)	–0.103	**–3.4
Cross terms (2, 3)	0.028	**–3.9
Cross terms (2, 4)	–0.006	*–2.3
Cross terms (2, 5)	–0.008	**–3.0
Cross terms (2, 6)	0.020	**3.7
Cross terms (2, 7)	0.032	**3.9
Cross terms (3, 4)	–0.035	–1.6
Cross terms (3, 5)	–0.021	**–2.6
Cross terms (3, 6)	–0.019	–1.2
Cross terms (3, 7)	–0.105	**–4.6
Cross terms (4, 5)	0.009	1.1
Cross terms (4, 6)	0.020	**2.5
Cross terms (4, 7)	–0.022	–1.1
Cross terms (5, 6)	–0.009	–1.5
Cross terms (5, 7)	0.052	**6.1
Cross terms (6, 7)	0.004	0.3
σ^2	0.952	8.0
σ_η	0.914	52.6
σ_μ	–1.865	–7.1

a One and two asterisks indicate a level of confidence of 95 per cent and 99 per cent, respectively.

Table 9.A.2 Auxiliary regressions for marginal cost and scale economy corrections

	Model in logarithms		*Model in natural values*	
	Coefficient	*t-value*[b]	*Coefficient*	*t-value*[b]
Production	–0.37	**–4.5	–1.34[a]	**–6.3
Production2	0.01	**2.7	2.49[a]	**4.6
Intercept	0.83	*1.9	0.20	**31.5
Adjusted R^2	0.19		0.07	
Number of observations	607		607	

a For presentational reasons expressed in billions of euros, instead of in thousands of euros, as elsewhere.
b One and two asterisks indicate a level of confidence of 95 per cent and 99 per cent, respectively.

Notes

1 Based on Bikker, J.A., M. van Leuvensteijn, (2008), Competition and efficiency in the Dutch life insurance industry, *Applied Economics* 40, 2063–2084.
2 Bikker (2012).
3 For an overview, see Bikker (2004) or Bikker and Bos (2005).
4 For life insurances, a second motive is the accumulation of assets. Some countries see many buyers of annuities eventually cashing out their contracts rather than annuitizing.
5 In the Netherlands, health insurance is part of non-life insurance, whereas in Anglo-Saxon countries, health insurance is seen as part of life insurance.
6 A typical endowment insurance policy pays a given amount at a given date if a given person is still alive, or earlier when he or she passes away. Of course, there are many variants to these archetypes.
7 The tax regime change might cause a structural break. However, re-estimation of our model for two sub-periods, before and after the change, did not give different results.
8 For a fuller discussion we refer to CPB (2005). See also Kamerschen (2004).
9 For a detailed analysis of the various effects we refer to CPB (2003).
10 Concentration ratios are discussed in Bikker and Haaf (2002). $HHI = \sum_{i=1}^{n} s_i^2$ where s_i represents the market share of firm *i*.
11 Acquisition costs are marketing costs and sales costs, which include commissions to insurance agents.
12 Incidentally, a new Dutch Financial Services Act ('Wet Financiële Dienstverlening') came into force at the start of 2006, pressing for more transparency in this market, which may also work to improve competition in this submarket.
13 See Consumentenbond, (2004), Consumentengeldgids ('Personal finance guide'), September, 34–37.
14 This interpretation would be different in a market with only few firms, so that further consolidation would be impossible. It would also change when new entries incur unfavourable scale effects during the initial phase of their growth path.
15 Note that sometimes scale economies are defined by the reciprocal of Equation (9.3), see, for instance, Baumol et al. (1982, page 21) and Resti (1997).
16 The first stochastic frontier function for production was independently proposed by Aigner, Lovell and Schmidt (1977) and Meeusen and Van den Broeck (1977). Schmidt and Lovell (1979) presented its dual as a stochastic cost frontier function.

17 This expression relies upon the predicted value of the unobservable, u_{it}, which can be calculated from expectations of u_{it}, conditional upon the observed values of v_{it} and u_{it}, (see Battese and Coelli 1992, 1993, 1995).
18 Note that the $E(c_{it}|u_{it}, X)$ differs from actual costs, c_{it}, due to v_{it}.
19 An alternative definition would be the inverse of EFF_{it}, $INEFF_{it} = \exp(u_{it})$, which is bounded between 1 and ∞.
20 Increased competition can force firms to consolidate (see our scale economies discussion). Claessens and Laeven (2004) found in a world-wide study on banking that concentration was positively instead of negatively related to competition.
21 Suppose that the negative profit firms are price fighters. In a well-functioning market the price fighters will influence profitability of the other firms.
22 Some insurance firms can approximate their value added by comparing their embedded value over time. These data are not publicly available.
23 The definition of production of life insurance firms is discussed further in Section 9.8.2.
24 The price of management, or wages, has been excluded by applying the two standard properties of cost functions, namely linear homogeneity in the input prices and cost-exhaustion (Jorgenson, 1986).
25 Of course, the accuracy of this optimal size is limited, as its calculated location lies far out of our sample range.
26 This figure is based on the OLS estimates, which provides the starting values of the numerical optimization procedure. As OLS minimizes the errors terms and maximizes the degree of fit, the latter will be lower in the SCF model.
27 This measure can be defined as $PCM = \sum_{i=1}^{n} s_i (p_i - m_i) / p_i$ where p_i denotes the firm's equilibrium output price and mc_i its marginal cost.
28 ISIS data concern both domestic and foreign activities. Pure domestic figures would be more precise but are not available.
29 For instance, firms in the Netherlands use more agents as selling channels than those in other countries (CEDA, 2004, page 144).
30 A similar picture emerges from figures of CEDA (2004), page 198.
31 This lagging adjustment of profitability does not disturb the international comparison, as this limitation also holds for the foreign data.
32 Note that the variable cost may change over the size classes due to scale efficiency (just as the marginal cost may do), so that the *average* variable cost may differ from the marginal cost. Apart from this theoretical dissimilarity, these variables are also measured differently in practice.
33 We have also estimated random effect models for profits (Table 9.7) and markets shares (Table 9.8). Their coefficients were quite similar to those of the fixed effect models, with even slightly higher values and higher levels of significance. This suggests that the estimates presented in Tables 9.7 and 9.8 are quite robust. We tested for random effect using the Hausman test, but this test appeared undefined, suffering as it did from the 'small sample problem'. All models include year dummies, also not shown in the tables.
34 The value of the PCS indicator in these estimations is around –0.85. Results can be obtained from the authors.
35 The elasticity of this variable is the coefficient (0.45) times the average of the unit-linked fund ratio (0.33; see Table 9.2), so 0.15.
36 In the basic model, the β_l values for *mc* are lower (around –1) than for average variable costs. For one year they are not even significant, see Table 9.A.2 in Appendix 9.II.
37 The elasticity, the first derivative of the auxiliary equation in logs, is –0.37 + 0.01 × 2 × average production in logarithms. For the auxiliary model in natural values it is equal to $\partial mc/\partial production$ × (*average production / average mc*) = (–0.134e–7 + (0.249e–14 × 247707.4 × 2) × 247707 / 0.18.

References

Aigner, D.J., C.A.K. Lovell, and P. Schmidt (1977) Formulation and estimation of stochastic frontier production function models, *Journal of Econometrics* 6, 21–37.

Altunbas, Y., E.P.M. Gardener, P. Molyneux, and B. Moore (2000) Efficiency in European banking, *European Economic Review* 45, 1931–1955.

Battese, G.E., and T.J. Coelli (1992) Frontier production functions, technical efficiency and panel data: with applications to paddy farmers in India, *Journal of Productivity Analysis* 3, 153–169.

Battese, G.E., and T.J. Coelli (1993) A stochastic frontier production function incorporating a model for technical inefficiency effects, Working Papers in Econometrics and Applied Statistics nr. 69, Department of Econometrics, University of New England, Armidale.

Battese, G.E., and T.J. Coelli (1995) A model for technical inefficiency effects in a stochastic frontier production function for panel data, *Empirical Economics* 20, 325–332.

Battese, G.E., and G.S. Corra (1977) Estimation of a production frontier model: with application to the pastoral zone of Eastern Australia, *Australian Journal of Agricultural Economics* 21, 169–179.

Baumol, W.J., J.C. Panzar, and R.D. Willig (1982) *Contestable Markets and the Theory of Industry Structure*, Harcourt Brace Jovanovich, San Diego.

Berger, A.N., and D.B. Humphrey (1997) Efficiency of financial institutions: international survey and directions for future research, *European Journal of Operational Research* 98, 175–212.

Berger, A.N., and L.J. Mester (1997) Inside the black box: what explains differences in the efficiencies of financial institutions, *Journal of Banking & Finance* 21, 895–947.

Berger, A.N., W.C. Hunter, and S.G. Timme (1993), The efficiency of financial institutions: a review and preview of research: past, present and future, *Journal of Banking & Finance* 17, 221–249.

Bikker, J.A. (2004) *Competition and efficiency in a unified European banking market*, Cheltenham: Edward Elgar.

Bikker, J.A. (2012) Performance of the life insurance industry under pressure: efficiency, competition and consolidation, DNB Working Paper No. 357, De Nederlandsche Bank, Amsterdam.

Bikker, J.A., and J.W.B. Bos (2005) Trends in competition and profitability in the banking industry: a basic framework, Suerf Series 2005/2. Vienna: The European Money and Finance Forum.

Bikker, J.A., and M. van Leuvensteijn, (2008) Competition and efficiency in the Dutch life insurance industry, *Applied Economics* 40, 2063–2084.

Bikker, J.A., and K. Haaf (2002) Measures of competition and concentration in the banking industry: a review of the literature, *Economic & Financial Modelling* 9, 5–98.

Bikker J.A., J.W.B. Bos, and L.G. Goldberg (2006) The efficiency and productivity of European insurance firms: what matters most for whom?, (mimeo), De Nederlandsche Bank, Amsterdam.

Boone, J. (2004) A new way to measure competition, CEPR Discussion Papers: 4330.

Boone J., R. Griffith, and R. Harrison (2004) Measuring competition, presented at the Encore Meeting 2004 'Measuring competition'.

Bos, J.W.B., and J.W. Kolari (2005) Large bank efficiency in Europe and the United States: are there economic motivations for geographic expansion in financial services?, *Journal of Business* 78, 1–39.

CEDA (2004) *European Insurance in Figures*, Comité Européen Des Assurances, June, http://www.insuranceeurope.eu/facts-figures/statistical-publications/european-insurance-in-figures.

Claessens, S., and L. Laeven (2004) What drives banking competition? Some international evidence, *Journal of Money, Credit and Banking* 36, 563–584.

CPB (2000) Measuring competition: How are cost differentials mapped into profit differentials? Working paper

CPB (2003) Tight oligopolies, CPB Document 29, CPB Netherlands Bureau for Economic Policy Analysis, The Hague.

CPB (2005) Competition in markets for life insurance, CPB Document 1, CPB Netherlands Bureau for Economic Policy Analysis, The Hague.

Christensen, L.R., D.W. Jorgenson and L.J. Lau (1973) Transcendental logarithmic production frontiers, *Review of Economics and Statistics* 55, 28–45.

Creusen, H., B. Minne, and H. van der Wiel (2004) Competition in the Netherlands in the 1990s: what do indicators tell?, presented at the Encore Meeting 2004 'Measuring competition'.

Creusen, H., B. Minne, and H. van der Wiel (2005) More competition in Dutch industries?, CPB Document, CPB Netherlands Bureau for Economic Policy Analysis, The Hague, http://www.cpb.nl/publicatie/het-meten-van-concurrentie-nederland.

Cummins, J.D., and M.A. Weiss (2000) Analyzing firm performance in the insurance industry using frontier efficiency and productivity methods, in: G. Dionne, (ed.), *Handbook of Insurance,* Boston: Kluwer Academic.

Fecher, F., S. Perelman, and P. Pestieau (1991) Scale economies and performance in the French insurance industry, *The Geneva Papers on Risk and Insurance* 16, 315–326.

Fecher, F., D. Kessler, S. Perelman, and P. Pestieau (1993) Productive performance of the French insurance industry, *Journal of Productivity Analysis* 4, 73–93.

Grace, M.F., and S.G Timme (1992) An examination of cost economies in the US life insurance industry, *Journal of Risk and Insurance* 59, 72–103.

Hauner, D. (2005) Explaining efficiency differences among large German and Austrian banks, *Applied Economics* 37, 969–980.

Hirschhorn, R., and R. Geehan (1977) Measuring the real output of the life insurance industry, *Review of Economics and Statistics* 59, 211–219.

Jorgenson, D.W. (1986) Econometric methods for modeling producer behaviour, in: Z. Griliches, M.D. Intriligator (eds), *Handbook of Econometrics*, Volume III, Elsevier Science, 1842–1905.

Kamerschen, D. (2004) A mnemonic for the major factors influencing the likelihood of collusion, *Applied Economics* 36, 1021–1024.

Kasman, A., and C. Yildirim (2006) Cost and profit efficiencies in transition banking: the case of new EU Members, *Applied Economics* 38, 1079–1090.

Leibenstein, H. (1966) Allocative efficiency versus X-efficiency, *American Economic Review* 56, 392–415.

Lozano-Vivas, A. (1998) Efficiency and technical changes for Spanish banks, *Applied Financial Economics* 8, 289–300.

Meeusen, W., and J. van den Broeck (1977) Efficiency estimation from Cobb–Douglas production functions with composed error, *International Economic Review* 18, 435–444.

Resti, A. (1997) Evaluating the cost-efficiency of the Italian banking system: what can be learnt from the joint application of parametric and non-parametric techniques, *Journal of Banking & Finance* 21, 221–250.

Schmidt, P., C.A.K. Lovell (1979), Estimation technique and allocative inefficiency relative to stochastic production and cost functions, *Journal of Econometrics* 9, 343–366.

Index

Page numbers in **bold** refer to figures, page numbers in *italics* refer to tables and page numbers followed by 'n' refer to notes.

Aigner, D.J. et al. 29, 33, 198n16 *see also* ALS model; frontier production functions
Allen, F. et al. 18
ALS model 29, *32–5*, *40 see also* Aigner, D.J. et al.; frontier production functions
American Sugar Refining Company (ASRC) *see* ASRC (American Sugar Refining Company)
Anderson canonical correlation likelihood ratio *see* Anderson correlation test
Anderson correlation test *109*, *111*, 125, *129–30*, *146–7*
antitrust regulation 101
ASRC (American Sugar Refining Company) 4; 1890-1914 96–7, 100–2, *101*; Lerner index 107, 109; market data 103–6, **105**; PCS indicator 98–100, 112–**13**, 114; sugar production 102–*3*
average ranking 85–**8**, *87*
average variable costs 1; life insurance 181, 189–**94**, *190*, **191**, *193*, 199nn32&36; loan markets 122, 132; PCS indicator 65

bank competition 8, *89*, 90, 132, 136n2
bank data 92n11, 144–6, *145*, 151–4, 154–7
bank types *126*, *145*
banks by country *126–7*, *145*
BankScope 79, 92n11, 124, 144
Basel Committee on Banking Supervision (Basel I, II and III) 10, 16, 20
Beck, T.A. et al. 18
Berger, A.N. et al. 20
Berry, S. et al. 50, 65
Bertrand competition 2; efficiency of firms 43; PCS indicator 50, 53, 55–6, 60–1, 66–7; regimes of competition 108
Boone, J.: interest rate pass-through 143; life insurance 180–1, 189; loan markets 119, 122, 131; PCS indicator 49, 50, 55; performance measures for banks 79; regimes of competition 97–9, 107, **113**
Boot, A.W.A. 13, 14
Box-Cox test 37, *38–9*, 121
Boyd, J.H. 18
Bresnahan (Lau) model 119–20
Bresnahan, T.F. 2, 46n2, 119–20
Breton, R. 19

Claessens, S. 8, 14, 136n3, 199n20
co-integration tests 150–1, 154–7, *156*, 166n33
collective contracts: life insurance 170, 173, 176, 181, 192; obstacles to competition 13, 15, 21nn5&10
commercial banks: balance sheet data 124–5; by country *126*, 128, 132–3; interest rate pass-through 144–*5*, 165n13; loan markets 123, 137nn12&13
competition regimes *see* regimes of competition
competitive behaviour: bank performance *78*; banks 140; competition regimes 99; efficiency of firms 26, 27, 29, 36, 40; life insurance 169, 171; loan markets 120; obstacles to competition 9, 14
concentration index *see* HHI concentration index
constant marginal costs 50, 57–8, 60, 65, 69, 98 *see also* marginal costs
consumer organizations 13, 175
consumer power 12–14, 15, 20, 170, 175–6, 195

cooperative banks: interest rate pass-through 144–*5*, 165n13; loan markets *119*, 123, 124–5, *126*, 128
cooperative behaviour 28, 36–7
Cornwell, C. et al. 30
corporate control 41
correlation coefficients **79**–*81*, **88**
correlation with competition *76*, 77
Corts, K. 50, 96, 99
cost categories 61–2
cost-to-income ratio 75–*6*, 78, 79, *82*, 86–*7*, 93n23
country-level competition 82–4, *83*
Cournot competition *see* Cournot model
Cournot model 2–3; competition regimes 98–9; efficiency of firms 25, 27; interest rate pass-through 144; loan markets 121; PCS indicator 50, 53, 55–6, 67, 69–70; performance measures for banks *78–80*, **79**, *82*, 84, 86–*7*, 93n18 *see also* Nash-Cournot equilibrium
Cournot-Nash equilibrium *see* Nash-Cournot equilibrium
cross-elasticity of demand, 40
Cuba 100–1, 103–4, 108, 110, ***113***

datasets 5–6; interest rate pass-through 141, 144–*5*, 146; life insurance 181, 186, 188–9; loan markets 125; PCS indicator 49, 61, 70; performance measures for banks 78–9, 92n11, 93n14; regimes of competition 97, 104–5 *see also* panel datasets
De Nicolo, G. 18
demand functions 56, 65
demand side factors: life insurance 170, 175–6, 195. *See also* supply side factors; obstacles to competition 8, 9–*10*, 11–14, 17, 20
Demsetz, H. 25
diagnostic framework 8, 9, 14, 15, 173
dominant firms 36, 44, 97, 114

ECB (European Central Bank) 4, 89, 118, 140, 151, 166n29
ECM (error correction model) 89, 93n28, 142, 148–50, 157–64, 165n15
efficiency hypothesis 3, 76–*8*, **77**, 88, 118, 120–1
efficiency of firms 25–46; conclusions *42*; determinants 40–1, 41–3, *42*; introduction 26–7; market share 36–40, *38–9*, *40*; market structure 27–9; production function 29–36, *32–5*; research data 44–6
elasticity-adjusted Lerner index 96–7, 99, 106–7, 107–***10***, 114, *115 see also* Lerner index; PCM (price-cost margin)
elasticity of residual demand 12, 175
empirical research 49, 70, 196
entry barriers: banks 144; competition measure 48, 55, 70; competition regimes 98; life insurance 173; loan markets 121; obstacles to competition 9–11, *10*, 13, 20
entry costs 49, 52–**4**, 57, *66*, 69–70, 98–9
equilibrium: efficiency of firms 25, 29, 36; interest rate pass-through 148–9; life insurance 157, 199n27; PCS indicator 51–5, 57–8, 61, 65–6, 70, 71n4; regimes of competition 98
error correction model (ECM) *see* ECM (error correction model)
euro area 4, 16, 118–37, 140–65; balance sheet data 124–5; bank data 144–6, 151–7, *152*, *153*, *155*, *156*; conclusions 132–3, 164; empirical evidence 157–64, *158*, *160*, *161*, *162*, *163*; interest rate pass-through model 148–50, 150–1; introduction 118–19, 140–2; literature 119–21, 142–3; marginal costs estimation results 133–6, *134–6*; PCS estimation results 125–32, *126*, *127*, *128*, *129–30*; PCS indicator 121–2, 123–4, 143–8, *145*, *147*
European Central Bank (ECB) *see* ECB (Central European Bank)

financial illiteracy (consumers) 8, 12, 14, 15, 16, 20
financial innovation 74
financial products 11–14, 20, 21nn5&13, 73, 169, 173
financial stability 8–9, 14, 17–20, 20–1, **74**, 89
firm costs 26, 27, 36
firm efficiency *see* efficiency of firms
firm market share 26, 37
firm-specific effects 29, 30–1
firms *see* low cost firms high cost firms
France: interest rate pass-through 141, *145–6*, 148, 152; life insurance 174, 185, *188*–9; loan markets 124, *129*, **131**, 133; performance measures for banks *83*
frequent interaction *10*, 173

frontier production functions 29–31, *32–5*, 40, 43

GDP (gross domestic product) 75, *89*, 166n29
General Method of Moments (GMM) *see* GMM
Genesove, D.: interest rate pass-through 143; PCS indicator 50; regimes of competition 96, 99, 100, 102, 103, 114
Germany 1, 4; interest rate pass-through 141, *145*, *146*, 148, 152; life insurance 165n13, 173–5, *174*, *188–9*; loan markets 124, 128–*9*, **131**, 133–*4*, 136n9; performance measures for banks *83*, 93n27
GMM (General Method of Moments) 111, 125, 128, 146–8, *147*, 165n12
Goldberg, P. 50
Gorter, J. 17
Graddy, K. 50, 99
Great Britain *see* UK
Greene, W.H. 31, *33*
gross domestic product (GDP) 75, *89*, 166n29
gross investment 25, 29, 40, *40*

H-statistic 88, 119, 120, 122, 132, 143 *see also* Panzar-Rosse model
HAC (heteroskedastic and autocorrelation consistent) variance estimations *see* Newey-West kernel
Hansen *J*-statistic *see* Hansen *J*-test
Hansen *J*-test: interest rate pass-through *146*–8, *147*; loan markets 125, 128–*30*, *129*, *135*; regimes of competition *109*, *111*–12
health insurance 16, 21n5, 198n5
healthy competition 17, 74–5
Heffernan, S.A. 137n20, 143
Hellmann, Th.F. et al. 19
Herfindahl-Hirschman concentration index (HHI) *see* HHI concentration index
heterogeneity: interest rate pass-through 150, 165n21; life insurance 173, 180; obstacles to competition 8, *10*–11, 15–16
HHI concentration index 2; interest rate pass-through 141, 144; life insurance 173–*4*, 180, 198n10; loan markets 119, 120, 121; performance measures for banks *76*, *82*, 84, *87*, *89*, 92; regimes of competition 97–8
Hicks, J. 76
high concentration 10, 14, 137n13, 173
high cost firms 26, 29
high efficiency firms 56
high entry barriers *10*, 173
high switching costs 11, 12, 175
homogeneity: bank competition 144; efficiency of firms 25, 27, 43; life insurance 180, 199n24; loan markets 123; obstacles to competition 15; PCS indicator 60

IMF (International Monetary Fund) 20
imperfect competition 9–*10*, 11, 143 *see also* perfect competition
incentive structures 2; efficiency of firms 25–6, 29, 41, 43–4; interest rate pass-through 140; life insurance 175; obstacles to competition 11, 12, 18–19, 20
incentives for managers 26, 29
indirect measures: life insurance 169, 171, 176, 178; loan markets 118, 120; performance measures for banks 73, *76*
inefficient firms 55–6, 118, 171
intensity of competition: life insurance 175; obstacles to competition 9, 11; PCS indicator 48–50, 54–5, 57–8, 59, 66–7
interest rate pass-through 140–66; bank data 151–*4*, *152*, *153*, 154–*7*, *155*, *156*; conclusions 164; empirical evidence 157–64, *158*, *160*, *161*, *162*, *163*; introduction 140–2; literature 142–3; model specification 148–50, 150–1; PCS indicator 143–4, 144–6, *145*, *146*–8, *147*
intermediation 13, 16–17, 20, 172
International Monetary Fund (IMF) 20
IPS (Im, Pesaran & Shin) test 150, 154, *156*, 157
Italy 4; interest rate pass-through 141, *145*–8, *146*, *147*, 152; life insurance *174*, *188*–9; loan markets 124, 128–**31**, 137n13; performance measures for banks 83

Japan 4, 124, 128, *130*–3, **131**, 173–*4*
Jimenez, G. et al. 19

Keeley, M.C. 19
kernel-based heteroskedastic and autocorrelation consistent (HAC)

variance estimations *see* Newey-West kernel
Klein, M. 142

Laeven, L. 136n3, 199n20
Lau, L. 2, 119–20
Lerner index 2–4; loan markets 120, 136n5; performance measures for banks *78*, 84, 93n13; regimes of competition 96–7, 99, 106–7, 107–10, 114, 115 *see also* PCM (price-cost margin)
life insurance industry 169–99; conclusions 195–6; data 181–3, 182; introduction 169–71; Netherlands 173–5, 175–6; PCS indicator 180–1, 189–92, **191**, 192–**4**, *193*; production of life insurances 171–2; profitability *188*–9; scale economies 176–8, 183–5, *184*; X-inefficiency 178–80, 185–8, *187*
liquidity 12, 20, 74
loan markets 4–5, 118–37; balance sheet data 124–5; competition measurement literature 119–21; conclusions 132–3; introduction 118–19; marginal costs estimation results 133–6, *134–6*; obstacles to competition 18–19; PCS estimation results 125–32, *126*, *127*, *128*, *129–30*; PCS indicator 121–2, 123–4
low cost firms 25–6, 29, 74, 83, 85, 100

managers: efficiency of firms 26, 29, 44; life insurance 170, 178, 186, 188; loan markets 120; PCS indicator 62
mandatory saving 15, 21n10
marginal costs 5–6; interest rate pass-through 143–4, 146, 165n12; life insurance 180–1, 189–92, 192–4, 196–8, 199nn27&32; literature 119–20; loan markets 121–2, 125, 132, 133–*6*, 136nn5&11, 137n12; PCS indicator 50, 57–8, 60–1, 65–6, 69, 71n10; performance measures for banks 84; regimes of competition 97–9, 102–3, 103–6, 106–7, 110–12, 112–14; scale economies 177, 183, 185; translog cost function (TCF) 123–4
market power: bank competition 142–3, 150; banks *78*, 84, 93n23; competition regimes 98; life insurance 170; loan markets 119–20, 133; obstacles to competition 8–9, 14, 17–19, 20
market share 1–3, 5–6; and efficiency 36–40, *38–9*, *40*, 43–4; efficiency of firms 25–6, 27–9, 41–3, *42*, 46n9; interest rate pass-through 141, 143–*5*, 165n12; life insurance 170–1, 180, 188, 192–**4**, *193*, 196; loan markets 120, *127*, 132, 136n11, 137n12; PCS indicator 121–2, 125; performance measures for banks 76, *78–9*, 84, 86, 88; regimes of competition 96–7, 99–100, 102–*3*, 103–4, *115*, 116n8
market structure: bank performance *76*–7, *78*, 84; efficiency of firms 27–9, 36, 40; life insurance 173; loan markets 120; obstacles to competition 8, 9, 14
MFI Interest Rate (MIR) statistics 151, 165n23, 166n24
MIR (MFI Interest Rate) statistics
monetary transmission *4*, 74, 89, 142–3
Monti-Klein model 142
mortgage rates 73, 152, *153*, *155*
Mullin, W.: interest rate pass-through 143; PCS indicator 50; regimes of competition 96, 99, 100, 102, 103, 114
multiproduct cases 59, 66

Nash-Cournot equilibrium 25, 27, 28, 46n4, 57, 98 *see also* Cournot model
Netherlands 4, 169–99; collective pension system 15; health insurance 16, 21n5, 198n5; interest rate pass-through 141, *145*, *147*, 153; life insurance 169–70, 172, 185–6, *188*–9, 195, 198n5; life insurance market *173–4*, 175–6; intermediation model 17, 21n3, 118, 128, 130, 133; loan markets 124, 128–**31**, *129*, *130*, 133; obstacles to competition 15–17, 21nn3&5&7&10; performance measures for banks 74
network properties 8, 11, 16, 20
Nevo, A. 50, 66
Newey-West kernel 108, 110, 128, 148, 166n30
Nickell, S.J. 25–6, 30, 46n1
non-transparency 8, 12, 175

obstacles to competition: competition and financial stability 17–20; conclusions 20–1; introduction 8–9; policy reactions to failure 14–17; structural problems 9–11, 11–14
OECD (Organisation for Economic Co-operation and Development) **75**, 79, 85–*6*, 92n11
Organisation for Economic Co-operation and Development (OECD) *see* OECD
output levels: interest rate pass-through 144; life insurance 176–7; loan markets

121, 123; PCS indicator 52–3, 55–8, 68; regimes of competition 98
output reallocation effects 49–50, 55–6, 58–9, 64, 67–9

panel datasets 5–6, 186
Panzar-Rosse model 6; loan markets 119, 132, 133; performance measures for banks *78–80*, *82*, 87–8, 90–2, 92n10, 93n18 *see also H*-statistic
PCA (principal components analysis) 81, 93nn14&16
PCM (price-cost margin) 2–3; efficiency of firms 25–7; interest rate pass-through 120, 121; loan markets 170, 188, 199n27; PCS indicator 48–50, 64–70, *66*, 70–1, 70n2, 71nn6&10; regimes of competition 96, 97–9, 106, 107–9, *115 see also* Lerner index
PCS (performance-conduct-structure) indicator 3–6, 19, 48–71; bank data 151*–4*, *152*, *153*, 154–7, *155*, *156*; comparison with PCM 64–70, 70–1; competition measurement literature 119–21; competition models 50–9, *78*–9, 79–84, 97–100, 121–4; elasticity-adjusted Lerner index 106–7, 107–14; empirical evidence 157–64, *158*, *160*, *161*, *162*, *163*; estimation results 125–32, *126*, *127*, *128*, *129–30*; interest rate pass-through 143–8, 149–51, 151–7, 157–64; introduction 49–50; life insurance 171, 180–1, 189–92, 192–4, 195–6, 199n34; marginal costs estimation results 133–6, *134–6*; new measure of competition 59–64, **60**; regimes of competition 96–7, 114; US sugar industry 100–3, 103–6
Pedroni co-integration tests 150–1, 154–7, *156*, 166n33
pension schemes 15, 21n12, 170
perfect competition: loan markets 119, 136n5; obstacles to competition 11, 14; PCS indicator 61; performance measures for banks 78, 90–1, 94n34; regimes of competition 114 *see also* imperfect competition
performance-conduct-structure (PCS) indicator *see* PCS (performance-conduct-structure) indicator
performance measures for banks 73–94; critical appraisals **79**–*81*, *80*, 81*–2*, 82–5, *83*; financial institutions **75–***6*, 76–**7**, *78*–9; indicators 85, 85–**8**, *86*, *87*, 88–*90*, *89*; introduction 73–5; loan markets 132; summary 91–2; validated measures 90–*1*
policy change 48, 192, 194
policy reactions to failure 8, 14–17
predictive validity 73, 85, 88, 88–*90*, *89*, 93n25
price-cost margin *see* PCM (price-cost margin)
principal components analysis (PCA) *see* PCA
product markets 26, 41, 119, 121, 172, 196
profit margins 1; life insurance 171, 183, 185, 188–9, 194–5, 196; loan markets 122, 137n13; performance measures for banks 73, 76, *78*, 81, 84, 89; regimes of competition 98, 102, 103
proxies *4*, 6; interest rate pass-through 143, 144, 146, 152; life insurance 177, 181, 183, 185, 189; loan markets 123, 125; performance measures for banks 75, 76, 78; profit-proxy 103–**5**, 111–12, 113, 114; proxy for profits 103–**5**, 111–12, 113, 114

quiet life hypothesis 76

R&D (research and development) 29, 41, 53, 61–2, 71n7
reallocation effects *see* output reallocation effects
regimes of competition 96–116; PCS and Lerner 106–7, 107–14; PCS indicator 96–7, 97–100, 114; US sugar industry 100–3, 103–6
relative costs 25–6, 28
reliability 74
research and development (R&D) 29, 41, 53, 61–2, 71n7
residual demand 12, 175
revenues 2; life insurance 181; loan markets 119, 122; PCS indicator 56, 61, 65, 67; performance measures for banks *78*

savings banks 6; interest rate pass-through 144–*5*, 165n13; loan markets 119, 124–*6*, 128, 132–3, *134–5*, 137nn12&13
scale economies: life insurance 170–1, 180–1, 183–5, 195, 196; loan markets 120, 125; measurement 176–8; PCS

indicator 189–**91**, *193–4*; performance measures for banks *76*, 90–*1*
SCF (stochastic cost frontier) function 179, 199n26 *see also* TCF (translog cost function)
Schmidt, P. 30, *33*
Scott, M.F.G. 40
SCP (structure-conduct-performance) model 2–3; loan markets 120; model comparisons **79**–84, *82*, *86–7*; obstacles to competition 9, 14; performance measures for banks 76–**7**, *78*, 88, 92, 93nn18&21
search costs 8, 12, 175
securitization 5, 19
selection effects 53
SEPA (Single European Payment Area) *see* Single European Payment Area
short-run efficiency 29, 30, 41–3, *42*
Sickles, R.C. 30
simple indicators 43, 73, 87
Single European Payment Area (SEPA) 16
small firms 36, *184*, 187–8, 195
solvency 10, 74, 83, 196
Spain 4; interest rate pass-through 141, *145*, *147*; loan markets 124, 128–**31**, *129*, *130*, 133, 137n13; obstacles to competition 19; performance measures for banks 83
stochastic cost frontier (SCF) function 179, 199n26 *see also* TCF (translog cost function)
stochastic frontier production function models *see* frontier production functions
strategy equilibrium 52
structural approach 65
structural changes 132
structural features 170, 173
structural links *10*, 11, 173
structural problems 8–9, 9–14
structural weakness 15, 20
structure-conduct-performance (SCP) model *see* SCP (structure-conduct-performance) model
sugar production *see* ASRC (American Sugar Refining Company)
supernormal profits 9, 10, 171, 173, 188
supplier power 13, 176, 195
supply side factors: life insurance 170–1, 173–5, *174*, 176, 195; obstacles to competition 8, 9–11, *10*, 13
systemic risk 17

Tabak, B. et al. 19
tariff structures 11, 96, 98, 100–1, 104
TCF (translog cost function): interest rate pass-through 144–*5*; life insurance 170–1, 189, 195; loan markets 122, 123–4, 133–*4*; scale economies 176–7, 183–5, *184*; X-inefficiency 179, 186
time-invariant effects 29, 30–1
time-variant effects 30–1, *33*
translog cost function (TCF) *see* TCF (translog cost function)
transparency *10*, 12, 173, 175, 198n12

UK 4; life insurance 173–5, *174*, *188–9*; loan markets 124, *126–8*, *130–2*, **131**, 133, 137nn19&20; manufacturing sectors 26, 43, 44; obstacles to competition 15; performance measures for banks *83*
unit root tests 150–1, 154, *156*, 157, 165n20
United Kingdom *see* UK
unused scale economies 90–*1*, 120 *see also* scale economies
US competition regimes *101*
US sugar market *see* ASRC (American Sugar Refining Company)

variable costs: efficiency of firms 27; interest rate pass-through 122, 132; life insurance 181, 189–**94**, *190*, **191**, *193*, 199nn32&36; PCS indicator 59, 61–2, 65, 67, 71; performance measures for banks 94n33; regimes of competition 102
Vickers, J.S. 25, 46n1, 55

Wald test: interest rate pass-through 149, *158–61*; loan markets 132, 137n18; regimes of competition 106, *110*, 112–14, *113*, 116nn7&8
Willig, R.D. 26
Wolfram, C. 50

X-efficiency 5; appendices *197*; life insurance 170–1, 178–80, 183, 186–*7*, 189, 195; loan markets 120; performance measures for banks *76*, *78–80*, **79**, 85–*7*, *86*, 92n11
X-inefficiency 5; life insurance 169, 178–80, 185–8, *187*, 195–6; loan markets 120; performance measures for banks 90–*1*

For Product Safety Concerns and Information please contact our EU representative GPSR@taylorandfrancis.com Taylor & Francis Verlag GmbH, Kaufingerstraße 24, 80331 München, Germany

Batch number: 10725798

Printed by Printforce, the Netherlands